# GOD WILLING?

# God Willing?

## Political Fundamentalism in the White House, the "War on Terror," and the Echoing Press

# David Domke

Pluto Press
London · Ann Arbor, MI

First published 2004 by Pluto Press
345 Archway Road, London N6 5AA
and 839 Greene Street, Ann Arbor, MI 48106

www.plutobooks.com

British Library Cataloguing in Publication Data
A catalogue record for this book is available from the British Library

ISBN 0 7453 2306 5 hardback
ISBN 0 7453 2305 7 paperback

Library of Congress Cataloging in Publication Data applied for

10  9  8  7  6  5  4  3  2  1

Designed and produced for Pluto Press by
Curran Publishing Services, Norwich, UK

Printed and bound in Canada by Transcontinental Printing

# Contents

# Figures

# Preface

This book is an analysis of the inter-connections among politics, religion, public discourse, and the press in the United States. This book also is a critique of the Bush administration's disregard for democracy in the months following the terrorist attacks of September 11, 2001. It was the former before it became the latter.

In January 2002 I began working with several graduate and undergraduate students at the University of Washington on a series of research projects examining the Bush administration's strategic communications after September 11. For the past decade I have analyzed how U.S. political leaders and news media shape public opinion, and this period promised to offer rich insights. President George W. Bush had captured the rhetorical high ground in his address to Congress and the nation on September 20, 2001, in which he painted the world in stark good versus evil terms, declared that other nations either would be with the administration in a "war on terrorism" or against them, and asserted confidently that "freedom and fear, justice and cruelty have always been at war, and we know that God is not neutral between them." Congress and much of the mainstream U.S. news media responded with deference and support. The president and administration seemingly had offered a compelling vision *of* the nation and *for* the nation; with this in mind, in our research we set out to identify and systematically track any communication strategies that had been prominently utilized in this process. A substantial public emphasis by the administration on themes of national identity and a clever approach of preempting potential criticisms of the "war on terrorism" emerged in our analysis, and this research eventually produced a series of articles in academic journals.

Over time, however, as this research continued through 2002 and 2003, something else began to emerge in the analysis. It became apparent to me that the president and administration's vision was more than strategically nationalistic and politically adroit. It also was religious. The administration's public discourse consistently:

- exhibited an antipathy toward complex conceptions of reality
- framed demands for immediate action on administration policies as part of the nation's "calling" and "mission" against terrorism
- issued declarations about the will of God for the United States and the values of freedom and liberty, and
- demonstrated an intolerance for dissent.

The combination of these communication themes with the religious conservativism of President Bush, Attorney General John Ashcroft, and others in the administration pointed in one direction—that of fundamentalism. Indeed, scholarship and commentary on religious fundamentalisms consistently highlight these kinds of beliefs and actions or present a picture wholly suggestive of them. I gradually became convinced that the administration, in making its case for war against a terrorist network headed by Islamic extremists, had capitalized upon the September 11 crisis to put forward its own blend of conservative religion and politics, what I call in this book political fundamentalism.

But that is not the end of the story. Analysis of this worldview emanating from the White House and its effects upon U.S. political and media systems between September 2001 and the president's calling of an end to "major combat" in Iraq in May 2003 left me with one conclusion: the administration's political fundamentalism subverted many of the country's most precious democratic ideals. The president and his team consistently utilized communication approaches that merged a conservative religious worldview and political ambition in pursuit of controlling public discourse, pressuring Congress (and the United Nations) to rubber stamp its policies, engendering a view of its actions as divinely ordained, and stifling dissent. The result was a dominance of the political agenda unmatched in recent American history. Just as important, at no time did the administration's public communications suggest an openness to consideration of whether the nation's policies might have contributed to the September 11 attacks or to the possibility that other Americans—or international allies— might effectively contribute to the shaping of the nation's response or subsequent campaign against terrorism. The administration did what it wanted, when it wanted, without concern for others—and its public communications were a key component of making this form of leadership attractive or at least palatable to a citizenry reeling from the trauma of September 11.

The administration had help in this process. Mainstream news media in the United States responded to the terrorist attacks with a predictable nationalism, predictable because a commercial press always has responded to externally initiated national crises by standing in line with political leadership (its sources) and advertisers (its financial benefactors). What *was* surprising is that such a deferential posture by the news media toward the administration rarely waned over the 20 months of analysis in this book: the mainstream press consistently echoed the administration's communications from September 11 to Saddam and Iraq—thereby disseminating, reinforcing, and embedding the administration's fundamentalist worldview and helping to keep at bay Congress and any serious questioning among much of the public. Even in press criticisms of the administration, which were present during this period, the administration's communication emphases resounded.

At the same time, Democrats in Congress also bear responsibility for the course of events because of their consistent acquiescence to the administration's rhetoric and demands. Had leading Democrats been able to articulate a compelling alternative moral vision for the nation, regularly asked tough questions of the administration, or at least insisted upon appropriate deliberations about some of the administration's post-September 11 policies, their views might have received substantial airing by news media and resonated with a considerable portion of the American public. But the administration's political fundamentalism was so certain, so determined, and so unrelenting that the mainstream press and Democrats in Congress abdicated their responsibilities as key checkpoints in American democracy—to the enormous detriment of the nation and the world.

This book, then, is about politics, religion, public discourse, and the press in the United States as it played out under the Bush administration in the aftermath of September 11. It is unfortunately the case that there will be a desire by some to dismiss this book as the product of an anti-religious, anti-conservative mindset. The reality could not be farther from the truth. My worldview, and that of a number of the individuals who assisted me on this project or offered insightful suggestions, has been and continues to be substantially shaped by the Christian faith. Further, I see great merit in both conservative and liberal thinking. This research was driven by one and only one agenda: a desire to rigorously examine the public communications and to understand the motives of George W. Bush and his administration in this momentous period in U.S. history. Political elites and news media have special, leading roles in the U.S. experiment in democracy, and it is always important to scrutinize how that power is being exercised. Whether the actions of the Bush administration, Congress, and the mainstream press in the period between September 11 and the Iraq war in spring 2003 were anomalous or indicative of a permanent shift in the relations among these institutions is unclear. I do know for certain, though, that what did happen during this time period had far-reaching implications for the nation and the globe. This book is an attempt to understand these developments and to contribute toward a democratic future, for the benefit of my students who have worked with me and for the current and future students who will teach us in the future.

# Acknowledgments

This project would not have been undertaken, sustained or completed without the contributions and support of many.

For their comments and suggestions early in my thinking, I am indebted to Gerald Baldasty, W. Lance Bennett, Robert Entman, John Gastil, Barbara Warnick, Hazel Dicken-Garcia, Dan Wackman, Susan Jeffords, Robert Tynes, and Hallack Greider. Each offered insights that significantly contributed to the direction of the manuscript, and also was enthusiastic when it was needed most. This project would not have progressed far without them.

A second group of individuals was kind enough to provide me with mid-course evaluations: Robert Jensen, Sandra Silberstein, Charles Scalise, Laurie Wheeler, James Caswell, and Greg Orwig. Each nudged me to think deeper about certain ideas, to refine my language, and to sharpen my focus. In a similar manner, friends who were kind enough to talk with me about this research at regular intervals included Tom Johnston, Melinda Priddy, K. C. Watkins, and Erin Shea.

A group of students at the University of Washington was with me in the beginning of this project, and another was there at the end. Throughout, I benefited enormously from the conceptual insights, energy, and hard work present in my collaborations with John Hutcheson, M. Andre Billeaudeaux, Philip Garland, Kevin Coe, Erica Graham, Sue Lockett John, and Victor Pickard. I learned from them at least as much as they from me. Another group of students worked diligently with me as research assistants, without whom I would still be working on this project: Ben Amster, Jae Shim, Ted Coopman, T. Johnson, Mari London, Margaret Stevens, Todd Egland, Jamal Siddiqui, David Ko, Jordan Thompson, and Trena Berton.

I was fortunate to receive grant support from the University of Washington's College of Arts and Sciences and the Department of Communication, through its Test Trust Fund, at key points in this research. This was invaluable.

Sections of Chapter 2 were presented in an article in *Journal of Communication* in its Summer 2004 issue, and sections of Chapter 3 were presented in an article in *Newspaper Research Journal* in its Winter 2003 issue.

At Pluto Press, my editor Julie Stoll helped me to see the deeper import of my analysis, and worked with me to move the project from its original fit for an academic audience to one (I hope) that contributes to scholarship and broader public discourse.

Two people in particular deserve additional mention. Kevin Coe and Robert Tynes provided tireless assistance on this project. They discussed ideas, combed through scholarship and popular discourse, analyzed administration communications and news coverage, offered insightful suggestions, read draft after draft, and did all of this on a timeline that fit my schedule. I am most grateful.

I am responsible for the ideas, data, and conclusions in this book, of course.

Finally, I am fortunate to have had the support of Lisa and William, who helped me simultaneously to grasp the importance of this project and consistently to gain much-needed perspective on just how important anything is.

# 1
# Religion, politics, and the Bush administration

President George W. Bush delivered the 2003 State of the Union address before Congress and an estimated U.S. television audience of 62 million, emphasizing goals and accomplishments of his administration as well as challenges posed by terrorism and other perceived threats. In particular, Bush devoted just over half of the address to the administration's "war on terrorism" and the need to confront Iraq and Saddam Hussein. Near the end, the president turned to discussion of the national character of the United States and its purpose in the world, declaring that "Americans are a free people, who know that freedom is the right of every person and the future of every nation. The liberty we prize is not America's gift to the world, it is God's gift to humanity." He then added, "We Americans have faith in ourselves, but not in ourselves alone. We do not know—we do not claim to know all the ways of providence, yet we can trust in them, placing our confidence in the loving God behind all of life and all of history. May He guide us now" (Bush, 2003a).

Four days later on the morning of February 1, the space shuttle *Columbia* exploded, killing all seven crewmembers. The president spoke to the nation from the White House that afternoon. Included in his comments were these words:

> In the skies today we saw destruction and tragedy. Yet farther than we can see, there is comfort and hope. In the words of the prophet Isaiah, "Lift your eyes and look to the heavens. Who created all these? He who brings out the starry hosts one by one and calls them each by name. Because of His great power and mighty strength, not one of them is missing." The same Creator who names the stars also knows the names of the seven souls

we mourn today. The crew of the shuttle *Columbia* did not return safely to earth. Yet we can pray that all are safely home.

(Bush, 2003f)

The explicitly religious language in these two addresses, in combination with the administration's push for war in the Holy Land-rich Middle East, prompted a spate of popular analyses of Bush's religious faith. *Newsweek* magazine devoted its March 10 cover to "Bush and God," the *Washington Post* took up the topic with stories and columns,[1] and *New York Times* columnists and guest writers weighed in.[2] In August, *Vanity Fair* contributed "God and man in the White House,"[3] and in September *Gentlemen's Quarterly* offered "George W.'s personal Jesus".[4] These writers and publications were of mixed mind regarding how much Bush's religious faith infused his politics and how it accorded with previous presidencies. It was clear, though, that this president's faith, and the implications of that faith for administration policy and global relations, had become a matter of considerable public interest. Bush's religious outlook was no longer merely a personal or even political matter; it had now been absorbed into the discourse of popular culture.

The argument here is that Bush's overtly religious language, what religion scholar Martin E. Marty termed "God talk" in one of the *Newsweek* articles,[5] was only part of the story. The much more important and far less obvious matter was that the administration had converged a religious fundamentalist worldview with a political language to create a *political fundamentalism* that offered familiarity, comfort, and a palatable moral vision to the U.S. public in the aftermath of September 11. This book offers a definition of political fundamentalism and then examines its application by the Bush administration and the response of mainstream U.S. news media, focusing on the period between the 2001 terrorist attacks and major combat in the Iraq war in spring 2003.

One indication of the remarkable success of the Bush administration in this endeavor was the presidential images that served to bookend the 20 months analyzed here. On the evening of September 11, 2001, Bush was relatively unpopular for a first-year president, faced a skeptical, anxious, and confused public, and delivered a somber address from the Oval Office. On May 1, 2003, the president was riding high in public approval, had headed the nation through two military campaigns, and delivered a "Mission Accomplished" address with pomp and full regalia from the deck of a U.S. aircraft carrier. Indeed, in April 2003 a full 80 percent of the U.S. public said that the president "is a strong and decisive leader" (Gallup, 2003)—an all-time high in the polling organization's measure of this trait.[6]

The leadership of Bush and the administration came with a significant price, however. Absent during the months from September 11 to the Iraq war in 2003 was a robust public discussion about the meaning of the terrorist attacks and the direction of the nation in its aftermath. The administration's political fundamentalism did much more than offer familiarity, comfort, and a moral stance; it also closed off a substantive societal—and international—conversation through a set of politically calculated, religiously grounded communication strategies. Instead of opening up the discourse and allowing a democratic dialogue to take place, Bush's rhetoric hijacked the discussion about the significance and implications of September 11, thereby denying to U.S. citizens important opportunities for national self-examination and a wide public hearing of diverse viewpoints — and also shutting out the world, much of which was extending unprecedented sympathy for U.S. citizens and the nation. Democracy was disregarded as the administration emphasized language and policies that limited potential avenues of political and social action, pushed incessantly for immediate adoption of administration policies by consistently raising the specter of another September 11, declared that U.S.-defined freedom and liberty were unchallengeable God-decreed norms for all peoples, and consistently silenced dissent by proclaiming it to be un-American and dangerous.

These administration communication approaches, in the midst and then aftermath of the September 11 crisis and substantially amplified by mainstream news media, effectively controlled public discourse and engendered a climate of nationalism in which the public treated presidential support as a patriotic duty and Congress felt compelled to adopt far-reaching domestic and foreign policies. Policies enacted between September 11 and spring 2003 included the U.S.A. Patriot Act, several economic recourses to a widely felt recession, the new Cabinet post of the Department of Homeland Security, a preemptive foreign policy doctrine, and the decision to apply this doctrine against Iraq—all of which occurred with far less public debate among political leaders, both in the White House and on Capitol Hill, than the nation deserved. The administration had created a national mood of spiritual superiority under the guise of a just sovereignty. It was a moral stance underpinned by threat, fear, and paranoia, and carried the connotations of the apocalypse; that is, of course, if Bush's prescriptions for deliverance were not followed. The ultimate irony is that in combating the Islamic extremists responsible for September 11, the administration adopted, pursued, and engendered its own brand of political fundamentalism—one that, while clearly tailored to a modern democracy, nonetheless functioned ideologically in a manner similar to the version offered by the terrorists.

This book examines several domains of the U.S. political and news environments closely to understand these developments. The public's surge of support following the September 11 attacks, what political scientists have termed "rally round the flag" behavior, is a necessary but not sufficient condition to explain the president and administration's remarkable political successes in late 2001, throughout 2002, and early 2003.[7] The president was given the opportunity to lead by the public and Congress, clearly; but he need look no further than his father's experiences in the early 1990s to know that his public standing would ultimately depend upon his ability to offer a resonant agenda in a convincing manner. For Bush the son to be successful, he would have to transform into a rhetorically compelling leader *and* he would need a nationalistic news media to widely amplify his message to the U.S. public. To be specific, the administration had to fashion and then set into motion what political scientist W. Lance Bennett has described as "propaganda, American style" (1988, p. 176), wherein the public is fed simple, stereotypical ideas from politicians via uncritical television and newspaper media—with the result that the public becomes either passive to or accepting of the message. The historical record suggests that Bush delivered and the mainstream press obliged.

This book focuses on how this occurred and what it means for the United States generally, and the U.S. political system in particular. The central argument is that the Bush administration offered a message ideally suited and strategically crafted for the times, one that leading news outlets consistently conveyed to a mass audience. Capitalizing upon the post-September 11 anomic state felt by many U.S. residents, the president and his administration brought a conservative religious worldview into the mainstream of U.S. politics. Religious worldviews, Rottenberg (2000) has argued, offer a "comprehensive faith-inspired vision about the nature of things and the meaning of history"

(p. 403) that guides the establishment of norms, decision-making and behavior.[8] The Bush administration's worldview is one grounded in religious fundamentalism—that is, it emphasizes absolutes, authority and tradition, and a divine hand in history and upon the United States.[9] Such a worldview is disastrous for a democratic political system, for it mandates an ideological shift away from open discussion, publicly responsive leadership, and humility, toward authoritarianism, publicly unmindful leadership, and arrogance. All of these were present in the Bush administration after September 11.

It is necessary to acknowledge, though, that worldviews are not easily identified. They are often unconscious in nature and articulated by people in language that rarely sheds clear light on one's foundational values and assumptions about reality. Lakoff (1996) has argued:

> [M]any people believe that they are consciously aware of their own worldviews and that all one has to do to find out about people's views of the world is to ask them. Perhaps the most fundamental result of cognitive science is that this is not true. What people will tell you about their worldview does not necessarily accurately reflect how they reason, how they categorize, how they speak, and how they act.
>
> (Lakoff, 1996, p. 36)

For this reason, research on political worldviews must establish clear criteria about what counts as evidence; Lakoff suggested analyses should be able to offer a unifying explanation for why and how individuals focus on certain topics and use certain words and phrases in arguing about these topics, and then should test this explanation by analyzing these individuals' communications because every "speech or book or article is a challenge to any would-be description" of a worldview (p. 30). This is the approach adopted here. The arguments offered about the administration's political fundamentalism are examined through systematic analysis of the public communications of the president and top administration officials (speeches, press conferences, congressional testimony, and so on) regarding several policies and goals between September 11, 2001, and the president's calling of an end to major U.S. combat operations in Iraq on May 1, 2003. In turn, to gain insight into how these communications disseminated and whether they ultimately were influential, news and editorial discourse of leading news organizations and public opinion polls are examined at several points during the same 20-month window.

## MODERN POLITICAL FUNDAMENTALISM: A CONCEPTUAL FRAMEWORK

Political fundamentalism is offered and defined here as an intertwining of conservative religious faith, politics, and strategic communication. It is conceptualized as consistent with, yet substantially distinct in societal implication from, civil religion—what Bellah (1974) defined as "a collection of beliefs, symbols, and rituals with respect to sacred things" that "while not antithetical to, and indeed sharing much in common with, Christianity, was neither sectarian or in any specific sense Christian" (p. 29).[10]

A common example of civil religion discourse in U.S. politics is the "God bless America" phrase that presidents have used to conclude national public addresses. Such language is present in the Bush administration, but so are several additional discourses that are far less common among U.S. political leaders and are suggestive of the central role that religion—conservative religious faith, to be exact—has served in this administration. Political fundamentalism also is of much greater strategic import than a basic presence of religious fundamentalism in U.S. politics, which, in the form of the "Christian Right" over recent decades, has drawn considerable national attention and strongly infused the Republican Party with a socially conservative agenda.[11] This movement has labored, however, to successfully broaden its message into a political fundamentalism—that is, to convert a self-proclaimed Christian rectitude, via strategic language choices and communication approaches, into righteous political beliefs.

The Bush administration achieved such an adaptation following September 11, transforming a religious paradigm into a political one *by choosing language and communication approaches that were structurally grounded in a conservative religious outlook but were political in content and application.* Insight into this process can be gained by drawing upon the concept of "structures of feeling," offered by cultural theorist Raymond Williams as a way to understand how meanings and values become embedded in social, political, economic, and cultural environs over time. Williams emphasized that social and political leaders' abilities to shape the "specific feelings, specific rhythms" experienced on a daily basis by individuals is crucial to the process by which certain ideologies become "formalized, classified, and in many cases built into institutions and formations" (1977, p. 132). The result of the Bush administration's policy and communication processes after September 11 was the formation of a worldview emanating from the White House that had deep and conservative religious roots yet felt political—and thus became more likely to be received favorably in the press and by the U.S. public. This is what is meant here by political fundamentalism.

It would be a mistake to think about political fundamentalism only in regard to the Bush administration, however. Political fundamentalism in a modern form has both a recent, albeit nascent, past and a likely future in the United States.[12] The dramatic social changes and turmoil of the 1960s and 1970s prompted a number of U.S. residents to turn to the stability offered by fundamentalist churches and doctrines, bringing conservative Christianity into the "cultural mainstream" by the mid-1970s.[13] At the same time, religious conservatives began to engage in substantive political action to address perceived declines in traditional morality and the nation's potential abdication of its role, in fundamentalists' view, as "the 'city on a hill' ordained by God as the light to the nations" (Ammerman, 1991, p. 40). Indeed, since it was founded, a conception of the United States as a "chosen nation" has been present among many Protestants.[14] In 1976, however, religious conservatives gained a new sense of political efficacy when devout Southern Baptist Jimmy Carter was elected to the White House. Concerted political organizing followed, and by the early 1980s the new Christian Right, as the movement became known, had created "a sophisticated political operation that was far more extensive and effective than any of its predecessors" (Lienesch, 1993, p. 7).

At the center of this movement was the Moral Majority, an organization developed by three conservative political organizers and headed by fundamentalist preacher Jerry Falwell.[15] The Moral Majority's agenda focused on family-related issues, particularly abortion, prayer in schools, and matters of sexuality and gender roles, including staunch opposition to the Equal Rights Amendment for women. In time, fundamentalists began to develop a network of pastors, churches, television programs, newsletters, and seminars that generated considerable revenue, while also spreading and reinforcing a renewed engagement by Christian conservatives in politics.[16] The Christian Right eventually opposed Carter over a number of matters, particularly his foreign policies. Falwell argued, for example, that the dissemination of Christianity to other peoples could not be carried out if other nations were communist—a perspective which provided a good reason to support a strong U.S. military and conservative foreign policy.[17] In this context, Ronald Reagan emerged as the favorite son of religious conservatives. Reagan offered the mix of conservative social and foreign policies desired by fundamentalist leaders—in particular, opposition to abortion, support for school prayer, and a conception of the Soviet Union as the "evil empire"—and he exhibited open enthusiasm for Christian conservatives, to whom he said in 1980, "I endorse you" (quoted in Sawyer, 1984).[18] Indeed, Reagan gave federal appointments to several leaders of the religious right.[19]

Just as important, the Reagan administration developed a language and set of communication strategies, under the leadership of Michael Deaver and David Gergen, that appealed simultaneously to fundamentalists and to a broader mass public. In the words of Ritter and Henry (1992), "the union between the sacred and the secular ... defined Reagan's public discourse" (p. 4). In particular, the president's tendency to paint the world in stark good versus evil terms, with the United States as the divinely chosen defender of freedom and liberty—a language that, as we will see, was closely paralleled by George W. Bush in the aftermath of September 11—helped Reagan gain the support of religious conservatives. Indeed, Falwell told Moral Majority members that they could "vote for the Reagan of their choice".[20] The network of religious conservatives began to coalesce in these years with a broader group of conservatives, which gave rise to widespread conservative talk radio and a significant interconnected association of think tanks and grass roots political organizing.[21] By the end of the 1980s, according to Lienesch (1993), the new Christian Right exercised power via "a labyrinth of lobbying groups and political action committees" (p. 3). This convergence of politics and religious conservatism within and during the Reagan administration might be considered the birth of a successful, modern form of political fundamentalism in the United States.

The presidencies of George H. W. Bush and Bill Clinton took different pathways, however. From the beginning, religious conservatives were skeptical of Bush, so much so that he was challenged in the Republican Party primaries by Christian Right leaders Pat Robertson in 1988 and Pat Buchanan in 1992. Bush governed more moderately than Reagan—even raising taxes—and his support for fundamentalists' core concerns was conceived as lukewarm and tenuous.[22] Clinton was opposed by political conservatives generally, and staunchly so by religious conservatives, who immediately assailed his decision upon entering office to repeal the ban on homosexuals serving in the military. By the 1990s the Moral Majority had given way to the Christian Coalition, which had broader public support and a more sophisticated communication approach.[23] Religious conservatives were generally less politically visible during these years than in the 1980s, but nonetheless continued to grow in importance, spreading well beyond the Southeastern United States to pervade institutionalized arenas of politics. When Republicans gained control of the House of Representatives in 1994, close to 60 percent of victorious congressional candidates received Christian Coalition backing.[24] The Christian Coalition subsequently propelled the impeachment process against Clinton,[25] and Conger and Green (2002) concluded, "Christian conservatives ha[d] become a staple of politics nearly everywhere" by the 2000 elections (p. 65).

In particular, religious conservatives had become a staple of the Republican Party. Lind (2001) argues that Christian conservatives formed one of a half dozen groups in Reagan's coalition of public supporters, whereas by 2000 the pre-eminence of religious fundamentalists had "relegated to the sidelines" all other factions in the earlier Reagan coalition.[26] In this environment, George W. Bush—viewed by many in the fold as ideologically not his father's son, but rather Reagan Jr.—became the clear choice of religious conservatives, a viewpoint solidified in the aftermath of September 11.[27] Data by the Pew Research Center (2003i) indicate that in 1987–8, 34 percent of white evangelical Protestants identified as Republicans and 31 percent as Democrats. Over time this gap had widened, and it reached unprecedented levels in summer 2003 when 43 percent of white evangelical Protestants identified as Republican, 22 percent as Democrat. The same partisan movement also was visible among white Catholics. In the late 1980s, 41 percent of such individuals considered themselves Democrats, compared with 24 percent Republicans. This gap shrank over time, and in summer 2003 for the first time more white Catholics identified as Republican (31 percent) than as Democrats (29 percent), a shift particularly pronounced among those who attend Mass regularly.

These trends toward political conservatism among religious white U.S. residents both contributed to and were reflective of landmark partisan developments among the broader U.S. electorate in the aftermath of September 11—developments that tilted the entire U.S. political landscape to the advantage of the Bush administration and Republican Party. At the national level, in the 2002 elections Republicans, on the strength of Bush's campaigning in many states and a new grass roots organizing approach, gained seats in both houses of Congress—the first time this had happened for a president in midterm elections since 1934—and control of the presidency and both houses of Congress, something that not even the Reagan administration achieved.[28] At the state level, a majority of state legislators are now Republicans for the first time in 50 years, and in spring 2003, almost as many U.S. adults (30 percent) called themselves Republicans as called themselves Democrats (32 percent), the narrowest gap since pollsters began measuring party identification among the public in the 1940s.[29] If the Reagan administration gave birth to a modern form of political fundamentalism, it became ascendant under the Bush administration in the aftermath of September 11.[30]

At the same time, fear-inducing terrorism unfortunately and inevitably is likely to occur again (in varying form, of course) in future years in the United States. The world of terrorism has breached the nation's shores and is not likely to be eliminated with certainty anytime soon, if ever—especially given the Bush administration's willingness, which it consistently emphasizes, to act preemptively with military might when diplomatic means do not unfold as desired. It is important, therefore, to situate an analysis of the Bush administration within the context of how political fundamentalism might "work," generally, in the U.S. political and media system. Indeed, it is possible to develop a broader, predictive conceptual framework that asserts that *political fundamentalism is likely to (re)emerge, gain a wide public presentation, and receive a favorable hearing in the United States* when four characteristics are present:

- a nation-challenging crisis occurs
- national political leaders are religiously conservative
- the same political leadership is skilled in strategic communications

- the news media give substantial emphasis to leaders'communications.

The convergence of all four of these provides an environment in which political fundamentalism has the potential for power and influence in the United States. Notably, at least three of these attributes are *not* perceived as the norm—that is, they are not the way things regularly are—in the U.S. political and media systems. Specifically, contemporary U.S. society is thought to be fairly resilient to nation-challenging crises due to (a) its emphasis on individual freedoms, democratic mechanisms, and wide-ranging civil rights, and (b) the lack of an "opposing" nation-state (such as the former Soviet Union) with substantive military resources. Second, because of its secular political system—with its constitutionally inscribed separation of church and state—and a primarily "objective" and secular media system, the United States seems relatively unlikely in times of normalcy to elect or strongly support individuals with highly conservative religious outlooks in the top national office. Third, U.S. elites certainly may be adroit at strategic communications, but a rigorously "on message" political leadership is relatively uncommon, in part because of ambitions among leadership and in part because of the invasive and competitive U.S. media environment.[31] Finally, U.S. mass media are primarily commercial in economic basis, and thus theoretically have great freedom to deviate from the viewpoints of political leadership.[32] These four characteristics nonetheless converged in the post-September 11 milieu and provide an explanatory framework for the political successes of President Bush and his administration between the terrorist attacks and Iraq war. These characteristics are elaborated in the following pages, and then an overview is provided of the analysis in ensuing chapters on ways in which political fundamentalism was enacted by the Bush administration after September 11 and the implications of these developments.

### Nation-Challenging Crisis

Marty and Appleby, who edited *The Fundamentalism Project*, a six-volume opus published in the 1990s, argued that "fundamentalisms arise or come to prominence in times of crisis, actual or perceived" (1991b, p. 822). When the world gets turned upside down, when anxiety dispels comfort, when social, economic, political, and cultural relations are in flux, religious fundamentalism becomes attractive because people seek a familiar framework in which to interpret events. As Ammerman (1991, p. 55) puts it: "In chaotic times and places, when individuals and communities are searching for moorings, the certainty and clarity of fundamentalism often seems appealing." Religious fundamentalisms, therefore, both are spawned and become more manifest and attractive in times of crisis. In the words of Ammerman again (p. 56): "Fundamentalism has been most politically active and culturally visible" in periods of major turmoil and subsequent renewal; the post-September 11 era encompasses both of these. There are all manners of crises, of course; the ones that are the most likely to have the greatest impact—that is, large effects of a lasting nature on many people—are crises that challenge the nation, because these can cut to the core of one's understanding and experience of the world. Specifically, an individual's conception of the nation, what scholars call "national identity," offers a form of collective identification that, in the words of Schlesinger (1991), is simultaneously "one of inclusion that provides a boundary around 'us' and one of exclusion that distinguishes 'us' from 'them'" (p. 301). A significant challenge to such collective boundaries is a necessary first step in the rise of political fundamentalism. When the public faces uncertainty about its national affinity, then the opportunity for significant ideological change or reversion becomes possible. Political leaders are aware of this, of course.

U.S. citizens have become accustomed to *intra*-national challenges such as racial and ethnic conflict, class disputes, religious bickering or worse, partisan political struggles, and so on. As unfortunate as these are, such dynamics might be viewed as more or less inevitable in a liberal democracy, which encourages or at least allows free speech, religious liberty, political protests, and the like. What has become rare for the United States over the past half-decade, and thus is unfamiliar to large segments of the population, is a serious external challenge to the nation-state; when this occurs, a necessary response of political leadership is to re-construct the sense of "imagined community" that—perhaps consciously, perhaps not—holds together disparate citizens.[33] Niebuhr (1967), for example, has argued that each nation has a positive "social myth" that distinguishes it from other nations, justifies its existence, and defends its interests; these myths frame historical events in positive lights and establish a sense of superiority over other nations. Such myths are propagated by national leaders and through political and cultural institutions such as schools, churches, and the mass media.[34] A defining characteristic of these narratives, almost without exception, is an emphasis upon particular moral qualities as integral to the nation. A nation-challenging crisis, then, prompts a (re)turn to consideration of nationality and morality, both of which predictably intersect with religion for many U.S. residents, thereby providing a pathway for political fundamentalism to be expressed and to be favorably received. For the Reagan administration, a severe economic recession and the Iran hostage situation combined to constitute a considerable crisis; for the current president, the stakes were even higher with the events of September 11.

The terrorist attacks on New York City and Washington D.C. presented a crisis of the gravest sort—thousands of U.S. residents dead on U.S. soil, the nation's economic epicenter devastated, and its political capitol imperiled. Even though the large majority of U.S. residents experienced the attacks only indirectly, via media coverage or through the death or injury of someone they knew, the psychological trauma of these events was substantial. In a public opinion survey one week later, 71 percent of U.S. adults said they felt depressed due to the attacks; of these, half said they were having difficulty concentrating on work or normal activities, and one-third indicated they were having trouble sleeping.[35] In a survey two months later, 31 percent of U.S. residents said their "own personal sense of safety and security" had been shaken a good deal or a great amount by the September 11 events, a finding slightly higher among women, people living in the Eastern United States, and those *under* the age of 45.[36] Nearly half also said their hope for the future had changed due to the attacks, and 41 percent said that their stress level had become elevated since September 11. And in a CBS News survey one year after the attacks, 50 percent of U.S. adults said they generally felt "somewhat uneasy" or "under danger" from terrorist attacks, 62 percent said they thought about September 11 at least every week, and a full 90 percent agreed that "Americans will always have to live with the risk of terrorism."[37]

Manifest effects such as these recede over time, of course; however, scholarship in political psychology suggests that such powerful cognitions and emotions can nonetheless be *primed*, that is, brought to mind, by new terrorism-related cues disseminated through the mass media, such as elevated threat levels, U.S. military campaigns, or even presidential addresses emphasizing concerns about terrorism.[38] These cues prompt the mental (and mass media) replaying of the September 11 events, and it is common in such instances for old fears to be renewed and re-lived. In November 2001, the editorial board of the *New England Journal of Medicine* noted:

> Although studies of prior disasters suggest that stress reactions diminish over time in the vast majority of people who have had indirect exposure, the September 11 attacks, the shocking televised images, and the profound ramifications are unprecedented. It remains to be seen whether stress reactions in people throughout the country will indeed diminish, especially with recurrent triggers from ongoing threats and further attacks.
>
> (Schuster et al., 2001, p. 1511)

Evidence does suggest subsequent events served as recurrent triggers. In October 2001, the percent of U.S. adults who said they were "very worried" that another terrorist attack would soon occur was 27 percent. This number declined in subsequent months, but in June 2002, following public notification that U.S. citizen Jose Padilla had been arrested on allegations that he planned to detonate a radioactive "dirty bomb" and as the president unveiled his proposal for a Cabinet-level Department of Homeland Security, this percentage spiked to 32 percent. This number fell into the 'teens in subsequent months before surging to 31 percent in December as U.N. weapons inspectors prepared to enter Iraq. When inspections moved ahead, the U.S. population relaxed, but when the administration's war rhetoric heated up in February 2003, anxiety about another terrorist attack shot up to 34 percent. In a related poll question at the same time, 22 percent said they were "very worried" that a family member might be a victim of a terrorist attack, also a post-September 11 high.[39] Further, in late March 2003 a full 67 percent of U.S. adults said that they felt sad when watching the Iraq war on television and another 58 percent said it was frightening to watch television coverage of the conflict.[40] In sum, for a significant number of U.S. residents the trauma of September 11 waxed and waned, but nonetheless remained through the Iraq war in 2003.

## Religiously Conservative Political Leadership

It is tempting for people in the United States to see the close inter-twining of religion and politics as a matter of consequence only for others—such as Arab nations in the Middle East, particular groups and locales in Southeast Asia, or strife-ridden regions in Africa. Of course, religion has often been an integral part of U.S. national poli-tics, from the founders' mix of Christianity and deism, to the late-nineteenth century "Social Gospel," to Christian Temperance moralism in the 1920s and 1930s, to the civil rights movement in the 1950s and 1960s, and to the rise of the Moral Majority and Christ-ian Right in recent decades. Indeed, in a September 2000 poll, 70 percent of U.S. adults agreed it was important "that a president have strong religious beliefs."[41] In short, a person of religious faith has been generally perceived as a good thing in U.S. politics. However, after September 11 George W. Bush offered a religious stripe rarely found in the White House—a staunch Christian conservative who, more than a few suggested, acted with the certainty that "God is on his side."[42] The president often has spoken of his "born-again" faith, and several other key members of the administration hold strong Christian beliefs, including Attorney General John Ashcroft, Commerce Secretary Donald Evans, and National Security Adviser Condaleezza Rice.[43] According to David Frum (2003), who worked as a Bush speechwriter in 2001–2, the presence of overt religiosity in the White House was such that "Bible study was, if not compulsory, not quite *uncompulsory*, either" (p. 4, his emphasis).

Notably, during the buildup to the Iraq war aides consistently claimed that the president's religious groundings did not "dictate policy" in the administration,[44] yet at times the president publicly cast his entire political agenda in a spiritual, particularly Christian, frame-work.[45] Indeed, it would be counter to the tenets of the president's faith for him *not* to ground the administration's policy decisions in his religious outlook. That Bush's politics are founded upon, not merely accompanied by, his faith is the view of many religious conser-vatives. When preparing to run for president in 1999, Bush met with leading pastors in Texas, asked for their prayers, and told them he'd been "called" to seek higher office.[46] During the campaign, when asked who he considered his favorite philosopher, Bush said, "Christ, because he changed my heart," a response that provoked cynicism and criticism among some in the press,[47] but resonated with others of devout faith.[48] Over time, U.S. religious conservatives so embraced Bush that, a *Washington Post* article opined, Pat Robertson's resignation as head of the Christian Coalition in December 2001 created little stir: "For the first time since religious conservatives became a modern political movement, the president of the United States has become the movement's de facto leader—a status even Ronald Reagan, though admired by religious conservatives, never earned" (Milbank, 2001, p. A-2). And on the eve of the 2004 presidential campaign, Robertson predicted on his *700 Club* television program on the Christian Broadcast Network that Bush would be re-elected in a "blowout" because whatever Bush does, "good or bad, God picks him up because he's a man of prayer and God's blessing him."[49]

What makes all of this important is that it seems almost inevitable that a religiously conservative president—already inclined to see the hand of God in most happenings—and his matching constituency would interpret any nation-challenging crisis occurring on his watch as his *raison d'être*. As a result, such political leaders become likely to view their present station in life as a God-ordained "calling," an outlook that imbues—in their eyes, at least—subsequent policies and actions with a magnitude of moral certainty.[50] As will become clear in this book, considerable evidence suggests that such an interpretation of the September 11 events and subsequent "war on terrorism" took hold among the Bush administration, particularly for the president. For example, in his address to Congress and the nation on September 20, 2001, the president declared:

> Great harm has been done to us. We have suffered great loss. And in our grief and anger, *we have found our mission and our moment.* Freedom and fear are at war. The advance of human freedom, the great achievement of our time and the great hope of every time, now depends on us.... Fellow citizens, we'll meet violence with patient justice—*assured of the rightness of our cause,* and confident of the victories to come.
> (Bush, 2001e, emphasis added)

Such a statement was an example of how the Bush administration adapted a conservative religious foundation that of a missionary project and righteousness—into a moral and resonant political language that also made clear the administration had little inclination for public debate about these matters. At the heart of this process was the manner in which a conservative religious worldview structured the administration's public communications—which leads to the lynchpin of the Bush administration's political fundamentalism.

## Strategic Political Communications

The presence of a nation-challenging crisis would foster among the U.S. public and governing leaders a swell of support for any administration; further, a religiously conservative administration's interpretation of the conflict as a defining "mission" and "moment" for the nation undoubtedly marked a significant start on a compelling narrative. At the same time, this support would not be offered in perpetuity. Whether an administration—religiously inclined or not—turned it into political capital would be ultimately dependent upon factors considerably of their own making, particularly the ability to engender favorable impressions of their competence, integrity, and vision. Bush's team, therefore, had to find ways to entice and persuade, not alienate. Insight into how they did so can be found in an understanding of the power of language and, in turn, communication. Language, as the primary medium of interchange between humans and reality, serves a constitutive role in shaping how individuals understand their social worlds.[51] Specifically, language, as the building block of all communication, simultaneously reflects various cultural forces while contributing to the relations, identities, and institutions which lie behind those structures. That is, choices about language and forms of communication do not occur merely after people have evaluated the world and wish to communicate about it; rather, language and communication patterns themselves are fundamental to the processes by which humans construct, understand, and act in their social worlds. Our words simultaneously represent and bring into being certain ways of thinking, feeling, and acting.

Put simply, language makes us who we are. One's interactions with and experience of intersecting social, political, and cultural relations gain meaning only through language. As a result, we might conceive of all communication about a topic, such as an address by the president, congressional testimony by an administration Cabinet member, or a news story or editorial, as drawing upon and, in some important degree, *constructing*, *reproducing* or *challenging* broader ways of understanding that define, describe, delimit, and circumscribe how a subject is "talked about."[52] That is, all communication

[ 17 ]

*forces* individuals to agree with, accept, or reject the ideas presented. Like it or not, we are compelled to adjust our understandings of the world and senses of identity whenever we encounter discourse. Further, in this process communications crafted for and disseminated by mainstream mass media take on particular importance because of their ability to suggest certain culture-wide norms, values, and expectations. Communication theorist Stuart Hall argues, in particular, that the representations and images promulgated in news media content suggest certain "common sense" ways of understanding the world that emphasize simplicity over complexity and often uphold existing power relations.[53] Messages disseminated widely through the press, therefore, are crucial to establishing the range of criteria for constructing, debating, and resolving social issues.

From this perspective, the public communications of the Bush administration might be viewed as the crucial mechanism in propagating a religiously grounded, politically focused ideology—that is, a political fundamentalism—as *the* appropriate approach to fighting terrorism. In a nation of omnipresent mass media and a citizenry whose "news interest" after September 11 rose to levels not seen for at least a decade and remained high through the Iraq war,[54] the president and his administration were remarkably effective at what political scientist Jarol Manheim has termed "strategic political communications"—that is, the crafting of public language and communication approaches with the goal to create, control, distribute, and use mediated messages as a political resource.[55] All politicians communicate strategically, yet some give strategy more thought and some, not always the same ones, are more effective than others.[56] Lakoff (1996) contends that U.S. political conservatives, in particular, are effective at strategic "moral politics" because they have spent substantial time in recent decades

> carefully working out their values, comprehending their myths, and designing a language to fit those values and myths so that they can evoke them with powerful slogans, repeated over and over again, that reinforce those family–morality–policy links [that conservatives believe in], until the connections have come to seem natural to many people in the United States, including many in the media. (p. 19)

The political conservatives most likely to effectively meld ideology with popular language, Lakoff suggested, are those who see a clear religious foundation to the moral order.[57] One such individual is George W. Bush, who long has been known for his discipline in adhering to a carefully crafted communication approach of being "on message"—that is, consistently focused on the few key points he wishes to make. Under the tutelage of long-time Bush strategist Karl Rove (and, previously, Karen Hughes), this on-message approach became a hallmark of the entire administration after September 11.[58] Quite simply, it was rare for a key administration member to publicly offer an opinion counter to or divergent from the president's.[59]

Message consistency across an administration is not easily accomplished, but it is noteworthy that it was a defining characteristic of the Reagan presidency in the 1980s.[60] At the same time, two components of the Bush administration's strategic communications after September 11 were distinct from previous administrations. One was the creation of what Lakoff and Johnson (1980) have called an "orientational metaphor"—in the case of this administration, the "war on terrorism"—that surpassed the strategic power of the Cold War frame in that it had a mass media-disseminated central organizing image, the terrorist attacks of September 11, which the administration and U.S. popular culture constantly referenced.[61]

A second notable aspect of the administration's strategic communications was the delivery by the president of more than a dozen televised national addresses between September 11 and May 1, 2003, an unprecedented pace among modern presidents. These addresses significantly facilitated control over public discourse in ways unmatched by previous administrations, and made it difficult for the far less unified Democratic Party to mount an effective counter-challenge.[62] In combination, these forms of strategic communication allowed the administration to enact discourses that were consistent across leaders, organized around a visually omnipresent central narrative, and were often delivered directly to the public. All of this was crucially important after September 11, when other politicians, journalists, and citizens were paying close attention to the administration's leadership cues.

**An Echoing Press**

In the United States, news media have considerable latitude to choose what to cover and how to cover it. The extent of government influence over media waxes and wanes across administrations, but it is the case that the mainstream press is thought to be largely *independent*. A primary reason for this independence, at least from government, is that U.S. news media tend to be commercial entities, funded centrally by advertising and marginally by subscriptions. In theory, this reliance on private monies provides the U.S. press with great freedom to choose when to criticize and when to support the government, various social institutions, or key cultural actors. All of this, however, assumes social and political milieus of "normalcy." Everything changes with the onset of a crisis, particularly one with the power to challenge the nation; in such contexts, habitual ways of working by the news media and unconscious allegiances to the home country become amplified in the news industry. With this in mind, a theory of an *echoing press* is offered here as a means to understand the role and actions of ostensibly independent news media in times of national crisis.

Citizens rally in support of U.S. political leaders during crises, in the process adopting a posture of support for an administration. Nationalism, also commonly labeled "patriotism," is accentuated. The solidity of this posture varies, of course, but a starting point of increased willingness to support the president engenders a general public opinion toward the administration that is moved less easily by valence news coverage—that is, positive or negative treatment—than in times of normalcy.[63] Further, in crisis periods a president and other administration leaders often speak directly to the public, so that news representations of an administration are no longer the sole, or perhaps even primary, means for individuals to form their political impressions. As a result, news *treatment* of the administration—that is, the degree of positive or negative support for the president suggested within news coverage—becomes less important than whether the administration can craft a resonant message, convey that message directly to the public, *and* have it amplified widely in the press.

This suggestion that news echoing of the administration's discourse trumps news treatment of the administration in times of crisis might be considered a modified version of the communication strategy espoused by Michael Deaver during the Reagan presidency. In one famous instance, retold in several places and borrowed here from Bennett (2003), CBS News correspondent Lesley Stahl put together a long report showing the gap between Reagan's carefully styled news images and his actual policies. Bennett continues the story:

Stahl was nervous about the piece because of its critical tone and the practice of the White House Communications Office to call reporters and their employers about negative coverage. The phone rang after the report was aired, and it was "a senior White House official." Stahl prepared herself for the worst. In her own words, here is what happened:

And the voice said, "Great piece."

I said, "What?"

And he said, "Great piece!"

I said, "Did you listen to what I said?"

He said, "Lesley when you're showing four-and-a-half minutes of great pictures of Ronald Reagan, no one listens to what you say. Don't you know that the pictures are overriding your messages because they conflict with your message? The public sees those pictures and they block your message. They didn't even hear what you said. So, in our minds, it was a four-and-a-half minute free ad for the Ronald Reagan campaign for reelection."

(Bennett, 2003, pp 148–9)

For the Reagan administration, therefore, the "Deaver Rule" decreed that how the press treated the administration was less important than whether the press presented the images chosen and crafted by the administration; that is, press criticisms of the administration were willingly tolerated if news media emphasized the administration's desired images. In the post-September 11 era, memory of the burning World Trade Center towers is readily primed among U.S. residents, to the rhetorical advantage of the Bush administration. In the context of this ever-present crisis image, the new "Rove Rule" might be that press treatment of the administration is much less important than whether the press gives consistent voice to the *words and ideas* crafted by the administration. That is, critical news coverage of the administration is willingly tolerated as long as the criticisms nonetheless echo the administration's preferred discourse.

And indeed, a combination of individual and institutional factors made it likely for U.S. news media after September 11 to consistently give voice to and stay focused upon the Bush administration's messages. First, since most journalists are citizens of the nation that they cover, they possess many of the same cultural values and beliefs as other members of the nation—values and beliefs that act as an ethnocentric filter through which news content is produced, particularly coverage of U.S. involvement in international events.[64] Second, journalists rely heavily upon government leaders as news sources generally,[65] and particularly so early in crises and in national security contexts.[66] These factors, then, suggest that Zaller's (1994b) claim that during crises "national unity [is] good politics" (p. 267) might be adapted to suggest that national unity is also good *business* for news institutions during such times. For example, after September 11 many leading U.S. news organizations, including national television networks, incorporated the colors of red, white, and blue into their promotions and identifying logos during this period. Similarly, in a less jingoistic display of national unity, others in the press might have emphasized the ideas of administration leaders and chosen to consistently frame news coverage around their perspectives rather than seek out alternative perspectives.

In the post-September 11 United States, one additional influence on the press was present. During the 1980s and 1990s the conservative right's sophisticated network of activists, operatives, and media pundits and talk show hosts increasingly leveled allegations of "liberal media" at mainstream news organizations and came to dominate political talk radio programming.[67] In this milieu, Fox News Channel was launched in 1996 with a stated agenda of providing a "fair and balanced" counter-voice to other media, and saw its public popularity and stature among conservatives soar during the 2000 election impasse; afterward, Republican Senate leader Trent Lott said, "If it hadn't been for Fox, I don't know what I'd have done for the news" (quoted in Kurtz, 2001a). Following September 11, Fox consistently surpassed cable rival CNN in the ratings by offering what some critics saw as an overly nationalistic picture of reality.[68] Fox subsequently has come to dominate cable television news, ending 2002 ahead of CNN and receiving the highest ratings in its history during the Iraq war.[69] In response, third-ranked cable network MSNBC undertook a number of strategies, several of which moved the network to the political right.[70] The importance of the rise of Fox and this shift among cable networks resides in the 24/7 nature of these media outlets, which substantially drives political rhetoric and shapes news discourse in other mainstream news media outlets.[71]

To be clear, then, the argument here is not that U.S. news media emphasized the same messages to exactly the same extent as the Bush administration after September 11; that would imply that the commercial, independent news media were merely government mouthpieces. Similarly, this perspective recognizes that news media do sometimes staunchly criticize administration ideas, particularly when other political leaders speak out against the administration.[72] However, the combination of the administration's strategic crafting of its public communications, the reticence of other political leaders to oppose the president, *and* the individual and institutional biases routinized in the news industry made it likely that any criticisms raised in news coverage remained within the parameters of thinking established by the Bush team. As a result, the mainstream press's probing of administration policies, ideas, and language would have been largely predictable—a dynamic that allowed the administration to preemptively delimit criticisms and to engender news coverage that consistently emphasized desired administration discourses. In a time of national crisis such as that triggered by September 11, then, the viewpoints proffered by a strategically adroit presidential administration are likely to be consistently echoed in the mainstream press as the "objective" picture of reality.

In sum, these four dimensions—nation-challenging crisis, conservative religious political leaders, strategic political communications by the same leaders, and an echoing press—provide a conceptual framework for understanding how political fundamentalism might (re)emerge, gain wide public presentation, and receive a favorable hearing in the United States. None of these is a sufficient causal mechanism by itself. For example, the onset of a nation-challenging crisis is a crucial instigating force, but it does not determine the response or the direction of political leadership. Entman (2003) has noted that the Bush administration in its reaction to September 11 "might have identified other enemies, chosen other ways of interpreting and responding to the attacks" than the avenues it pursued (p. 416). At the same time, the presence of conservative religious views among political leaders may aid an administration in the crafting of a familiar, moral vision, but such individuals might never figure out how to infuse such an outlook into policies and public communications without neglecting or repelling wide numbers of the public. Indeed, this was the fate of several U.S. presidential candidacies by religious conservatives in recent decades, several of whom became non-contenders because their political message was perceived as too far to the right, extremist, overtly flaunting Christian fundamentalism, and alienating.

The other two components of the framework are similarly insufficient to enact political fundamentalism. An administration's strategic communications clearly can influence both news coverage and public opinion, yet rarely can political leaders significantly mobilize a nation toward dramatic goals without a crisis context. Indeed, the onset of a nation-challenging crisis triggered by an external actor was a crucial foundation upon which the Bush administration capitalized. In like manner, political leaders can strategically use religious language or draw upon religious outlooks in attempting to define issues in moral terms, but unless such rhetoric is consistent with policy expectations such an approach is politically doomed among the religious conservatives most likely to find these actions attractive—as devout Southern Baptist Jimmy Carter learned when he chose policy directions opposed by many in this camp. Thus, strategic political communication, while crucial, cannot solely account for a rise of political fundamentalism.

The final component of the conceptual model is the press. While financially independent from government for the most part, mainstream news media in the United States nonetheless rely far too much upon political and cultural elites as sources in their news coverage, and upon established institutions for advertising support, to lead the way on most matters of public interest. That is, the press has great ability to amplify or to challenge the ideas of particular political actors, but has little inclination or ability to mount a sustained political campaign. The nature of the news media is to follow and to replicate, but not to generate ideologies. As a result, political fundamentalism can certainly be disseminated through the press, but has almost no chance of originating there.

## AN OVERVIEW OF THE EVIDENCE AND IMPLICATIONS

A convergence of all four of these conceptual components—crisis, conservative religious political leaders, strategic political communications by the same leaders, and an echoing press—may seem improbable in the United States. But it certainly seems less improbable than prior to September 11, 2001, the date when the world's sole superpower learned that a nation-challenging crisis was only a moment away. With this in mind, this opening chapter offers a framework that shows the entry point at which political fundamentalism would likely (re)emerge, gain wide public presentation, and receive a favorable hearing in the U.S. political and media systems. The following four chapters contain close study of the inter-relationships among the final three components of this framework to uncover how the Bush administration so effectively capitalized upon the September 11 crisis. Systematic analysis of a wide range of administration members' addresses, remarks, and exchanges with news media revealed four distinct and patterned characteristics of their communications that were grounded in a conservative religious worldview, but were strategically presented and applied in political terms. In each chapter, one of these characteristics is defined and discussed, and then evidence is offered of (a) its consistent presence in the administration's public communications between September 11 and May 2003, and (b) the echoing response of a large segment of U.S. news media to these communications. The characteristics are as follows:

*A binary conception of reality.* Religious fundamentalism sets black-and-white boundaries through the establishment of rigid norms and behavioral codes. That is, it conceives of the world as a place of absolutist rules and relations that serve as guideposts for how people think, talk, and live. This archetypal component of fundamentalism is at the core of an administration headed by a president who once said, "In Texas, we don't do nuance."[73] To be specific, the Bush administration offered a conception of political reality that emphasized *binaries*, an unbending form of thinking and language that parses people, institutions, behaviors, and ideologies into opposing "camps." In the words of Burke (1945/1969), a binary conception is "the placement of one thought or thing in terms of its opposite" (p. 403); that is, the world is consistently presented as a place of clearly demarcated and opposing groupings, with no opportunities for alternative ground. Chapter 2 examines the presence of two binaries in the president's discourse and news coverage after September 11—good versus evil and security versus peril—and argues that these conceptions of reality reflected and contributed to a sense of moral certitude among the Bush administration that was used to justify limits on civil liberties, a dismissal of United Nations conventions, and major preemptive military action while also helping to engender consistent public support for the president and the administration's "war on terrorism." The use of binaries in the administration's rhetoric effectively made all, including those in the press and the public, either a friend or an enemy; and in a time of high fear, being a foe was far from desirable.

*An obsession with time.* For religious fundamentalists, the possibility that the world may end, as Ammerman (1991) phrased it, at "any moment," infuses ideas and behavior with an over-riding urgency. Indeed, the biblical words of Jesus declare that believers should "keep on the alert; for you do not know when the appointed time [of Christ's return] may come." For Christian fundamentalists, this constant perception of limited time impels *imminent action* and, in a related manner, *unremitting calls for more action* on behalf of their causes. Further, this urgency imperative becomes simultaneously heightened and solidified when circumstances, such as a crisis or conflict, prompt people to see their actions as "part of God's plan for history" (Harding, 1994, p. 58). Individuals then attach an eternal dimension to their words and actions, with the result being an increased willingness to enter into an *enduring commitment*, during which one derives sustenance from seeing one's self and role as part of a long-running drama. It is a chance for commoners to enter the mythic realm of their own faith. That President Bush viewed his role as part of a divine unfolding of events with eternal consequences is apparent; that he included himself into the mythologizing of recent history is part of the problem. Chapter 3 offers evidence of these time fixations throughout the administration's discourse and news coverage, and argues that they allowed the administration simultaneously to push for immediate action on specific "war on terrorism" policies and to justify this desire as a requisite step in a long-term, God-ordained process. Further, the implication—sometimes made explicit—was clear: to not act quickly or to not endure in the campaign against terrorism was to risk another September 11. Indeed, death and the apocalypse were perpetually imminent.

*A belief in a universal gospel.* Religious fundamentalists conceive of their beliefs as providing what Lawrence (1989) has called "mandated universalist norms" that cross cultural and historical contexts. As a result, these beliefs are to be shared with all peoples—a perspective made clear by the biblical command of "go therefore and make disciples of all the nations." This outlook among fundamentalists compels them to impose "what they take to be God's will upon other people" because others are viewed as certain to benefit (Perkin,

2000, p. 79). Hence all of their actions become part of "the mission" and they become the missionaries, the keepers of the only truth imaginable. A belief in universal norms and the necessity of acting in ways that defended and extended these principles was particularly manifest after September 11 in the communications of President Bush, who consistently presented *freedom* and *liberty* as the noblest motivations, highest aspirations, and God's wishes for all peoples. Evidence is offered in Chapter 4 of how this universal gospel of freedom and liberty, offered by the president and echoed by the press, functioned as a central rationale for the administration's foreign policies, particularly in justifying the new preemptive doctrine and the Iraq war. This emphasis, in turn, facilitated the necessary reconstruction of what Niebuhr (1967) has called a nation's positive "social myth": a culturally embedded narrative that distinguishes a nation from others, justifies its existence and establishes a sense of superiority over others. In reconstructing this myth, the Bush administration helped to restore U.S. citizens' positive self-image but in so doing closed off potential discussion of the preemptive doctrine, especially questions about whether such actions are imperialistic and antithetical to a nation espousing democratic ideals.

*An intolerance for dissent.* Considerable scholarship has linked religious fundamentalism with authoritarian decision-making and behavior. One way in which this linkage manifests itself is that, in Garvey's (1993) words, "the most ambitious fundamentalists would prefer to stamp out all forms of dissent" (p. 24). For the Bush administration, this urge to suppress dissent was apparent in two ways. First, the administration consistently exhibited a unified *voice* in public communications, a carefully undertaken approach that helped to control public discourse. The message never veered, which meant the choices for rebuttal were always limited. Second, the administration infused its public communications with requests for other political actors to *act with political unity*, particularly in support of the administration's goals. While an emphasis upon unity within diversity long has been a staple of U.S. presidential rhetoric,[74] the Bush administration's emphasis on unity in a context of crisis provided a platform from which the White House could adroitly characterize any strong disagreement as not in the interests of U.S. citizens. Indeed, the administration accompanied these approaches with imposition of a significant *cost* for dissent, both among individuals internal to the administration and for other political actors who chose not to stand with the president. Chapter 5 focuses on how the administration's emphasis upon political unity and harsh rebukes of those who dissented worked together to encourage support for the administration, and to suggest that anyone who held opposing views was unpatriotic and potentially placing people in the United States at risk.

Chapter 6 reflects upon the collection of evidence, in three central sections. First, it argues that the Bush administration offers an instructive case study—consistent with the proposed conceptual framework—of how political fundamentalism can gain wide support in the United States. The particularly key attribute was the administration's ability to craft a strategic communications approach, grounded in a conservative religious worldview that effectively controlled public discourse in the anxious world of terrorism. Five characteristics of the administration's language and communications strategies are discussed, with a focus on how these capitalized upon and contributed to the other dimensions in the conceptual framework. The chapter's second section scrutinizes the role of news media in these processes, with the argument that in a nation-challenging context, commercial mass media—although ostensibly independent—are drawn to the discourses of political conservatives, particularly those that are religiously grounded. Specifically, the routines and practices that dominate mainstream journalism prompt reporters to see great news value in the language of political fundamentalism, while the financial imperatives of commercial mass media accentuate the merits of appealing to U.S. political conservatives. These characteristics make news media highly likely to echo political fundamentalist discourse. The final section of the chapter explores how cultural leaders might craft a moral discourse that counters the predominance of political fundamentalism, and why it is crucial for U.S. citizens and others that they do so. In the words of Lakoff (1996), political progressives in particular currently do not have "an adequate language to reflect their moral politics" (p. 386). Drawing upon both the legacy of liberal-democratic principles and insights from the Bush administration's strategic communications in the aftermath of September 11, four suggestions are made for how such a language might be crafted.

Chapter 7 offers conclusions, focusing on implications of the administration's political fundamentalism for democracy, both in the

United States and globally. The central argument is that fundamental-ism in the White House is remarkably similar in its rhetorical forms to that of the network of terrorists the administration claims to be fighting. Both offer closed ways of thinking, link temporal actions with eternal consequences, claim the universality of their norms, and are intolerant toward dissent. The administration, in particular, has built its discourses and actions upon fear, embedding this as the predominant U.S. emotion since September 11. Indeed, whether an administration with a worldview rooted in religious fundamentalism can engage in reasoned, open, and public deliberation is doubtful. The book concludes by arguing that the dispelling of fear is the necessary foundational step in the reclaiming of democracy, and suggests that a wide number of U.S. institutions, but particularly Congress and the mainstream news media, need to play central roles in this process. Most substantially, only when the mainstream press function as a bulwark against governmental oppression, rather than a buttressing of it, will a renewal of democratic ideals be possible.

# 2
# Marking boundaries

In the aftermath of September 11, 2001, George W. Bush became the unchallenged voice of the U.S. government. In a remarkably short period of time, the president evolved from a politician routinely mocked for his linguistic shortcomings to one hailed for his "steel and eloquence" ("Bush exudes strength," 2001). This transformation occurred in full public view, as Bush spoke several times to national television audiences in the weeks following the terrorist attacks. Perhaps the most important of these communications was his national address before a joint session of Congress on September 20, during which the president declared, "Every nation, in every region, now has a decision to make. Either you are with us, or you are with the terrorists" (Bush, 2001e). This statement had clear rhetorical power at the time, and subsequently became something even more important—the foundational policy of the Bush administration's "war on terrorism." As the president said in October 2002, "The doctrine that says, 'Either you're with us or with the enemy,' still holds. It's an important doctrine. It's as important today as it was 13 months ago" (Bush, 2002m).

This declaration by the president was notable for one other reason—it is an archetypal example of an either/or construction of reality. As will be discussed in this chapter, such *binary* constructions are simultaneously grounded in a fundamentalist worldview while being well suited for a U.S. political culture dominated by mass media. What made the president's binary communications so important was that they presented a limited, rigid view of the world and forced decisions between two options that, in actuality, were not the only possible outcomes. Binaries were at the heart of the Bush administration's political fundamentalism following September 11. With this in mind, a conception of *binary discourse* is offered in this chapter and used to examine both the president's national addresses from his inauguration in January 2001 to his calling of an end to "major combat operations" in Iraq on May 1, 2003, and the editorial response of 20 leading U.S. newspapers to these communications. This analysis is a particularly appropriate place to begin examination of the administration's public communications because these national addresses reached large audiences and thereby provided a constant backdrop for the thoughts and actions of other U.S. political actors and residents. For example, 82 million U.S. residents watched the president's address before Congress on September 20, the second-largest audience in 2001 after the Super Bowl, while the 2003 State of the Union had an audience of 62 million.[1] In short, the president had significant access to a large portion of U.S. public opinion during these addresses. Whether he could sway the public in the administration's favor, though, depended upon the ideas and words that he chose to emphasize.

## FUNDAMENTALISM, BINARIES, AND STRATEGIC COMMUNICATION

Religious fundamentalism "excels" at being a "boundary-setter" by establishing rigid norms and behavioral codes.[2] That is, it conceives of the world as a place of absolutist rules that serve as guideposts for how people *should* think, talk, and act. In the words of Nagata (2001), a fundamentalist conception of reality "simplifies complex issues, makes black and white out of gray zones and attempts to restore certainty" in an uncertain world (p. 494). Similarly, Lakoff (1996) has argued that a religiously grounded conception of the moral order is the foundation on which ideologically "prototypical" political conservatives—such as some in the Bush administration—see the world in black or white terms (see pp. 65–107). This boundary-marking characteristic of fundamentalism was at the core of this administration after September 11, when it offered a conception of political reality that parsed people, institutions, behaviors, and ideologies into opposing "camps." Such binary thinking and language, in the words of Burke (1945/1969), might be defined as "placement of one thought or thing in terms of its opposite" (p. 403).[3] This rhetorical move, when carefully constructed, can railroad an audience's thinking into an "all or nothing," "us versus them" mentality. When forced into only two choices, the easiest path is to choose either this or that rather than to push for the exploration of potentially other, more complex solutions. Binaries, then, allow a speaker to seize control over audience cognition—particularly when the audience is predisposed to a position of support, as was the case for the U.S. public toward President Bush after September 11—and to convert that power subsequently into maximal gain.

The centrifugal binary for religious fundamentalists is good versus evil. A conception of reality as a struggle between these opposing forces is at the core of Christian thought, found throughout the Bible in notions of light versus darkness, pure versus impure, and righteous versus sinful. Marty and Appleby argue:

> [A] very sharp line can be drawn in the fundamentalist world, a line where good and bad, true and false, right and wrong get bartered and defined. Closely associated with the end-time thought of fundamentalisms is the embracing of a dualistic worldview which sharply divides the world into God's versus Satan's, Good versus Evil. The dualisms are extreme for a reason: they help fundamentalists see the enemy clearly and without flinching.
>
> (Marty and Appleby, 1992, p. 29)

In the words of Hunsberger (1996), religious fundamentalists "believe they are opposed by powerful, evil forces in this world, including other religions, which must be vigorously fought" (p. 48). In the everyday United States, this worldview commonly engenders among Christian conservatives a hostility toward—rather than merely disagreement with—those who are perceived to represent impurity or evil, including homosexuals, criminals, and "radicals" challenging the government.[4] An irrational sense of threat underlies these perceptions, which nonetheless become viewed as divinely desired acts in the mind of the believer. Notably, since "good" language is commonplace in U.S. politics, particularly in regard to the character of the United States, the key discursive indicator of a binary conception of reality among fundamentalists is an emphasis upon "evil."[5] Claims about evil are found almost solely among conservative politicians, particularly religious ones who see the naming of someone or something as evil to be a statement against the perceived creeping moral relativism of U.S. society. In the aftermath of September 11, the president, according to long-time close friend U.S. Commerce Secretary Don Evans, drew upon his religious groundings to formulate "a very clear sense of what is good and what is evil" (in Fineman, 2003, p. 25), a viewpoint that Bush consistently communicated in public settings.

A conception of the September 11 acts and actors as evil hardly required a fundamentalist worldview, of course—although it is difficult to imagine a political liberal being the first to make such a claim (former President Bill Clinton, a Democrat, used the word "evil" only twice in his seven State of the Union addresses). Stronger evidence that a fundamentalist worldview undergirded the Bush administration's policies and communications between September 2001 and spring 2003 would be the presence of *multiple binary constructions*. And indeed, after September 11 the president employed a second binary of security versus peril, which pitted an external danger reminiscent of the Soviet threat that Ivie (1990) labeled the "prevailing image" of Cold War discourse against matters of U.S. national security.[6] This binary was an ideal rhetorical complement to good versus evil: Both have great moral power and were boundary-marking communications, but security versus peril tempered the explicit religious foundation of good versus evil. Use of them together, then, allowed the administration to offer a broader political, rather than clearly religious, fundamentalism. At the same time, both binaries foundationally highlighted fear, perhaps the most widely shared sentiment by U.S. residents after the attacks; that the president incorporated fear into his *core* discourses in the "war on terrorism" speaks volumes about how the administration viewed the world and sought to capitalize upon this sense of collective vulnerability. Finally, both binaries were adequately expansive to provide the administration with a crucial discursive bridge from the September 11 events to the domestic policy creation of a Department of Homeland Security and foreign policy turn toward Iraq.

Binary constructions are not merely intriguing conceptions of reality, however: They constrain political discourse in important ways. First, they function to eliminate or marginalize potential thought and action by suggesting that only certain avenues are worthy of consideration.[7] Second, binary constructions inevitably create a hierarchy among the paired objects. Derrida (1972/1981) has contended that the opposing sides of a binary construction do not have a "peaceful coexistence," but rather tend to exist as a "violent hierarchy" in which "one term governs the other ... or has the upper hand" (p. 41). Similarly, Carr and Zanetti (1999) have argued that binary constructions powerfully suggest, "if one position is right, then the other must be wrong" (p. 324). Such a choice-limiting form of communication had great importance between autumn 2001 and spring 2003, when several decisions were faced. The administration had to choose an appropriate response to the terrorist attacks, and other nations had to decide whether or to what extent they would support this response. Congress had to vote on the U.S.A. Patriot Act almost immediately, and then in 2002 took up the formation of a Cabinet-level Department of Homeland Security and a resolution granting the president authority to disarm Iraq by force. And the U.S. public had to decide how to live with a suddenly elevated sense of fear and anxiety, which re-emerged at moments over time. In this context, the president and administration, by consistently positioning political goals and ideas in terms of seeming opposites, suggested that their position was appropriate and that any others were wrong or, at a minimum, out of political bounds. To step outside the Bush administration's binary markers implied risk, threat, and—with the omnipresent shadow of September 11—possibly death.

One way to gain insight into the administration's binary discourse is through examination of the president's national addresses. The crisis context initiated by September 11 and sustained through the Iraq threat, in combination with the strategic political value of these binaries, made it likely that the president employed the good/evil and security/peril binaries more often after September 11 than before. At its core, the president's discourse likely included placement of binary concepts in direct opposition to one another (for example, "us" versus "them," as in the president's declaration on September 20, 2001), which may have occurred in the same sentence or more broadly within a thought expression. Such overt juxtaposition of the concepts was necessary to make clear the binary being established, to make sure that the public "got the message." The rhetorical weight of such presentations almost certainly would diminish if omnipresent, however. As a result, the use of explicitly juxtaposed binary concepts by the administration likely was subsumed within a broader communications approach in which the concepts on either side of the binary were consistently highlighted as time passed. For example, once the binaries had been established, general emphasis over time by President Bush on the concept of "evil" even without explicit linkage to "good," or vice versa would have subtly reinforced a binary conception. Indeed, we will see later in this chapter that President Bush after September 11 was more likely to do both of these: place the opposing sides of good/evil and security/peril in direct opposition, and give a sustained presence to each side of the binaries independently across time.

## BINARY DISCOURSE AND AN ECHOING PRESS

Commercial news media have considerable individual, institutional, and economic motivations to become especially attuned to the views of political leaders during times of national crisis. These factors do not mean that news media automatically become what Zaller and Chiu (1996) have termed "government's little helper" during nation-challenging periods, but the combination of these forces certainly encourages mainstream news media to favorably respond to a presidential administration—provided that the administration offers leadership. In the eyes of many people in the United States, including a number employed in the news media, President Bush did just this with his September 20, 2001, address to the nation. Consider the perspective of *Washington Post* columnist Richard Cohen:

> In *Band of Brothers*, the Stephen Ambrose book and the HBO television series, the sergeants of Easy Company stage something of a mutiny. Having lost faith in the leadership abilities of their commanding officer, Herbert Sobel, they demand that he be replaced, saying they would not follow such a man into combat. Until Thursday night, that's about how I felt about George W. Bush.
>
> Until his televised speech to a joint session of Congress, the president had been occasionally wobbly, somewhat tentative and diminished in stature. He seemed unsure of himself, somehow shrunken in his clothes and—understandably—scared by the responsibilities he suddenly faced and for which he was, by background and intellectual habit, almost totally unprepared. Little by little, though, he gained confidence. He seemed emboldened by the heroism of others—those New York City firefighters, for instance. They did what they had to do because it was their job to do it. So it was to be with Bush and so, at least in that speech to the nation, did he rise to the occasion. ...
>
> [A] speech is more than words. It is theater. Winston Churchill understood that. His words set an unsurpassed standard for eloquence. But his effect also mattered—his delivery,

his pauses and his determination to venture out into still-smoking London. He became the face of Britain.

This—or something like it—was what Bush displayed Thursday evening. He seemed steadfast. He seemed determined. He seemed confident. He was the master of the moment, as much the leader of that room as a conductor is of his orchestra. He seemed—this is our American word for it—"presidential." ...

[T]he man who was a middling student, a boozer and towel-snapper, an incurious and intellectually inert business-man and governor who back-slapped his way into the presidency, emerged Thursday night as something we terribly needed. He was always the president. Now he is the commander in chief.

(Cohen, 2001)

Cohen's viewpoint about Bush's address was widely shared: In surveys conducted afterward, 81 percent of U.S. adults said their reaction toward the address was "very favorable" and 73 percent said the president provided them with "a better understanding of the way the terrorists will have to be fought" (NBC News Poll, 2001; *Newsweek* Poll, 2001). Clearly, Bush's rhetoric had worked. He had essentially unified a previously divided (post-2000 presidential election) nation and had extraordinary political capital at his disposal.

Having been so successful with this national address, Bush subsequently delivered nearly a dozen more before the "end" of major combat in Iraq in spring 2003, an unprecedented number by a U.S. president in the age of television. How the news media responded to his addresses—specifically, his binary discourse—over these months was of considerable importance. In particular, did news coverage echo his words and focus on his perspectives, thus disseminating and helping to entrench the administration's political fundamentalism among the U.S. public?

Binary constructions are certainly well suited for a media environment, for several reasons. First, binaries are simple and pithy, which allows them to be communicated and understood easily. Garvey (1993) suggests that simplicity helps to give religious fundamentalism "potential for mass appeal" because it offers "a kind of stripped-down" belief system "that travels light and fast" (p. 16), which is ideal for a sound bite, rhetoric-driven media and politics system *and* for restricting the range of public discourse. The use of binary oppositions also inherently suggests competition between two forces—exactly the sort of conflict that makes for a good news story.[8] Finally, binary conceptions, in part because they often are rooted in fundamentalism, almost without exception have moral power, which give them a resonance with the mass public and a sustaining news value, both crucial components in the ability of political elites to shape public sentiment.[9] For these reasons, then, a presidential emphasis on a binary conception of reality was likely to be echoed by the mainstream press. In fact, it would be quite odd for the press not to accept a message so well crafted to the needs of the news industry. The administration knew this full well.

One important arena of U.S. news coverage to examine for its response to the president is that of newspaper editorials. Scholars contend that editorial boards have a central role in interpreting events,[10] often serving as a source of "opinion leadership" for both citizens and members of Congress.[11] Indeed, Dalton, Beck, and Huckfeldt (1998) found that partisan cues in newspaper editorials, more than such cues in news content, influenced public views about presidential candidates. Editorials are a prime example of one of the more refined theories about media effects in which the public turns to opinion leaders in their community for an interpretation of world and political events, thereby saving their own cognitive energies for myriad other tasks of modern life. It is vital, therefore, to examine how newspaper editorial boards—as the *institutional voices* of the mainstream press—responded to the president's communications. Situated uniquely as key opinion leaders for both citizens and political leaders, editorial boards were likely to have been sensitive to both the nationalistic sentiment and heightened security concerns that arose in this nation-challenging crisis context. All of this increased the likelihood that news media generally and newspaper editorials, in particular, aligned closely with President Bush's communications after September 11; thus, if the president employed a binary discourse, editorials likely followed suit. This was the case, as we will see shortly.

## ANALYSIS OF DISCOURSE

Analyzed first were a total of 17 major addresses by the president, beginning with his inauguration on January 20, 2001, and ending with his address on the aircraft carrier U.S.S. *Abraham Lincoln* on May 1, 2003, in which he declared an end to significant combat in

Iraq. Editorials from 20 major U.S. newspapers were then analyzed for the two days following each of these addresses.

Presidential texts were compiled in two steps. First, from the National Archives and Records Administration's *Weekly Compilation of Presidential Documents*, a comprehensive collection of presidential public communications, all "addresses to the nation" during the dates of interest were retrieved, with one exception. The president's brief address on the evening of the explosion of space shuttle *Columbia* was excluded because of its brevity and narrow scope. Two more addresses were then added: the president's remarks at the National Cathedral in Washington D.C. on September 14, 2001, and his address to the United Nations General Assembly on September 12, 2002. The former was included because it occurred close to the attacks, its content ranged beyond a basic eulogy (unlike the *Columbia* address), and it was televised by broadcast and cable networks. The latter, also nationally televised, was included because of its significance in the buildup to war in Iraq—it was the first time that the president publicly articulated his desire to gain international support and remove Saddam Hussein.

Editorials that ran during the two days following each address were collected from 20 U.S. newspapers, selected because they are leading news outlets and offer geographic diversity. Editorials were retrieved from the Nexis database for the following newspapers: *Albuquerque Journal, Atlanta Journal and Constitution, Boston Globe, Chicago Sun-Times, Columbus Dispatch, Daily News* (New York), *Denver Post, Houston Chronicle, New York Times, Omaha World-Herald, Oregonian* (Portland), *Plain Dealer* (Cleveland), *San Diego Union-Tribune, San Francisco Chronicle, Seattle Times, Star Tribune* (Minneapolis), *St. Louis Post-Dispatch, Tampa Tribune, Times-Picayune* (New Orleans), and *Washington Post*. Content was retrieved by the search string of "editorial and (Bush or president)" in the headline, lead paragraph or key terms. This search retrieved 2,404 documents; irrelevant content (such as material that was not editorials or referred to presidents other than Bush) was discarded, leaving 326 editorials. The discarding of many texts is common in content analyses that utilize the Nexis database, because the goal is to create a search string that casts a wide net in finding news content, and then to dispose of irrelevant content manually.

The analysis of presidential addresses focused on the ideas present in each paragraph; that is, each paragraph in each address was examined for the presence of the binary categories (discussed below). This content analysis approach allowed identification of not just the presence of the binary concepts but also their *prevalence* in each address, so that relative emphases could be tracked over time. The paragraph breaks present in the addresses were followed. For newspaper editorials the analysis focused on the entire editorial due to the general brevity of editorials as well as their common focus on specific topics or themes. In addition, collection of editorials across 20 newspapers provided confidence that any meaningful shifts in editorial discourse would be captured. Also, because the newspapers were geographically diverse, regional differences would be accounted for, so that the analysis did not overly reflect a Northern, Southern, Western, or Midwestern perspective on events.

Presidential paragraphs and editorials were first analyzed for the presence of "complete" binaries—that is, when both sides were present *and* situated in such a manner that the juxtaposition of the terms was apparent. Often the terms were placed in the same sentence; in other cases, the terms were positioned together within a broader thought expression that nonetheless anchored the ideas as oppositional. This analysis was derived from these definitions:

*Good/evil*: This binary was considered present if the term good, or similar terms characterizing a moral goodness such as right, righteous, light, best, just, great, or honorable, was set in opposition to the term evil, or other similarly connotative terms such as wrong, dark, worst, unjust, cruel, sadistic, wicked, ruthless, or barbaric. Traditional "American values" adapted from Hutcheson et al. (2004) were also counted as good because of President Bush's usage of these values as inherently good. These values included freedom, life, liberty, democracy, justice, and innovation. Contrasts to "American values," such as the phrase "enemies of freedom," were thus counted as evil, as was the term "fear," which the president often placed in opposition to the U.S. value of freedom.

*Security/peril*: This binary was considered present if the term security, or similar terms such as safety, protection, or safeguard, was set in opposition to the term peril, or similar terms such as threat, risk, danger, or hazard. References to potential future attacks also were considered as peril, because of the inherent peril that existed with such a possibility. Notably, security was counted when it appeared in mention of the Office or Department of Homeland Security because the Office, then Department of Homeland Security emerged in response to September 11, so these institutional titles must be viewed as part of the administration's security discourse.

Three additional analyses were undertaken. First, presidential paragraphs and editorials were examined for any reference to either side of the binaries, which allowed over-time tracking in presidential addresses and newspaper editorials of emphasis on these distinct themes. Second, references to the September 11 attacks in presidential paragraphs and newspaper editorials were identified. Finally, whether the binaries were criticized in editorials was examined because it was possible that news media would both (a) use the language of the president and (b) be critical of such discourse. Any criticism in editorials of either side of the binaries was identified.[12]

## BINARIES: THE EVIDENCE

Both President Bush and newspaper editorials consistently made reference to the events of September 11. For the president, this suggested that the terrorist attacks served as a central organizing mechanism in a broader discursive approach, providing the foundational basis for invocation of the good/evil and security/peril binaries. Figure 2.1 shows that Bush referred to these events in all but two of the post-attacks addresses analyzed and that a sizeable percentage of editorials regularly did so, although these numbers diminished over time—similar to the way an echo would dissipate. The president did not mention September 11 when issuing his ultimatum to Saddam Hussein on March 17, 2003, or in his announcement of military action in Iraq two days later—notable instances that, it will be argued later in the chapter, were strategically motivated. The evidence, then, suggests that the president utilized the terrorist attacks as a key rhetorical weapon in organizing his discourse, and that editorials followed this emphasis closely. Let us turn, then, to analysis of the binaries.

### Good/Evil Binary

President Bush was much more likely to place the concepts of "good" and "evil" in direct opposition following the terrorist attacks. Comparison of the president's language in three addresses

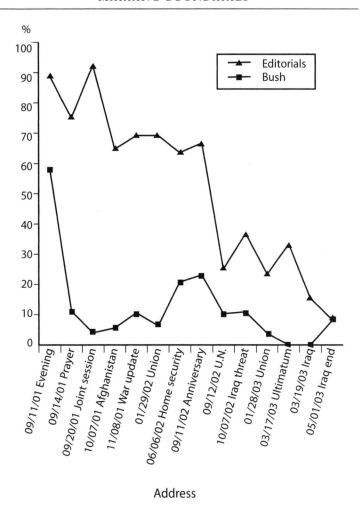

**Figure 2.1** September 11 references in Bush addresses by paragraph and in newspaper editorials in the two days following addresses

prior to the September 11 attacks with that used in 14 addresses afterward revealed that 2.4 percent of presidential paragraphs prior to September 11 contained "good" and "evil" language in a juxtaposed manner, compared with 6.5 percent of paragraphs after the attacks.[13] This means that the rate of the president's usage of this binary nearly tripled after September 11. In addition there was at least one clear juxtaposition of "good" and "evil" in each and every presidential address by Bush, except for his speech announcing military action in Iraq on March 19, 2003, which was the briefest address at 11 paragraphs.

Newspaper editorials also more commonly placed "good" and "evil" in direct opposition following the terrorist attacks: 1.7 percent of analyzed editorials prior to September 11 juxtaposed "good" and "evil" language, compared with 9.7 percent of editorials after the attacks.[14] Thus, the presence of this binary in newspaper editorials increased nearly six-fold. In sum, the president and newspaper editorials were significantly more likely to place "good" and "evil" in *direct opposition* after the September 11 attacks. Indeed, these emphases on the good/evil binary by the president and in newspaper editorials after September 11 made it almost certain that U.S. residents and the world "got the message" that anything less than outright support for the "war on terrorism" would be interpreted in hostile terms.

Turning to separate examinations of "good" and "evil" language—that is, regardless of whether these concepts were placed in direct opposition—Figure 2.2 shows distinct trajectories for these ideas across the president's addresses and newspaper editorials. "Good" terminology only increased marginally in *both* Bush's speeches (from 19 percent to 23 percent of paragraphs) and newspaper editorials (from 27 percent to 31 percent of these texts).[15] In contrast, the president's use of "evil" language increased more than three-fold after the terrorist attacks, rising from 4 percent to 14 percent of his paragraphs, while editorial emphasis on this concept increased from 22 percent to 38 percent over time.[16] These patterns are consistent with the expectation that "evil" language is the clear discursive indicator of a good/evil binary conception of reality, since "good" language is more common in U.S. political and news discourse. Normally, "good" would dominate the news, unless the press was being effectively steered towards greater use of the other half of the binary, "evil." This, of course, was exactly what happened. In addition, only two editorials offered criticisms of the president's emphasis on these concepts, with both narrowly focused on the president's "axis of evil" reference in the 2002 State of the Union address.

At the same time, despite the lack of increase in "good" terminology by the president after September 11, over-time analysis of "good" and "evil" in Bush's addresses indicated that both concepts had a sustained presence and seemingly were utilized together in a strategic

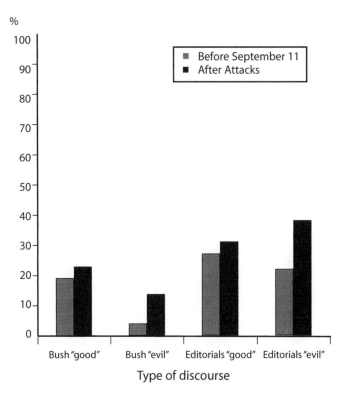

**Figure 2.2** "Good" and "evil" discourse in Bush addresses by paragraph and in newspaper editorials in the two days following addresses

manner, especially following September 11. The address-by-address correlation between the percentage of paragraphs containing "good" language and percentage of paragraphs containing "evil" language in the president's addresses was statistically very strong, indicating a close relationship between the presence of these ideas.[17] The supporting data are presented in Figure 2.3, which shows that the two sides of the binary moved in remarkable synchronicity, strongly suggesting a concerted discourse.

In addition, there was a distinct correspondence between the president and editorials that contained the "evil" discourse but far less of a link between the two for the "good" discourse.[18] These data, arrayed in Figures 2.4 and 2.5, show that editorials consistently echoed the president's emphasis upon "evil" but were

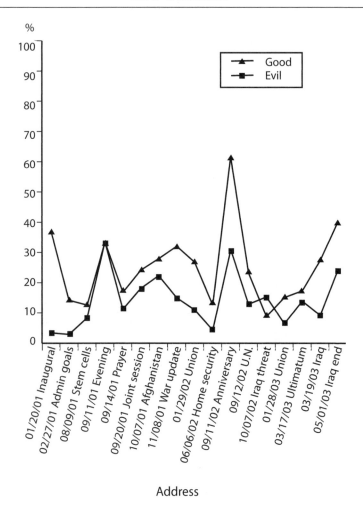

**Figure 2.3** "Good" and "evil" discourse in Bush addresses by paragraph

less consistently aligned with his accentuation of "good." Again, this is in line with the expectation that "evil" language would be the more noticeable entry in U.S. politics, and therefore more likely to be widely disseminated and closely paralleled by newspaper editorials.[19] It also may be noteworthy that the editorials analyzed following Bush's May 1, 2003, address calling an end to "major combat" in Iraq were generally less responsive (although

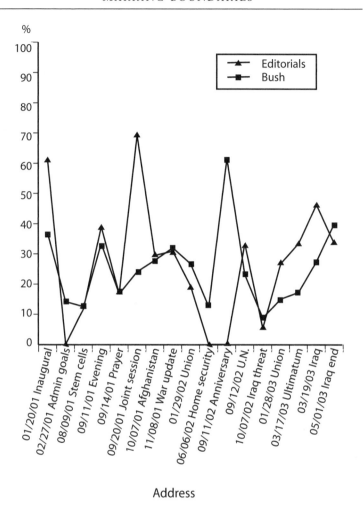

**Figure 2.4** "Good" discourse in Bush addresses by paragraph and in newspaper editorials in the two days following addresses

still responsive) to his claims of "good" and "evil," a particularly distinct occurrence for the latter concept. Perhaps the president's claims about finished business in Iraq were relatively less persuasive in the eyes of the press because Saddam Hussein remained at large at the time.

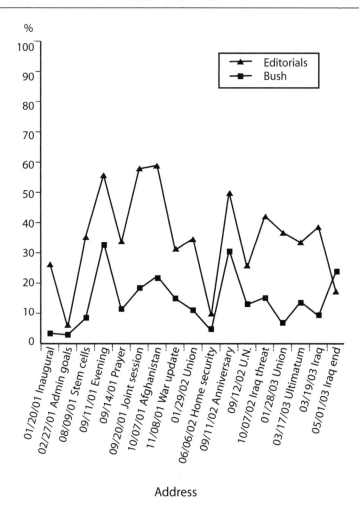

%

**Figure 2.5** "Evil" discourse in Bush addresses by paragraph and in newspaper editorials in the two days following addresses

Excerpts (a) from the president's addresses provide insight into these strategic emphases on "good" and "evil" ideas, and (b) from newspaper editorials are indicative of the press's echoing of this terminology. On the evening of September 11, 2001, for example, the president said, "Today our nation saw evil, the very worst of human nature. And we responded with the best of America" (Bush, 2001a). Speaking before Congress and a national television audience on September 20, Bush again juxtaposed "good" and "evil" concepts, adding a clear religious stamp: "Freedom and fear, justice and cruelty have always been at war, and we know that God is not neutral between them" (Bush, 2001e). Months later in his 2002 State of the Union address, Bush sounded an optimistic note: "I know we can overcome evil with a greater good" (Bush, 2002a). The president continued this rhetorical path in his State of the Union address the following year: "America is a strong nation and honorable in the use of our strength," and he characterized Saddam Hussein as such: "If this is not evil, then evil has no meaning" (Bush, 2003a). Slightly more than three months later in announcing an end to "major combat operations" in Iraq, the president said, "Those we lost were last seen on duty. Their final act on this earth was to fight a great evil and bring liberty to others" (Bush, 2003e).

Some editorials adopted the president's discourse directly. The *Cleveland Plain Dealer* noted "George W. Bush has cast the war against international terrorism as a fight that pits 'good versus evil.'" The newspaper went on to agree with the president's characterization: "There are times and issues when right and wrong are colored in shades of gray, when men and women of good conscience may differ. This is not one of them" (September 16, 2001). Similarly, the *San Francisco Chronicle* reiterated Bush's naming of Iraq, Iran, and North Korea as an "axis of evil," adding that these "regimes ... have the motive and the means to export horror" (January 30, 2002). On the eve of the war in Iraq, the *St. Louis Post-Dispatch* recalled the president's claim that he would "enforce the just demands of the world" (March 18, 2003). Other editorials picked up Bush's discourse without directly attributing it to him. An editorial in the *Daily News* (New York), for example, argued that Saddam Hussein's "sadistic regime holds the [Iraq] nation hostage" (March 19, 2003). And six weeks later the *New York Times* noted that there never was any question "whether American troops would succeed, or whether the regime they toppled would not be exposed to the world as a despicable one" (May 2, 2003). After the September 11 attacks, then, the president in his national addresses and with the assistance of newspaper editorials emphasized the good/evil binary, with a particular ratcheting up of "evil" rhetoric.

## Security/Peril Binary

President Bush was much more likely to place the concepts of "security" and "peril" in direct opposition following the terrorist attacks. Comparison of the president's language in addresses prior to the September 11 attacks with that used in addresses afterward revealed that less than 1 percent of presidential paragraphs prior to September 11 contained "security" and "peril" language placed in juxtaposition, compared with 5.7 percent of paragraphs after the attacks—a greater than six-fold increase.[20] In addition, juxtapositions of "security" and "peril" were present in most post-September 11 presidential addresses. They were present in Bush's address on the evening of the attacks and in his September 20 address to the nation. However, the two ideas disappeared during the military campaign in Afghanistan, and then reappeared in all of the remaining addresses (with one absence: the September 11, 2002, anniversary address).

Newspaper editorials also far more commonly placed "security" and "peril" in opposition following the terrorist attacks: 3.4 percent of analyzed editorials prior to September 11 juxtaposed "security" and "peril" language, compared with 19.5 percent of editorials after the attacks. This is almost a six-fold increase.[21] In sum, both the president and newspaper editorials were significantly more likely to place "security" and "peril" in direct opposition after the terrorist attacks.

Turning to separate examinations of "security" and "peril" language—that is, regardless of whether these concepts were placed in direct opposition—Figure 2.6 shows that the president's use of "security" and "peril" terminology increased after the attacks and editorials paralleled that trend. The president's use of "security" terminology rose from 2 percent to 19 percent and "peril" language increased from 5 percent to 22 percent.[22] Editorials showed a similar shift after the September 11 events: editorials containing "security" terminology increased from 20 percent to 51 percent, while those with "peril" language rose from 14 percent to 58 percent.[23] In addition, there was no criticism of the president's emphasis on these concepts in the editorials. The press seemed unreservedly to accept Bush's framing of the situation as imminent doom, which necessitated both a defensive, almost paranoid, homeland stance and an offensive global posturing.

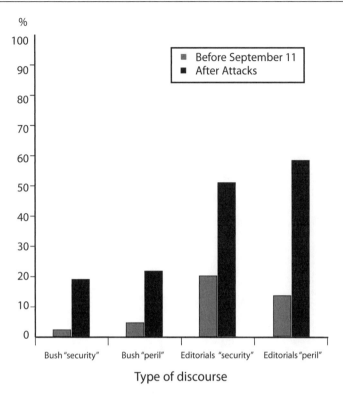

**Figure 2.6** "Security" and "peril" discourse in Bush addresses by paragraph and in newspaper editorials in the two days following addresses

Further, over-time analysis of "security" and "peril" indicated that both concepts had a sustained presence in Bush's addresses and appear to have been utilized together in a strategic manner, especially following September 11. The address-by-address statistical correlation between the percentage of paragraphs containing "security" language and percentage of paragraphs containing "peril" language in the president's addresses was, like "good" and "evil," statistically very strong, indicating a close relationship between the presence of these ideas.[24] The data, presented in Figure 2.7, indicate that the sides of the binary moved in high synchronicity, again strongly suggestive of a concerted binary discourse by the president.

In addition, there was a strong correspondence between the president and newspaper editorials both for "security" language and for

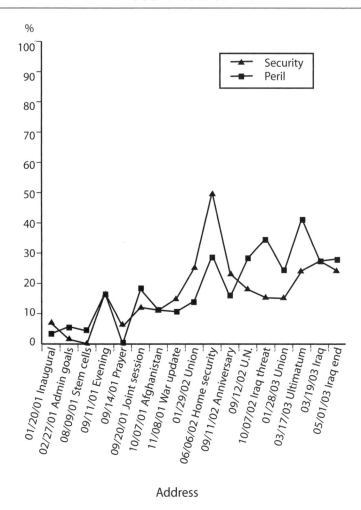

**Figure 2.7** "Security" and "peril" discourse in Bush addresses by paragraph

"peril" terminology.[25] These data are arrayed in Figures 2.8 and 2.9. Editorial echoing of Bush's "security" discourse was consistent and substantial. Editorials also closely paralleled the president's "peril" discourse across most addresses—with the striking exceptions of Bush's National Cathedral address on September 14, 2001, and his "war on terrorism" update of November 8, 2001. Interestingly, as with "good" and "evil" discourse, editorials after Bush's May 1,

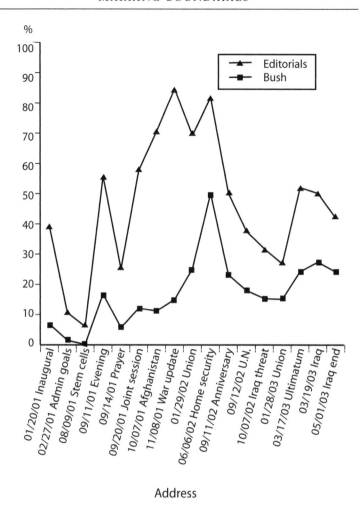

**Figure 2.8** "Security" discourse in Bush addresses by paragraph and in newspaper editorials in the two days following addresses

2003 address calling an end to major combat in Iraq were much less likely to adopt his "peril" language, although an echoing emphasis upon "security" remained. In this instance, perhaps the press interpreted the dislodging of Saddam from power to be adequate to blunt concerns about potential peril from Iraq—provided that U.S. security vigilance remained high.

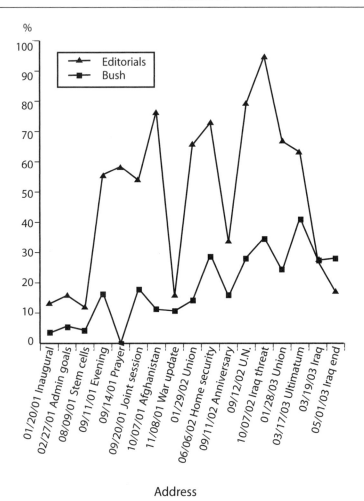

**Figure 2.9** "Peril" discourse in Bush addresses by paragraph and in newspaper editorials in the two days following addresses

Excerpts from the president's addresses provide insight into these strategic emphases on "security" and "peril" ideas, and from newspaper editorials are indicative of the press's adoption of this terminology. The president invoked the security/peril binary immediately following the attacks, assuring the nation on September 11 that the government was taking "every precaution to protect our citizens at home and around the world from further attacks" (Bush, 2001a). Ten days later, before Congress and the American public, the president claimed the United States was "a country awakened to danger," adding, "Our nation has been put on notice: We are not immune from attack" (Bush, 2001e). Security and peril were consistent emphases by Bush throughout the period of analysis. On November 8, 2001, he noted, "After September 11, our govern-ment assumed new responsibilities to strengthen security" (Bush, 2001i). More than a year later in the 2003 State of the Union address, when speaking about the possibility of Iraq aiding terror-ists, the president said, "We will set a course toward safety. Before the day of horror can come ... this danger will be removed" (Bush, 2003a). And in announcing military operations in Iraq on March 19, 2003, the president declared:

> The people of the United States and our friends and allies will not live at the mercy of an outlaw regime that threatens the peace with weapons of mass murder. We will meet that threat now, with our Army, Air Force, Navy, Coast Guard, and Marines, so that we do not have to meet it later with armies of firefighters and police and doctors on the streets of our cities.
>
> (Bush, 2003d)

A similar discourse was present in editorials. For example, the *New York Times* said, "Every routine, every habit this city knew was frac-tured yesterday. If a flight full of commuters can be turned into a missile of war, everything is dangerous" (September 12, 2001). A few months later the *San Diego Union-Tribune* restated the president's claim that "the government is doing all it can to safeguard the public" (November 9, 2001). In mid-2002 the *Minneapolis Star Tribune* claimed, "Terrorism has replaced the cold war as the most dangerous threat to U.S. national security" (June 8, 2002). And just prior to the war in Iraq, the *Seattle Times* wrote, "We are fighting to remove Saddam and his sons from Iraq and thereby increase the safety of the United States and our friends" (March 18, 2003). The *Portland Oregonian* argued:

> We believed and continue to believe that President Bush is addressing the essential security interests of the United States. In fact, we think he is addressing the essential security interest

of much of the rest of the world, too, even if some members of the United Nations' Security Council see it differently.

(*Oregonian*, March 21, 2003)

And the *New Orleans Times-Picayune* said, "Any war is a grave and terrible event. In this case, the goal is worthy: keeping a dangerous regime from developing and using the world's most destructive weapons" (March 20, 2003). After the September 11 attacks, therefore, the security/peril binary was emphasized both in the president's national addresses and in corresponding newspaper editorials. The Bush team was intent on delivering threat-laden messages and the U.S. press was more than willing to disseminate them.

### Differential Binary Emphases

Usage of multiple binaries allowed the president to be selective with his emphasis of good/evil or security/peril to fit strategic goals of the moment. Figure 2.10 shows the combined total of "good" and "evil" language (one line in graph) and combined total of "security" and "peril" language (other line in graph) in each presidential address. Bush placed relatively greater emphasis upon "good" and "evil" language in the first eight addresses analyzed, which included five in the period immediately following September 11; good/evil clearly was the primary binary across these addresses. Beginning with the 2002 State of the Union, "security" and "peril" language increased substantially and soon became predominant in Bush's addresses— with the understandable exception of the September 11, 2002, anniversary address. Thus, from the State of the Union 2002 through the commencement of U.S. combat operations in Iraq, security/peril was the primary binary. Interestingly, "good" and "evil" surged upward in the president's address on May 1, 2003, as he spoke of a post-Iraq war future. These data, then, indicate clear periods of differential emphasis by President Bush upon these binaries over time.

The increase in presidential emphasis upon "security" and "peril" beginning with the 2002 State of the Union suggests the need for a second look at Bush's over-time emphasis upon the two sides of this particular binary. These data, shown earlier in Figure 2.7, are suggestive of *two distinct periods of the president's usage of these binary concepts*. The first three addresses of 2002 might be viewed as the administration's "homeland security" policy campaign, beginning

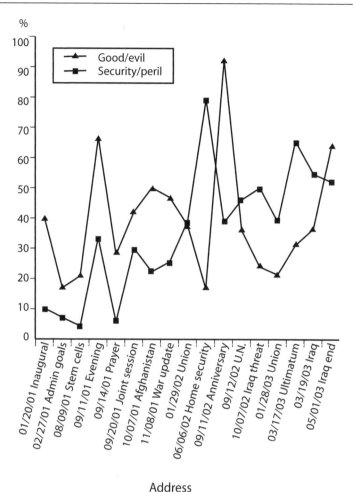

**Figure 2.10** Total (a) "good" and "evil" discourse and (b) "security" and "peril" discourse in Bush addresses by paragraph

with the president's claim in the State of the Union that "Our first priority must always be the security of our nation" (Bush, 2002a). The next national presidential address came in June, when he announced a reformulated version of the Department of Homeland Security in a speech replete with "security" language. And on the one-year anniversary of September 11 Bush again emphasized security more than peril. The six following presidential addresses, in contrast, might be viewed as the "Iraq war" policy campaign. The first of the six was the president's address to the U.N. General Assembly on September 12, which voiced the administration's desire to disarm Iraq—by force if necessary. The five subsequent addresses all focused largely on the "Iraq threat," culminating with Bush's closing of "major" military operations in Iraq.

With these policy emphases seemingly tied to strategic usage by the president of specific *sides* of the security/peril binary, two periods were distinguished among the post-terrorist attack presidential addresses: a "homeland security" campaign period (first three addresses of 2002) and an "Iraq war" campaign period (last two addresses of 2002 and four in 2003). Analysis with these data strongly suggests that the president highlighted a particular side of the security/peril binary to fit a specific administration policy goal. "Security" language was nearly twice as present in Bush's addresses during the "homeland security" campaign period (in 31 percent versus 16 percent of paragraphs) than in the other post-attack addresses,[26] while in remarkably similar data "peril" language was twice as present in Bush's addresses during the "Iraq war" campaign period (in 30 percent versus 15 percent of paragraphs) than in the other post-attack addresses.[27] In sum, the evidence is indicative of strategic usage by the president of these two binaries *and* for specific functions (that is, emphasizing particular sides of a binary) during the 20 months of analysis.

## COMFORT AND FAMILIARITY, AT GREAT COST

These data provide a clear picture of the usage by President Bush of binary constructions, and the adoption in newspaper editorials of this language after the terrorist attacks of September 11, 2001. Several points merit discussion about what these communication patterns mean.

The evidence strongly suggests that the president employed a binary discourse with three key attributes. First, Bush used the terrorist attacks as a central organizing object in his national addresses. Frequent references to September 11 had great political value, bringing to mind the trauma experienced by many people in the United States (see Schuster et al., 2001) *and* the president's effective rhetorical responses in the days and weeks afterward. In essence, the administration utilized September 11 as a discursive weapon to trigger fears among the public and support for the president, the two foundational pillars upon which the administration's political fundamentalism could emerge and flourish. Bush did not refer to September 11 in only two addresses—his ultimatum to Saddam and the announcement of military action in Iraq, delivered two days apart in March 2003. The president undoubtedly was aware of criticisms that the administration had not adequately made its case linking Iraq to the terrorist attacks; avoiding references to September 11 as he committed troops to combat in Iraq allowed Bush to sidestep this critique, both at the moment and in subsequent contexts such as the 2004 election. These omissions speak loudly about the strategic nature of this discourse and the omnipresent political calculations of this administration. Notably, had the central organizing object been something else with less clear moral dimensions—such as education or tax cuts, which were two other administration interests—the president's ability to speak in binary terms with credibility would have been more difficult. Indeed, a nation-challenging crisis is ideal, to use an unfortunate term, for a binary discourse. With such an opportunity available, the Bush administration capitalized.

Second, the data show that the president consistently employed multiple binaries in his communications. Specifically, the president strategically emphasized two binaries, good/evil and security/peril, which functioned together well. The former provided an explicit window on the religious groundings of the president and administration, indicative of a conservative religious outlook that conceives of reality as "clearly divided under the hegemonies of Good versus Evil" (Marty, 1992, p. 21). In large part because the morality is tightly bounded, this binary offered to the U.S. public a sense of comfort and confidence in anxious times—hence the president's greater emphasis upon this binary in his addresses immediately following September 11—while also lending credibility to security/peril by suggesting that sinister people and forces were active and an ever-present threat to U.S. lives. At the same time, the administration's political fundamentalism incorporated security/peril, a second binary that avoided the overt religiosity of good/evil while offering specific policy applications. Indeed, the data indicate that the president emphasized security/peril over good/evil when the administration began to publicly cast its focus toward Iraq with the 2002 State of the Union address, a rhetorical shift that gave the appearance of a return to affairs of the state and secular needs, even though a fundamentalist worldview remained the unseen modus operandi.

Third, the results indicated that the president consistently utilized interdependent binary forms in his communications. Following the attacks the president employed directly oppositional good/evil and security/peril placements in roughly one of every 15 to 20 paragraphs in his addresses, providing an increased and consistent presence for both. At the same time, because too much repetition by the administration of these juxtapositions risked diminishing their rhetorical value, they were subsumed within a broader communications approach in which each side of the binaries was given a sustained presence across a number of national addresses. Indeed, *once the binary juxtapositions were established after September 11* consistent emphasis upon any one of the concepts of "good," "evil," "security," or "peril" was most likely sufficient to bring to mind the opposing sides of the binaries. For example, by the time the president began to emphasize the "peril" of Iraq in 2002 it was almost unnecessary for him to add that U.S. "security" had to be strengthened; the public could be counted on to complete this already established binary. That is, the logic and language of the binaries were transferred over time from the president to the public, with the considerable assistance of leading media outlets. As a result, the parsing of the world into opposing camps in the post-September 11 struggle against terrorism may have begun in the White House, but in subsequent months this conception of reality became widely inculcated among the U.S. public—to the advantage of the Republican Party and almost no one else.

The evidence in this chapter also suggests that binary discourse is well suited for a political culture dominated by mass media, because it (a) inherently suggests competition and conflict, the heart of most political news coverage; (b) provides the simple rhetorical flourishes that news media outlets desire—and that television news, in particular, requires; and (c) has moral staying power, as suggested by the decades-long, binary-rich Cold War era.[28] These findings show that the press—at least the institutional voices of the press—uncritically aligned with the president's good/evil and security/peril constructions. Particularly revealing is that editorials, *following Bush*, exhibited a much greater increase in "evil," "security," and "peril" language but not "good" language after the September 11 attacks. That editorials consistently took cues from the president had grave implications, given the editorial mechanisms of interpretation and public education. When the language of the press so closely followed the discourse of the president, citizens and other political leaders who monitor the perspectives in these leading news media could not help but interpret these editorials as messages of support for the president and his (and his party's) agenda. Such cues in editorials, research by Dalton et al. (1998) has suggested, may be particularly influential upon public opinion in elections. Therefore, regardless of journalists' intent, the echoing press found in the United States in the aftermath of September 11 was, functionally, far from a neutral press. Instead of journalists as objective critical thinkers, mainstream reporters and editors acted as guard dogs for and perpetuators of the administration's agenda.

A union of religious fundamentalism and political strategy was present, then, in the binary discourse manufactured by the administration and disseminated widely in the mainstream press after September 11. These patterns of political communication offered comfort and familiarity to the U.S. public, but at tremendous cost for democratic debate and decision-making. To be specific, these constructions parsed people and ideologies into opposing camps, closed off certain avenues of thought and action, and at minimum reinforced a moral certitude among the Bush administration that helped to justify the imposing of restrictions on civil liberties, dismissal of United Nations conventions, and undertaking of preemptive military action. In doing all of this, the binaries simultaneously were grounded in a boundary-marking conservative religious worldview while offering a powerful form of strategic political communication. In short, in a manner that looked, sounded, and felt political, the president offered a conception of reality that Marty and Appleby (1992) have argued religious fundamentalists *always* offer: one that lacks "degrees of moderation" in thought and action, lest there be "confusion in the battle" (p. 29). This way of understanding and communicating about the world may be cognitively simplistic, but it is also powerful because it eliminates the desire and perceived need for deeper critical thinking—which was and remains so desperately needed about these matters. It was upon this foundation of a binary conception of reality, so comforting in the post-September 11 world and yet so rigid and harmful to public discourse, that the Bush administration built three additional dimensions of its political fundamentalism.

# 3
# A "mission" and a "moment," time and again

George W. Bush placed a telephone call from the White House to New York City Mayor Rudy Giuliani and New York Governor George Pataki on September 13, 2001. The importance and symbolism of this phone conversation prompted the nation's television networks to broadcast it live from the Oval Office. The strategic value of this conversation prompted the administration to let them do so. The president was standing at his desk, not sitting— thereby adopting a posture more likely to suggest leadership. Following the conversation, the president took a few questions from news media as the cameras continued to roll. One question, which became the final one, inquired about what kind of prayers the president was "thinking" and "where your heart is for yourself as you work" on the United States' response to the terrorist attacks. In reply, the president said:

> Well, I don't think about myself right now. I think about the families, the children. I'm a loving guy, and I'm also someone, however, who's got a job to do, and I intend to do it. And this is a terrible moment. But this country will not relent until we have saved ourselves and others from the terrible tragedy that came upon America.

What caught public attention in these comments was that the president's voice cracked with emotion as he said, "I'm a loving guy," and then gathered conviction as he turned to matters at hand ("Excerpts from president's remarks on investigation into attack," 2001). Many in the news media interpreted these words as a window into the president's compassion and determination.[1]

There also was something else of great import in these words, a dynamic that became a central component of the Bush administration's political fundamentalism after September 11: *an obsession with time*. In his comments in the Oval Office, the president paired a commitment of an enduring nature, reflected in his claim that "this country will not relent until we have saved ourselves and others from the terrible tragedy that came upon America," with a need for immediate action—despite his grief, he had a "job to do" at that "terrible moment." This pairing was not happenstance for a president ever on message. One week later, on September 20 before Congress and a national television audience, Bush offered a similar pairing, albeit a rhetorically more memorable one: "[I]n our grief and anger, we have found our mission and our moment." The argument in this chapter is that an omnipresent fixation on time, both long- and short-term, is rooted in religious fundamentalism while simultaneously providing a strategically powerful crisis language that helped the administration maintain control of the post-September 11 agenda and short-circuited congressional and public consideration of administration-proposed policies. It is unsurprising, therefore, that such discourse consistently emanated from the Bush administration after September 11. Further, the expectation of an echoing press in times of national crisis suggests that any time-focused emphases by the administration would receive considerable voice in news coverage. This too was the case.

## FUNDAMENTALISM, TIME, AND STRATEGIC COMMUNICATION

A pervading consideration among religious fundamentalists is the possibility, in the words of Ammerman (1991), that the world may end at "any moment." Such a conception engenders a constant awareness of how one spends one's time, since all of one's thoughts and behaviors are considered potentially to have eternal consequences.[2] The tight linkage of the temporal with the eternal has a simple yet profound implication: in the eyes of religious conservatives, *who people are* is inextricably tied to *what they do*, for *what they do* at every single moment may contribute to their ultimate relationship with God. This omnipresent awareness of the importance of how individuals spend their time impels action. This is thought to be in accordance with the instructions of Jesus in the biblical book of

Mark that believers should "keep on the alert; for you do not know when the appointed time [of Christ's return] may come," a claim echoed in several places elsewhere in the New Testament. For devout Christians, sloth is considered a deadly sin and an obstacle to divine providence, as reflected in the fundamentalist adage of earlier generations, "idle hands are the devil's workshop."

This imperative for action becomes heightened and solidified when circumstances, such as a crisis or conflict, prompt individuals to see their actions as "part of God's plan for history" (Harding, 1994, p. 58). Indeed, some evidence suggests the Bush administration regarded its role to be part of a divine unfolding of events, even before September 11; at a minimum, the president seemed to do so. In the 2000 presidential campaign, Bush said "our nation is chosen by God and commissioned by history to be a model to the world of justice" ("A sampler," 2000). In February 2003, at the National Prayer Breakfast gathering, Bush expressed a similar view about the course of developments:

> We can also be confident in the ways of providence, even when they are far from our understanding. Events aren't moved by blind change and chance. Behind all of life and all of history, there's a dedication and purpose, set by the hand of a just and faithful God. And that hope will never be shaken.
>
> (Bush, 2003b)

Communications such as these, Marty (2003) argued one month later, suggested that Bush had an "evident conviction that he's doing God's will" (p. 32). In turn, a belief that thoughts and events have a divinely scripted quality increases the likelihood that individuals will pursue a chosen course of action for as long as deemed necessary— regardless of obstacles encountered. In the words of Ammerman, the belief in a Second Coming of Christ at an unknown time "lends both urgency to evangelistic task and comfort to persecuted believers" (1991, p. 6).

The fundamentalist obsession with time, then, tends to become manifest in two beliefs: (a) that action in the here and now is imperative, and (b) that one's commitment to a certain course of action, if perceived to be God-inspired, should be of an enduring nature. These religiously based, time-fixated perspectives were employed in the political arena by the Bush administration in strategically powerful ways after September 11. It was commonplace, for example, for the president and other key administration members to push for *imminent action* on proposed policies, claiming that every day lost was a day closer to another terrorist attack or new threats. Such discourse fit the "moment" side of the "mission and moment" dualism established by the president following the terrorist attacks; in the view of the administration, the United States' moment to act was now. This unremitting push for quick action was accompanied in the administration's communications by consistent emphasis upon an *enduring commitment* to a campaign against terrorism, which fit the "mission" side of the administration's time obsession: framing the struggle against terrorism as a mission—a word with a clear religious subtext—suggested that to endure was to follow, in Harding's (1994) words, "God's plan for history." When combined, these time-fixated emphases became politically potent: They allowed the administration to push for immediate action on specific policy goals, with others' questions dismissed, and to justify these desires as unchallengeable steps in a God-ordained, long-term process. Further, the implication—sometimes made explicit—was clear: to not act quickly or to not endure in the campaign against terrorism was to risk another September 11.

This chapter presents evidence of how these conceptions of time became manifest in the administration's communications about key "war on terrorism" policies between autumn 2001 and spring 2003. Notably, by itself the creation of a "war on terrorism" implied a need for both quick action and a long-term commitment, suggestive of how this guiding metaphor of the administration was, at minimum, congruent with a religious fundamentalist worldview. This chapter, though, focuses specifically on ways in which the administration made explicit its obsession with time in discourse about anti-terrorism *policies*, because in these contexts such fixations had potentially far-reaching implications. In particular, the time-based discourses helped the administration to steamroll through and over the system of checks and balances built into U.S. governmental decision-making, mechanisms put in place in part for crisis contexts such as this when leaders might use events to justify the suspension of democratic debate. The Bush administration did the next best thing: It declared any congressional delays in passing its policies to be potentially catastrophic and in conflict with providential wishes for the nation. Such administration communications, rooted in a conservative religious worldview, put and kept Congress on the defensive and ultimately forced it to rubber stamp most of what the administration asked for to combat terrorism.

Administration communications about key policies were examined, beginning with initial public presentation of the "war on terrorism" after September 11 and concluding with the administration's presentation and justification of a preemptive foreign policy approach in 2002. The president's national addresses were the most visible of the administration's public communications and thus were the focus of analysis in Chapter 2. However, nearly every day the president and other key administration leaders spoke publicly—to citizens and residents, before Congress, with news media, and so on. The daily communications of the president, Secretary of Defense Donald Rumsfeld, Secretary of State Colin Powell, and Attorney General John Ashcroft were examined, providing insight into whether political fundamentalism was infused throughout the discourse of a number of administration actors. If several members of the Bush team espoused a similar time-based rhetoric, then the existence of a purposeful, designed, political communication strategy for the entire administration can be assumed, as opposed to merely the presence of a personal speech-spinning style of an individual president. And indeed, the grander plan was the case, as we will see later in this chapter.

Whether the administration's messages were echoed in the mainstream press also was a point of interest in this analysis. Chapter 2 showed that the president's binaries were echoed and substantially amplified in a wide range of U.S. newspaper editorials. A similar echoing in the press might be expected with the administration's obsession with time, for at least three reasons. First, in times of crisis the press simply considers it important to widely disseminate administration communications (in the very least as a public service), and second, consistent declarations by the administration of the need for imminent action on policies and for an enduring commitment in the campaign against terrorism both have considerable news value. The push for urgent action neatly fit journalists' interest in political strategy and competition, while the latter offered a "benchmark" timeline that could be used by journalists and others to evaluate the success of the administration's goals.[3] Furthermore, news is a time-based industry that thrives on the "now." To say that the world and the United States can only be saved from impending doom if a Bush policy is accepted straight away is to offer the press prime fodder for news copy: history-making, and immediacy. Indeed, an echoing of the administration's fixations on time was present in news content, which for this analysis was expanded to include a combination of newspaper articles, newspaper editorials, and television news coverage.

## ANALYSIS OF DISCOURSE

Administration communications and news content were examined about four important administration policies: (1) the "war on terrorism" plan, presented publicly soon after the terrorist attacks and addressed regularly thereafter in presidential addresses; (2) the U.S.A. Patriot Act legislation, proposed by the administration within weeks of September 11 and passed by Congress in late October 2001; (3) the new Cabinet-level Department of Homeland Security, proposed by the administration in June 2002 and passed by Congress in November 2002; and (4) the creation of a preemptive foreign policy, presented publicly in June 2002 and codified in September 2002. Data are explained in this section according to the type of evidence: (a) emphasis in the discourse upon an enduring commitment against terrorism; (b) emphasis in the discourse upon a need for imminent action on administration policies; or (c) both.

### Enduring Commitment

Two areas of administration communications were examined for potential evidence of an emphasis upon an enduring commitment in the struggle against terrorism. Analyzed first was the language of President Bush and other administration leaders in laying the groundwork for a "war on terrorism," particularly its initial stages, between September 11 and the beginning of the U.S. military campaign in Afghanistan on October 7, 2001. Analyzed second were the president's national addresses, beginning with the announcement of military action in Afghanistan on October 7, 2001, and continuing through the calling of an end to "major combat" in Iraq on May 1, 2003.

To identify administration communications about the "war on terrorism" in the period immediately following September 11, all news content in the front sections and in special "nation challenged"/"war on terrorism" sections of the *New York Times* and *Washington Post* was analyzed between September 12 and October 7, 2001. This was a remarkable amount of coverage— more than 1,000 articles in the *Post* alone. The focus of analysis was each *source* in each article, because the focus was on what expectations were discussed in news content and who in the administration talked about them. Only sources that discussed at least one of the identified expectations (explained below) were included in the analysis. Each source quoted or paraphrased was counted separately, and the entirety of each source's statements in an article was taken into account when determining that person's viewpoints. Three source categories are of interest here: (1) President Bush, (2) Cabinet members Secretary of Defense Rumsfeld and Secretary of State Powell, and (3) other U.S. government or military leaders, which included all other federal government or military spokespersons. Any administration "talking points" were expected to be present in this news content, for two reasons: First, journalists rely heavily upon government leaders as news sources early in crises before moving on to other sources, and second, these newspapers have by far the greatest amount of U.S. political coverage.[4] As a second step of analysis, *Times* and *Post* editorials were examined during the same period, with a specific interest in whether any emphasis in administration communications about an enduring commitment against terrorism, as represented in these outlets' news pages, was echoed on their editorial pages.

Analysis of news content in these newspapers identified five distinct administration expectations between September 11 and October 7. While not all were clearly tied to the notion of an enduring commitment against terrorism, as a group they provided insight into the relative points of concern of the administration. All themes were evaluated as absent or present, based on the following definitions.

*U.S. military casualties*: This theme was considered present if news sources or editorials discussed potential deaths of U.S. military or the administration's discussion of this subject:

*Afghanistan civilian deaths*: This theme was considered present if news sources or editorials discussed potential Afghan civilian deaths from wartime activities, including lack of food, or the administration's discussion of this subject.

*Duration of "war on terrorism"*: This theme was considered present if news sources or editorials discussed the potential duration of the U.S. campaign against terrorism or the administration's discussion of this subject. As a second step, this emphasis was further analyzed for language explicitly suggestive of an enduring commitment by the administration, defined as a commitment having no clear end or for as long as necessary.

*Rebuilding of Afghanistan*: This theme was considered present if news sources or editorials discussed the possibility of rebuilding Afghanistan after the war or the administration's discussion of this subject.

*War on Islam?* This theme was considered present if news sources or editorials discussed the possibility of Muslims being targeted or the administration's discussion of this subject.[5]

Presidential addresses to the nation also were examined for the presence of language explicitly suggesting an enduring commitment against terrorism by the administration. The addresses were the same as those analyzed in Chapter 2, with the exception that this analysis began where examination of the administration's discourse in the *Times* and *Post* left off—on October 7, 2001, resulting in analysis of 11 addresses.

## Imminent Action

Two areas of administration communications were examined for potential evidence of an emphasis upon a need for imminent action on key policies. Analyzed first was the language of administration leaders about domestic anti-terrorism legislation proposed shortly after September 11 by the administration, which provided government authorities with far-reaching oversight powers to prevent and protect against terrorist activities. Congress passed this legislation, eventually given the acronym the U.S.A. Patriot Act, on October 25, 2001. Analyzed second were the president's communications about the Department of Homeland Security: an administration-proposed Cabinet-level position presented to the nation on June 6, 2002, and eventually passed by Congress in November 2002. In addition, for both time periods a range of newspaper articles, newspaper editorials, and television news were analyzed to see if the administration's messages were echoed in the press.

Administration discourse was collected in two steps. First, for the U.S.A. Patriot Act, communications by President Bush were gathered from the National Archives and Records Administration's *Weekly*

*Compilation of Presidential Documents*, a comprehensive collection of presidential public communications. Retrieved texts included addresses, exchanges with news media, and public interactions with Congress. Every document from September 11 through October 25, 2001, was read; selected were those in which the president discussed, either explicitly or implicitly, anti-terrorism legislation or components of it. This procedure yielded 18 relevant texts. Also analyzed were the public communications of Attorney General Ashcroft about this legislation, because he was the law's architect and the administration's primary "point person" in discussions with Congress. Ashcroft's communications were collected from the Department of Justice website, which provides public communications by the attorney general. All communications about anti-terrorism legislation were collected between the same dates, yielding 13 relevant texts. For the Department of Homeland Security, the NARA database was searched using the string of "Bush and Homeland Security" between June 6 and November 4, 2002, the day prior to congressional elections which granted to the Republican Party control of Congress and made the legislation's passage a foregone conclusion (it eventually was passed November 25). This search also returned documents generally about homeland security; although these were part of the same discourse, this analysis was limited to communications specifically discussing the proposed Cabinet-level position. This procedure yielded 121 texts.

Searching newspapers and television news transcripts in the Nexis database identified news coverage for the same dates as administration communications. For the U.S.A. Patriot Act, articles and editorials were collected from 15 newspapers, selected because they are leading news outlets and offer geographic diversity: *Albuquerque Journal, Denver Post, Houston Chronicle, New York Times, Omaha World-Herald, Oregonian* (Portland), *Plain Dealer* (Cleveland), *San Diego Union-Tribune, San Francisco Chronicle, Seattle Times, St. Louis Post-Dispatch, Star Tribune* (Minnesota), *Tampa Tribune, Times-Picayune* (New Orleans), and *Washington Post*. News articles and editorials were collected using the search string of "(terror or anti-terror or Ashcroft) and (legislation or law or bill)." This search yielded 1,620 texts, of which 209 were deemed relevant. Using the same search string, television news transcripts were collected from the daily evening newscasts of the Columbia Broadcasting System (CBS), the American Broadcasting Corporation (ABC), and National Broadcasting Corporation (NBC). This search yielded 106 stories, of which 21 were relevant. The vast majority of discarded texts focused on general accounts of law enforcement response, additional events linked to the terrorist attacks (for example, bioterrorism, anthrax attacks), other legislation under consideration (for instance, reinsurance legislation, state legislation) or the military conflict in Afghanistan.

Analysis of news coverage about the Department of Homeland Security focused on newspaper editorials and television content. Editorials were analyzed in the same 15 newspapers examined for the U.S.A. Patriot Act plus five more with regional importance—the *Atlanta Journal and Constitution, Boston Globe, Chicago Sun-Times, Columbus Dispatch*, and *Daily News* (New York). Editorials were collected using the string of "homeland security and editorial and not letters," the latter category eliminating numerous letters to the editor, which often carried the label of "editorial" in the Nexis database (there were very few letters about the anti-terrorism legislation in 2001). This search yielded 190 texts, of which 81 were deemed relevant. Television news transcripts again were collected from the daily evening newscasts of CBS, ABC, and NBC, using the search string of "homeland security and (bill or act or legislation or proposed department)." This search yielded 113 texts, of which 51 were deemed relevant. Editorials and television news transcripts were eliminated if they did not address the proposed Department of Homeland Security legislation in some manner. Most discarded texts focused on homeland security in general or mentioned the proposed department merely in passing.

Administration communications about these two policies were first analyzed, with two themes emerging that were indicative of the notion of "imminent action." Analysis focused on each specific communication (a) by the president or attorney general (for example, an address, testimony before Congress, press conference), or (b) in news coverage (for instance, news story or editorial). Both themes were evaluated as absent or present, and were defined as follows:

*Calls for action by Congress:* This theme was considered present if a desire was expressed for congressional action on the legislation (U.S.A. Patriot Act or Department of Homeland Security). Examples of this discourse included "I call on Congress," "I urge Congress," and "Congress needs to act."

*Time urgency:* This theme was considered present if a desire for speed or time sensitivity in regard to the proposed legislation was explicitly expressed. Examples of time urgency discourse included "quickly," "immediately," and "we do not face unlimited time."[6]

## A Preemptive Foreign Policy

The president's public presentation of a preemptive foreign policy doctrine was the final component of administration discourse analyzed in this chapter. A policy of preemptively using U.S. military forces to prevent future attacks was both a point of discussion under President George H. W. Bush and then advocated to the Clinton administration by some who would subsequently gain key posts in George W. Bush's administration, in particular Deputy Secretary of Defense Paul Wolfowitz.[7] After September 11 the idea of preemption gained an increased hearing in the administration, and in March 2002 content from an internal administration document, the "Nuclear Posture Review," was leaked to the news media.[8] The administration's first public proclamation of a preemptive policy posture came in the president's commencement address at the U.S. Military Academy in West Point, New York, on June 1, 2002.[9] And in September 2002, the administration issued a *National Security Strategy* document in which the preemptive policy was discussed in detail.[10] For this analysis, the president's West Point address and the *National Security Strategy* document were examined for evidence of emphases upon both "imminent action" and an "enduring commitment" against terrorism.

## AN OBSESSION WITH TIME: THE EVIDENCE

Emphasis upon an enduring commitment in the struggle against terrorism is presented first here, followed by emphasis upon the need for imminent action on administration policies. Both are then analyzed in the president's justification for a preemptive foreign policy doctrine.

### Enduring Commitment

Administration leaders publicly unveiled plans, goals, and expectations for a "war on terrorism" in the near-month between the September 11 attacks and the beginning of the U.S. military campaign in Afghanistan on October 7, 2001. Analysis of the

*New York Times* and *Washington Post* during these dates indicated that President Bush, administration Cabinet members
Donald Rumsfeld and Colin Powell, and other government and
military leaders emphasized five predominant expectations—
regarding U.S. casualties, Afghan civilian deaths, war duration,
rebuilding of Afghanistan, and targeting of Muslims. These
patterns of discourse are presented in Figure 3.1.

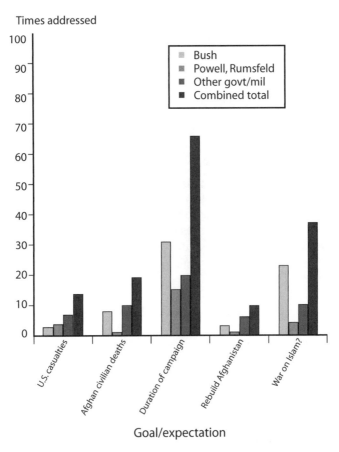

**Figure 3.1** Discourse by administration leaders and other government
and military leaders about goals/expectations for the "war on terrorism"
in *New York Times* and *Washington Post* news content,
September 12–October 7, 2001

In the *Times* and *Post* news coverage, which is indicative of daily interactions between political leaders and the press, the administration's expectation that received the greatest discussion was the duration of the military campaign (present a total of 66 times in this news content), followed by the likelihood of targeting Muslims or Islam more broadly (37 times), Afghan civilian deaths (19 times), U.S. casualties (14 times), and rebuilding of Afghanistan (10 times). The duration category was the most directly tied to the concept of "enduring commitment" and thus merited closer examination. Before turning to that analysis, however, it is noteworthy that the administration's emphasis on three other categories—Afghan civilian deaths, U.S. casualties, and rebuilding of Afghanistan—also implicitly suggested an enduring administration commitment against terrorism. Specifically, administration officials argued that Afghan civilian deaths and U.S. military casualties were unfortunate but unavoidable costs of *necessary* military action, while discussion of rebuilding Afghanistan suggested a long-range commitment by the U.S. government. These administration-emphasized goals and expectations received considerable discussion in *Times* and *Post* editorials, in a manner that paralleled the relative emphases placed by the administration on the topics. Across this period of 26 days, war duration was discussed in 12 editorials, the possibility of targeting Muslims was discussed in 11, Afghanistan civilian deaths was a topic in 10, and U.S. casualties were discussed in 8. The only administration emphasis to receive negligible attention in these newspapers' editorials was the rebuilding of Afghanistan, which was discussed in one editorial.

Closer examination of the war duration discourse showed that President Bush and Secretaries Rumsfeld and Powell often were explicit about the importance of a long-term commitment against terrorism by the administration—defined as a commitment having no clear end or for as long as necessary. Of the 46 instances in which these administration leaders were quoted or paraphrased in the *Times* and *Post*, in 28 (61 percent) they indicated an enduring commitment by the administration. Excerpts from the *Times* and *Post* provide insight into these communications. For example, the president said:

It's going to take a long time to win this war. The American people are going to have to be more patient than ever with the efforts of our combined efforts—not just ourselves, but the efforts of our allies—to get them running and to find them, and to hunt them down. ... I think this is a long-term battle—war. There'll be battles, but this is long term.

*(New York Times,* September 16)

In his September 20 address to the nation, the president declared that the struggle against terrorism would require "time and resolve," would be "a lengthy campaign unlike any other we have ever seen," and had now become the nation's "mission." These words were present in several *Times* and *Post* articles, and helped to set the prevailing frame about war duration. On September 23, a *Post* article said, "This one, the president declares, won't be brief," while a *Post* article two days later said, "Bush has warned that this war will be long, often invisible, and may not have a clear end."

The message of an enduring commitment ran consistently among other administration members too. A *Post* story on September 18 said:

But Powell said the nation should be prepared for a "long-term campaign" against worldwide terrorism that will include legal, political, diplomatic, law enforcement, and intelligence-gathering components—as well as military action. "What we have to do is not only deal with this present instance but the whole concept of terrorism, deal with it as a scourge upon civilization and go after it," he said.

*(Washington Post,* September 18)

On September 26, a *Times* article said, "Much of Mr. Rumsfeld's briefing was devoted to describing the complicated campaign against terrorism, a war without a formal opening or ending, and one that will not be without American casualties." And on October 7, the day in which military action would begin in Afghanistan, a *Times* article said:

More generally, Mr. Rumsfeld has likened the fight against terrorism to the strategy the United States had for containing Soviet power during the cold war.

"The cold war, it took 50 years, plus or minus," Mr. Rumsfeld said during his trip this week to Cairo. "It did not involve major battles. It involved continuous pressure. It involved cooperation by a host of nations.

"And when it ended, it ended not with a bang, but through internal collapse," he added. "It strikes me that might be a more appropriate way to think about what we are up against here, than would be any major conflict."

(*New York Times*, October 7)

In short, there was a clear administration emphasis in the days after September 11 on the necessity of a long-term struggle against terrorism. The war duration topic dominated administration discourse in the *Times* and *Post*, and much of this explicitly declared an enduring commitment against terrorism.

This message was resoundingly echoed in a number of *Times* and *Post* editorials that discussed the potential duration of the "war on terrorism." For example, on the day following the president's September 20 address to the nation, the *Times* said:

President Bush summoned a shaken but determined nation last night to wage a global struggle against terrorism. In a firm and forceful address, Mr. Bush rose to the challenge of making what may be the most critical speech of his life. Urging the American people to be both brave and patient, the president rallied Congress, the nation and its allies abroad to what promises to be a long and painful fight against a ruthless enemy.

(*New York Times*, September 21)

Ten days later, on September 30, a similar sentiment was expressed in the *Post*: "The Bush administration has wisely counseled patience; it needs time to gather intelligence, prepare its forces, forge coalitions. It has wisely told Americans that the military tool will be only one of many to be wielded in a long campaign." And on October 7 as military operations drew near, the *Post* opined that "the al Qaeda campaign will likely be long, hard and bloody," then concluded: "Hope for success now must lie not so much in massive force or high-tech weapons as in the likelihood that Sept. 11 has created the willpower among Americans to accept sacrifices and defeats and persevere until victory is achieved—first in Afghanistan, and eventually wherever terrorist networks find a home." In short, the administration made clear its plans for an enduring commitment against terrorism in the days following September 11, and this message reverberated in editorials by the nation's two leading newspapers.

An emphasis upon enduring commitment continued to resound across U.S. political culture in subsequent months because President Bush in his national addresses consistently reiterated this theme. On October 7, in announcing military strikes in Afghanistan, the president said, "In the months ahead, our patience will be one of our strengths: patience ... and understanding that it will take time to achieve our goals; patience in all the sacrifices that may come" (Bush, 2001h). In his next address, a "war on terrorism" update on November 8, Bush declared: "We will persevere in this struggle, no matter how long it takes to prevail" (Bush, 2001i). In his first State of the Union in January 2002, the president said: "Our war on terror is well begun, but it is only begun. This campaign may not be finished on our watch; yet, it must be and it will be waged on our watch. We can't stop short" (Bush, 2002a). In the September 11, 2002, anniversary address, the president noted that "we will not relent until justice is done and our nation is secure," then returned to the language of a "mission" against terrorism: "We're prepared for this journey. And our prayer tonight is that God will see us through, and keep us worthy. Tomorrow is September the 12th. A milestone is passed, and a mission goes on" (Bush, 2002h). And as the nation approached conflict with Iraq, Bush in his ultimatum address to Saddam Hussein on March 17, 2003, said, "Our goal will not be achieved over night, but it can come over time" (Bush, 2003c).

The final presidential address analyzed was delivered six weeks later on May 1, when Bush called an end to "major combat" in Iraq (Bush, 2003e). Two points are notable about this address. First, the president made explicit the administration's enduring commitment by positioning the conflict with Iraq as only one "battle" in a larger, ongoing struggle, and second, the president again returned to language suggesting the nation was engaged in a "mission" against terrorism. In regard to the former, the president said, "The battle of Iraq is one victory in a war on terror that began on September 11, 2001, and still goes on," and twice more characterized the Iraq conflict as a "battle." In regard to the latter, the president declared: "The use of force has been and remains our last resort. Yet all can know, friend and foe alike, that our nation has a mission: We will answer threats to our security, and we will defend the peace. Our mission continues." These excerpts are exemplary examples of the careful, strategic ways in which the Bush administration approached language and communication during these historic days.

Characterization of the Iraq conflict as a "battle" rather than a "war" was an intentional decision; administration strategist Karl Rove told a college audience in subsequent days, in response to a question about the *war* with Iraq, that "First of all, it's the battle of Iraq, not war," adding "This is part of the war on terrorism."[11] At the same time, the continuing use of "mission" terminology in the administration's discourse suggested a need to stay the course and subtly engendered a religious subtext to the endeavor. All of this was political fundamentalism at work as the Bush team injected evangelical desires into statecraft.

### Imminent Action

The U.S.A. Patriot Act and the creation of a Cabinet-level Department of Homeland Security both were proposed by the Bush administration. The former was developed in the days after September 11 under the guidance of Attorney General Ashcroft and sought far-reaching government powers to counter terrorist activities.[12] Among other provisions, this legislation proposed to give federal agents the ability to detain non-citizens, increase wiretaps, initiate email and Internet surveillance, and intensify the monitoring of student visas. This bill was introduced into Congress in early October 2001 and passed on October 25. The Department of Homeland Security initially was suggested, under a differing name, in a February 2001 report by the U.S. Commission on National Security/21st Century (2001), headed by former senators Warren G. Rudman and Gary Hart. Congressional Democrats called for a governmental agency on homeland security following September 11, but the president instead issued an executive order creating the Office of Homeland Security, reporting directly to the president. Over time, the administration reformulated and broadened the idea of a new department, and in a national address on June 6, 2002, the president proposed legislation enacting the Department of Homeland Security as the largest new federal department since the creation of the Defense Department after the Second World War. The legislation was introduced into Congress later that month. Debate was contentious at times and a bill had not been passed by the November elections, when Republican Party successes assured passage.

The administration placed great emphasis upon the importance of imminent action in discourse about these pieces of legislation. Data in Figure 3.2 show that the president and attorney general issued calls for Congress to act on the U.S.A. Patriot Act in 67 percent and 85 percent of their public communications about this legislation, respectively, and the president increased his push for congressional action to 90 percent of his communications about the Department of Homeland Security. Further, explicit requests of time urgency were present in one-third of the president's communications and 85 percent of Ashcroft's about the Patriot Act, and in fully half of the president's communications about the Department of Homeland Security. Three patterns, then, emerge in these data. First, emphasis upon imminent action was present in administration communications across both policy goals. Second, the president was more likely to call upon Congress to act and to emphasize time urgency in his discourse about the Department of Homeland Security. And third, the president was much less likely than Ashcroft to emphasize time urgency in discourse about the Patriot Act. All of these had strategic functions that will be discussed later in the chapter.

Some excerpts provide insight into how the importance of imminent action—in the forms of calls for congressional action or explicit claims of time sensitivity—on these pieces of legislation was made manifest in the administration's communications. In discourse about the U.S.A. Patriot Act, Bush on September 25 called upon Congress to "listen to the wisdom of the proposals that the Attorney General brought up, to give the tools necessary to our agents in the field to find those who may think they want to disrupt America again" (Bush, 2001f). Ashcroft was more blunt; speaking on the same day before the Senate Committee on the Judiciary, he said: "The American people do not have the luxury of unlimited time." For good measure, he later added, "Every day that passes with outdated statutes and the old rules of engagement is a day that terrorists have a competitive advantage. Until Congress makes these changes, we are fighting an unnecessarily uphill battle" (Ashcroft, 2001c). Two days later, Bush said that he understood "it takes time for legislation to work through the halls of Congress," but that the United States needed "to improve security right now" (Bush, 2001g). Ashcroft said on October 2 that there would be "plenty of time to review things in the future" (Ashcroft, 2001d), and on October 12, he said:

Congress needs to send a message to terrorists that they will find no safe haven in America. Again, our anti-terrorism task forces

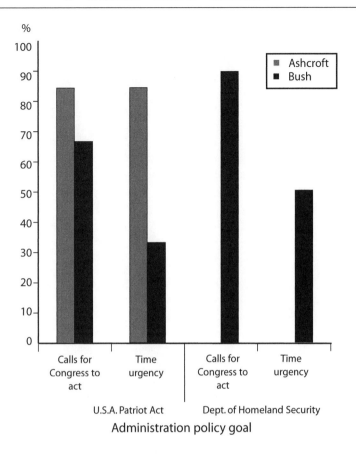

**Figure 3.2** Emphases on "imminent action" by administration leaders in public communications about administration policy goals

need tough new laws now to defeat terrorists. I ask the congressional leadership to send the president a bill to sign right away. Please don't delay; we need these anti-terrorism tools now.

(Ashcroft, 2001e)

In sum, calls for imminent congressional action were consistently present in the administration's discourse about the U.S.A. Patriot Act.

These emphases continued more than eight months later in the president's communications about the Department of Homeland

Security. On June 7, 2002, the day after his national address proposing the new Cabinet position, Bush said:

> We're just going to have to keep the pressure on the people in the United States Congress to do the right thing. I believe it is going to happen. This morning we had a group of Senators and House Members from both parties ... talking about how to get this bill started in Congress and through Congress as quickly as possible. And so I'm confident it's going to happen, particularly when the American people understand it is in our national interests that we bring these agencies under one— under one head.
>
> (Bush, 2002c)

On August 3, the president said, "The biggest issue that I confront is to make sure the homeland is secure. The biggest issue, the biggest challenge that we face, the President and the Congress, is to prevent the killers from taking American life again." As a result, "I've asked Congress to reorganize much of our government under one Cabinet agency called the Office for Homeland Security. It is vital Congress gets it right" (Bush, 2002e). In autumn, as Democrats in the Senate, lobbied by a key constituency, questioned the administration's desire to not allow federal employees in the new Department to unionize, Bush said on October 5 that "for the sake of the security of our country, I ask the Senate to be reasonable, to be realistic, and to understand their job is to leave a legacy behind that will allow those of us who have gotten the position you've elected us to, to do the jobs you expect us to do" (Bush, 2002n). And on October 28 when it was clear the Senate would not pass a bill before the elections, the president said that the House of Representatives had heeded his wishes, but that "the Senate hadn't. The Senate hadn't moved—another reason we need to change the leadership in the Senate so we can get a—so we can have a Homeland Security Department where this president and future presidents are able to put the right people at the right place with the right equipment at the right time, to protect the American people" (Bush, 2002r). In sum, analysis of the administration's communications about the U.S.A. Patriot Act and Department of Homeland Security revealed consistent emphasis upon a push for imminent action by Congress.

Turning to analysis of news coverage about these policies, two interesting patterns are apparent in Figure 3.3. First, news coverage gave considerable voice to the same themes as administration leaders, but not as extensively as Bush and Ashcroft in 2001 or Bush in 2002. Second, the administration's messages had a fairly sizable, and in most cases similar, presence *across* media forms. Specifically, for the U.S.A. Patriot Act, calls for action by Congress and an explicit emphasis upon time urgency were present in most instances in close to half of the coverage analyzed across newspaper articles, editorials, and television news. For the Department of Homeland Security, more than half of newspaper editorials and television news stories included calls for action by Congress, while a quarter to a third of this news

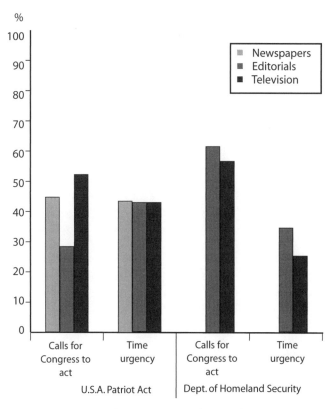

**Figure 3.3** Emphases on "imminent action" in news coverage about administration policy goals

coverage contained an explicit emphasis upon time urgency. These findings are indicative of an echoing, but not governmental mouth-piece, press.[13]

Some excerpts provide insight into how the themes became manifest in news coverage. For the U.S.A. Patriot Act, calls on Congress appeared in television coverage such as a September 24 NBC story, which reported, "On Capitol Hill today the attorney general pushe[d] laws he says will help fight terrorism: tougher immigration rules and broader authority to conduct wiretaps." The story then cut to a soundbite from Ashcroft: "Each day that so passes is a day that terrorists have a competitive advantage. Until Congress makes these changes, we are fighting an unnecessarily uphill battle." Similarly, a CBS news story on October 2 reported the administration's desire for quick congressional passage of the bill, highlighting that the "attorney general came here to the Capitol today to tell members they simply have to move faster" on the anti-terrorism legislation. A *Denver Post* editorial a few days later opined:

> Ashcroft's impatience with Congress is perfectly understand-able. The Justice Department has pledged to do everything it can to restore a sense of safety to the U.S. citizenry and it recog-nized very early that it can't do that job without additional powers. Each day that passes carries with it some risk that current laws won't be up to the task.
>
> (*Denver Post*, October 6)

A *New York Times* article on October 12 reported a Senate vote on a preliminary version of the law, then noted that Ashcroft "pushed hard for immediate action on the bill, even as civil liberties groups pleaded for more deliberate hearings." And a *San Diego Union-Tribune* article on October 13 reported that the president had "issued a statement urging Congress to iron out the minor differences between [House and Senate] bills and get the legislation to his desk as soon as possible."

These themes received continued emphasis months later in news coverage about the Department of Homeland Security. An NBC news story on June 8 quoted the president: "We face an urgent need and we must move quickly, this year, before the end of the Congressional session." An editorial the next day in the *St. Louis Post-Dispatch* said, "Congress should move quickly to examine Mr. Bush's proposal and enact most of it." On July 16, a CBS news story reported, "Ten months after the twin towers came crashing down, President Bush today laid out clear lines of authority and responsibility for his new Department of Homeland Security, and he appealed to Congress not to stand in his way." The story then quoted Bush: "But I'm confident that members of both parties and members of both chambers know that the security of our nation is the goal." As disagreements mounted in the Senate, the New York *Daily News* on September 5 argued that "Congress is dithering over the proposal, and Democrats are balking at the sensible White House plan to create a cabinet post vested with greater hiring and firing authority. Dither and balk, dither and balk. There's a war on. A little urgency would be appreciated." And on October 30, the *Washington Post* editorialized that Congress was lacking "the necessary sense of urgency" on the legislation, adding, "The homeland security bill should be passed in the lame-duck congressional session." In sum, the administration emphasized a desire for imminent action on both the U.S.A. Patriot Act and Department of Homeland Security legislation, and this message was echoed in a wide segment of news discourse.

## A Preemptive Foreign Policy

An obsession with time was also manifest in the president's justification of a preemptive foreign policy, which subsequently became known as the "Bush Doctrine." Notably, the idea of *even considering* a preemptive foreign policy may be viewed as predicated upon a worldview that sees action in the present to be of paramount importance: to not act is viewed as dangerous, a risk instead of an opportunity. With this in mind, two key communications by the president were examined in which the preemption doctrine was presented, elaborated, and justified: the president's commencement address at West Point on June 1, 2002, and the administration's *National Security Strategy* document, issued in September 2002. These are presented in chronological order, focusing on evidence of emphasis upon an enduring commitment against terrorism and the need for imminent action.

In the West Point address, the president utilized subtle religious language, consistent with the "mission" discourse, to preface his emphasis upon the administration's enduring campaign against terrorism: history had "issued a call" to the graduating military cadets, he said, then noted that "Our war on terror is only begun, but in Afghanistan it was begun well." A few sentences later, he added, "The dangers have not passed. This government and the American people are on watch, we are ready, because we know the terrorists have more money and more men and more plans." Bush then turned to the importance of imminent action. He began by noting that for "much of the last century, America's defense relied on the Cold War doctrines of deterrence and containment." However, he said, "new threats require new thinking," which he soon followed with three paragraphs presented in their entirety here, with italicization of places in which an emphasis upon imminent action was explicit:

We cannot defend America and our friends by hoping for the best. We cannot put our faith in the word of tyrants, who solemnly sign non-proliferation treaties, and then systemically break them. *If we wait for threats to fully materialize, we will have waited too long.*

Homeland defense and missile defense are part of stronger security, and they're essential priorities for America. Yet the war on terror will not be won on the defensive. We must take the battle to the enemy, disrupt his plans, and confront the worst threats before they emerge. In the world we have entered, *the only path to safety is the path of action. And this nation will act.*

Our security will require the best intelligence, to reveal threats hidden in caves and growing in laboratories. Our security will require modernizing domestic agencies such as the FBI, so *they're prepared to act, and act quickly, against danger.* Our security will require transforming the military you will lead—a military that *must be ready to strike at a moment's notice* in any dark corner of the world. And our security will require all Americans to be forward-looking and resolute, to *be ready for preemptive action* when necessary to defend our liberty and to defend our lives.

(Bush, 2002b)

The message was clear: action in the present, particularly urgent action, was a necessary component of the battle against terrorism. This fit the "moment" side of the administration's obsession with time—now was the moment to act, "and act quickly, against danger." Having thus emphasized the importance of imminent action in justifying a preemptive doctrine, the president returned briefly to emphasis upon the administration's enduring commitment: "We will lift this dark threat from our country and from the world," noting that "the war on terror will require resolve and patience." In sum, in this address an obsession with time, particularly the need for imminent action, was at the heart of the president's justification of the administration's development of a preemptive doctrine. How else, Bush seemed to argue, could the darkness of evil be eradicated from the shadowy, sinister regions of the world? There was no other way but the one suggested by the administration—*now* and *forever*.

Similar language and a similar ordering of these time-fixated dimensions were evident in the administration's *National Security Strategy* document, issued three months later. This document began with a substantial prefatory statement by the president, followed by 31 pages of formal policy discussion. The president's statement, which essentially summarized the remainder of the document, is the focus of this analysis. Not long into his statement, Bush said, "Defending our Nation against its enemies is the first and fundamental commitment of the Federal Government. Today, that task has changed dramatically." For example, "Terrorists are organized to penetrate open societies and to turn the power of modern technologies against us." As a result, Bush contended, "To defeat this threat we must make use of every tool in our arsenal—military power, better homeland defenses, law enforcement, intelligence, and vigorous efforts to cut off terrorist financing. The war against terrorists of global reach is a global enterprise of uncertain duration." These comments defined the scope of the threat and affirmed the administration's enduring commitment against it. Shortly thereafter, the president turned to the importance of imminent action as justification for a preemptive doctrine; again, italics indicate those places in which an emphasis upon imminent action was explicit:

[A]s a matter of common sense and self-defense, America *will act against such emerging threats before they are fully formed.* We cannot defend America and our friends by hoping for the best. So we must be prepared to defeat our enemies' plans, using the best intelligence and proceeding with deliberation. *History will judge harshly those who saw this coming danger but failed to act. In the new world we have entered, the only path to peace and security is the path of action.*

Again, the language of imminent action was central to the administration's justification of a preemptive policy. Following this paragraph, the president discussed several specific policy challenges facing the administration, nation and world, and then concluded with these sentences: "Today, humanity holds in its hands the opportunity to further freedom's triumph over all these foes. The United States welcomes our responsibility to lead in this great mission." The implication was that Bush and the United States would walk the world into the Promised Land.

## NO TIME FOR OTHERS, OR FOR DEMOCRACY

These data indicate that an obsession with time was present in the public communications of the Bush administration—across differing policy discussions, over time, and by a range of administration leaders—and that this emphasis was echoed in a wide segment of news coverage. The ways in which a time fixation became manifest in the analyzed communications were instructive of how the administration crafted and communicated a political fundamentalism after September 11. In the days immediately following the terrorist attacks, the president framed the "war on terrorism" as the nation's *mission* and *moment*, an uncomplicated pairing within which the administration defined its campaign against terrorism. The strategic nature and political value of these ideas were apparent across the months from September 2001 to the close of major combat in Iraq in May 2003. Specifically, the administration employed the "mission" language to emphasize the importance of an enduring commitment and suggest that this commitment was according to providential plan. In turn, the administration used the "moment" language to push for imminent action on specific policies—*administration* policies, to be clear—and justified this desire as a requisite component of a long-term process. The wide presence of these time-fixated conceptions in the administration's communications and, albeit to a lesser degree as might be expected, in news coverage was an indication of how carefully the administration crafted its messages, how rigorously administration leaders stayed on message, and how useful these religious-cum-political ideas were in helping the administration grasp and maintain control of the political agenda.

Consistent emphasis on these ideas suggested that the administration was proceeding with judicious speed in fighting terrorism—that is, aware of the difficult challenge, yet constantly seeking progress. Such a perception was particularly engendered by the administration's ordering of discourse, begun in the days and weeks after September 11 when the administration laid the groundwork for a lengthy "war on terrorism." Analysis of the *New York Times* and *Washington Post* during this period suggested that the administration's overriding concern was to set public expectations that the campaign against terrorism would be an enduring commitment—long, arduous, and without a clear ending. In turn, this message was echoed powerfully on these newspapers' editorial pages.

Public opinion polls in autumn 2001 suggest that the administration communications, both directly in presidential addresses and via the press, molded public expectations. When U.S. adults were surveyed on September 21–22 whether they thought "the war against terrorism will be a long war, or a short one," 92 percent chose the former option. In the same survey, when asked whether they thought "the war against terrorism will be a difficult one, or a comparatively easy one," 94 percent chose the former option. The administration's message stuck, too: in late November, even after U.S. military successes in Afghanistan, 87 percent said the struggle against terrorism would a long one and 95 percent continued to expect a difficult campaign.[14] An overwhelming majority of U.S. citizens had been rhetorically primed to accept the administration's worldview.

Establishment of plans for an enduring commitment against terrorism, further solidified with suggestions of a divine leading, provided a foundation upon which the administration subsequently introduced new policies or plans—emphasizing the importance of immediate action in each case. In autumn 2001, the administration pushed for implementation of the U.S.A. Patriot Act and undertook military action in Afghanistan. In March 2002, the administration leaked to the press its internal *Nuclear Posture Review* document, hinting at preemption. In June 2002, the administration proposed the Department of Homeland Security and the president publicly spoke of a preemptive doctrine. In September 2002, the administration issued its *National Security Strategy* document, officially presenting the preemptive doctrine, and turned public attention to Iraq with the

September 12 address to the United Nations, attention that lasted through 2003.

For the overwhelming majority of this period of analysis the administration either pursued action or emphasized in its public communications the need for imminent action—on administration policies. The administration's lack of interest in sharing the political agenda was made clear by its dismissal of a homeland security agency when Senate Democrats pushed the idea shortly after September 11. Once the administration had reformulated the idea and could claim it as its own, the new Department became a matter of vital national security that deserved immediate action by Congress. Action to combat terrorism was not the goal, therefore; rather, action that combated terrorism *and* politically benefited the administration, promoted its worldview, and shut out others from receiving public credit was.

These communications are suggestive of a religious fundamentalist worldview that holds in complementary tension a sense of urgency and a sustaining comfort that individuals should endure in difficult tasks that are perceived to be providentially guided. Faith is essential, and the Bush team was playing with it. Perhaps most importantly, however, was that the political fundamentalist obsession with time had several deleterious implications. First, in committing the United States to a campaign of enduring length against terrorism, the administration set in motion a trajectory of events that could not be easily altered. Such a far-reaching commitment deserved much greater public discussion than it received in the *few days* between the terrorist attacks and the administration's public unveiling of the "war on terrorism." Certainly, an effective response was needed to address the threats at hand; however, the administration's policies obligated the nation to a course of action of essentially indeterminate length even though there had been almost no opportunity for public discussion of the rationale or implications. Democratic debate was circumvented.

Second, the administration's "mission" language subtly imbued this campaign with a divine leading, which at a minimum reinforced the Bush administration's stay-the-course resolve when it encountered criticisms. For example, criticisms about civil liberties restrictions, treatment of military detainees at Guantanamo Bay, and the need for war in Iraq were largely dismissed by the administration—with, again, little substantive public consideration. And third, the administration's unremitting pushes for action on administration policies effectually suggested that for members of Congress to not act quickly was to risk another September 11. The message was that congressional questions would not only present unpatriotic delays, but also well might cause more death. In the words of the president in his March 17, 2003, ultimatum to Saddam Hussein: "Instead of drifting along toward tragedy, we will set a course toward safety. Before the day of horror can come, before it is too late to act, this danger will be removed." These emphases in the administration's political fundamentalism helped them capture and maintain control of public discourse and the political agenda—democratic ideals be damned.

Two specific findings regarding the administration's discourse of imminent action offer additional insight into the strategic usage of these time-fixated emphases. First, the president was much less likely than the attorney general to emphasize time urgency in public communications about the U.S.A. Patriot Act (and somewhat less likely to call for action by Congress). It is certainly the case that many matters commanded Bush's attention in the days after September 11, whereas Ashcroft focused primarily on the domestic response to terrorism. However, during this same period the president had no difficulty staying on message about a likely lengthy duration to the "war against terrorism." One plausible interpretation, therefore, is that the president gave less emphasis to a need for imminent action because a publicly expressed desire on his part to enact the legislation in quick fashion implicated the administration's lack of preparation for the terrorist acts; indeed, matters of anti-terrorism had been a lesser priority for the Bush administration prior to September 11, even though the threat of an attack was very real.[15] As a result, the politically savvy thing to do was to have Ashcroft, not Bush, be more active in the public push for this legislation. Support for this interpretation is suggested by the second notable aspect of the administration's action discourse: Bush's emphasis on both indicators of imminent action increased substantially in his communications about the Department of Homeland Security, a new Cabinet-level position presented nearly nine months, not weeks, after September 11, and thus more likely to be publicly perceived as a forward-looking administration plan. These findings further suggest that action combating terrorism *and* profiting the administration were the goals of these discourses.

Finally, these administration themes were noticeably echoed in the press. As a result, across these differing policies an obsession with time was often present in administration communications and given considerable voice in leading news coverage. For example, calls for action by Congress were present in more than a third of the analyzed news coverage of the U.S.A. Patriot Act and more than half of the analyzed news coverage of the Department of Homeland Security. Further, discussion of time-urgency concerns was just as present in news coverage of the U.S.A. Patriot Act; this theme was less evident in Department of Homeland Security coverage, but nonetheless still was a consequential component of the discourse. Just as important was that these time-fixated emphases had a meaningful presence in each of the media forms analyzed—newspaper articles, editorials, and television news. The common presence of these ideas across a wide range of media outlets, over time, and in the context of differing policies clearly helped to circulate and reinforce a political fundamentalism that worked to the favor of the administration. Members of Congress almost certainly felt pressure to restrain debate and to vote for these pieces of legislation, even if they had concerns. Indeed, analysis of U.S. Senate debates about the Patriot Act revealed that several senators expressed significant questions but said that a need for speedy congressional action justified affirmative votes.[16] That the administration's strategic communications and an echoing press contributed to this climate is clear, and unfortunate.

# 4
# The universal gospel of freedom and liberty

President Bush was scheduled to visit the Emma Booker Elementary School in Sarasota, Florida, on the morning of September 11, 2001, to promote the importance of reading and literacy. Shortly after arriving at the school, the president was informed of the terrorist attacks in New York City. He made a brief announcement and was immediately flown to Barksdale Air Force Base in Louisiana, where he made his first substantive public statement about the attacks. He began with these words: "Freedom, itself, was attacked this morning by a faceless coward, and freedom will be defended" (Bush, 2001b). So commenced the administration's resounding post-attacks emphasis upon the values of freedom and liberty—two ideas, used in an interchangeable manner, that over the next 20 months rhetorically and politically bolstered the administration's military actions, new security-focused legislation, and preemptive foreign policy doctrine. In justifying these, the president and administration consistently claimed that freedom and liberty represented the noblest motivations and highest aspirations of all people, and that the United States had a responsibility to promote and defend them. The centrality of these values to the administration was highlighted in the naming of military campaigns "Operation Enduring Freedom," which began in Afghanistan in 2001, and "Operation Iraqi Freedom," undertaken in Iraq in 2003.

Freedom and liberty long have been core elements of U.S. national identity, dating to the mythic founding of the nation as a republic that would serve as a beacon of democracy.[1] In the months following the terrorist attacks, public emphasis upon these values by the administration facilitated the necessary re-construction of what Niebuhr (1967) has called a nation's positive "social myth": a culturally embedded narrative that distinguishes a nation from others, justifies its existence, and establishes a sense of collectivity.[2] A defining characteristic of such narratives is the presence of claims that particular moral qualities are integral to a nation's identity and superior to those found elsewhere. In attempting to renew a sense of national collectivity and to mobilize public opinion in the aftermath of September 11, the Bush administration emphasized freedom and liberty as the central attributes of U.S. national identity. The focus of this chapter is on how these values were presented in presidential communications and, in turn, often echoed by news coverage—as defining moral qualities of the nation that were desired by God for all peoples, with the United States as the promoter and defender of the values. The core beliefs that the United States was seeking to spread were not nationalistic in nature but God's *universal gospel*, the administration said in essence, so do not challenge us. Such claims about the universality of freedom and liberty and that the United States has a standing order to uphold and spread these principles were simultaneously rooted in religious fundamentalism while engendering political capital in this period of crisis.

## FUNDAMENTALISM, FREEDOM AND LIBERTY, AND STRATEGIC COMMUNICATION

An omnipresent consideration for religious fundamentalists is the "Great Commission" biblical mandate, in the book of Matthew, of "go therefore and make disciples of all the nations." The felt responsibility to live out this command, both locally and globally, has become intertwined for conservative Christians with support for the principles of political freedom and liberty. In particular, the individualized religious liberty present in the United States (particularly available historically for European-American Protestants, of course) is something that fundamentalists long to extend to other cultures and nations.

In the 1980s, fundamentalist preacher and leader Jerry Falwell argued that the dissemination of Christianity could not be carried out if other nations were communist—a perspective which provided a good reason to support a strong U.S. military, conservative foreign policy, and the spreading of individual freedoms.[3] This entwining of faith and politics solidified among contemporary U.S. religious fundamentalists the long-held view of the United States, in the words of Ammerman (1991), as a "chosen nation," specifically "ordained by God as the light to the nations" (pp. 40, 46).[4] In short, freedom and liberty are central components of a fundamentalist worldview, inexorably linked with the practice and dissemination of what Marty and Appleby (1992) call "the one true faith—as each fundamentalist believes his or her faith to be" (p. 26).

In turn, fundamentalists' certainty that their faith version "is absolutely and uniquely right," in the words of Barr (1977, p. 338), engenders a conception of their beliefs as universal in appeal and benefit. That is, a fundamentalist understanding of the world is considered to provide what Lawrence (1989) terms "mandated universalist norms" that cross cultural and historical context and therefore, as the biblical command makes clear, are to be shared with all nations. Indeed, Cox (1987) argues: "Fundamentalists not only insist on preserving the fundamentals of the faith, but envision a world in which these fundamentals would be more widely accepted and practiced. They want not only to 'keep the faith,' but *to change the world* so the faith can be kept more easily" (p. 289, emphasis added).

A belief in universal norms and the necessity of acting in ways that defended and extended these principles was particularly manifest after September 11 in the public communications of President Bush, who presented freedom and liberty as the noblest motivations, highest aspirations, and God's wishes for all. This universal gospel of freedom and liberty—emphasizing values with both religious and political heritages—functioned as the centerpiece of what religion scholar R. Scott Appleby termed the administration's offering of "a theological version of Manifest Destiny" (quoted in "Divine Intervention," 2003, p. 14). This twenty-first century adaptation of manifest destiny differs little from earlier U.S. versions: the goal remains to vanquish any who do not "willingly" adopt the norms and values of white, religiously conservative Protestants. The administration's discourse declared that to question this goal or the means used in pursuit of it was to question God.

Examination in this chapter of the president's national addresses shows that Bush's discussion of freedom and liberty became more strident in several ways following September 11. First, the president placed greater emphasis on these values, becoming more likely to highlight freedom and liberty as defining moral attributes and part of the positive "social myth" of the United States. Such discourse was an important step in renewing a sense of collective national identity. Second, the president more often presented these values as "mandated universalist norms"—that is, desired by and valuable for all peoples, and, therefore, noble motivations for U.S. goals and actions. Notably, the administration showed great cheek in emphasizing such claims while pursuing a number of policies that for many people produced outcomes of *less* freedom and liberty. In particular, as we will see, emphasis on freedom and liberty, both generally and as universal norms specifically, were important in the administration's justification of the preemptive foreign policy doctrine and its application in military action in Iraq. Finally, the president stamped these values as God-ordained after September 11. That is, the values were declared to be divinely desired for all peoples, a set of *explicit* claims by Bush regarding God's wishes. The president was not asking for divine favor; he was making definitive claims regarding God's will—and he had the power to act upon such certainty in ways that reshaped the globe.[5] It was a potent combination.

Analysis in this chapter also shows that editorial boards of a wide segment of mainstream U.S. newspapers followed much of Bush's language about freedom and liberty—with one notable exception. The central role of freedom and liberty in conceptions of U.S. national identity, and the reality that most journalists at U.S. newspapers are U.S. citizens, made the press likely to follow the president's discourse about these values, both generally and as universal norms specifically. However, newspaper editorial boards did not give voice to explicit presidential claims about providential desires regarding freedom and liberty, perhaps due to a cynicism among journalists about politicians' religious language that often is not shared by members of the public.[6] Evidence of a press that echoed presidential discourse about freedom and liberty generally and as universal norms specifically, but disregarded explicit religious claims by the president about these values, underscores the strategic importance for the Bush administration of crafting a *political* fundamentalism.

## ANALYSIS OF DISCOURSE

Analyzed first were (a) presidential national addresses and (b) editorials from a wide segment of U.S. newspapers following each address. Then examined were the president's address at the U.S. Military Academy in June 2002 and the administration's *National Security Strategy* document published in September

2002, both of which were instrumental in the public presentation and justification of the administration's preemptive foreign policy.

## Presidential Addresses and News Editorials

The presidential addresses and news coverage examined were the same as in Chapter 2. Seventeen addresses were analyzed, beginning with Bush's inauguration on January 20, 2001, and ending with his address on the aircraft carrier U.S.S. *Abraham Lincoln* on May 1, 2003. Editorials in the two days following each address were collected from 20 U.S. newspapers, selected because they are leading news outlets and offer geographic diversity. Content was retrieved from Nexis by the search string of "editorial and (Bush or president)" in the headline, lead paragraph, or key terms. Content that referred to presidents other than Bush was discarded, leaving 326 editorials.

The analysis of presidential addresses focused on the ideas present in each paragraph; that is, each paragraph in each address was examined for the presence of each thematic category (discussed below). This content analysis approach allowed identification of not just the presence of the ideas but also their prevalence in each address, so that relative emphases could be tracked over time. The paragraph breaks present in the addresses were followed. For newspaper editorials the analysis focused on the entire editorial due to the general brevity of editorials as well as their common focus on specific topics or themes. In addition, collection of editorials across 20 newspapers provided confidence that any meaningful shifts in editorial discourse would be captured. Also, because the newspapers were geographically diverse, regional differences would be accounted for.

Presidential addresses and editorials were analyzed for the presence or absence of three components, which were defined as follows:

*Freedom/liberty discourse*: This category was counted as present if either of these terms or related root words appeared. Both nouns and adjectives were included as long as the meaning was appropriate (that is, word combinations such as "risk-free" and "casualty free" were not included); identified examples included "freedom-loving," "free market," "free trade," and "enemies of liberty." To be clear, this category identified explicit "freedom" and "liberty" language. References to the *ideas* of freedom and liberty that did not mention the terms (such as "People everywhere want to be able to choose who will govern them") were not included, because these passages would force the coders to perform too much interpretation. Looking only for exact references made the coding much more reliable. Hence, this analysis was a conservative estimate of the amount of "freedom" and "liberty" discourse.

*Mandated universal norms*: This category was considered present when either of two claims about freedom or liberty appeared. First, any claim that these values were deserved by, desired by, or would benefit humanity, peoples, nations, religions, or cultures was an indication that this theme was present. For example, the president in the 2003 State of the Union said, "Americans are a free people, who know that freedom is the right of every person and the future of every nation." Second, any justification of U.S. policies or military action as motivated by the defense or promotion of freedom or liberty was also a sign that this theme was present. For example, Bush in his September 11 anniversary address in 2002 said, "We fight [the "war on terrorism"] not to impose our will but to defend ourselves and extend the blessings of freedom." In tandem, these claims were indicative of a conception of freedom and liberty as valuable for and deserved by all peoples.

*God's desire*: This category was considered present when claims were made about providential wishes regarding freedom and liberty. Only explicit linkages of these values with "God," a "Creator," or with identified Bible passages were included in this coding (there were no sacred texts of other faiths quoted, of course). Abstract references to religion, faith, providence, callings, or history were not included, even though these often connote a religious conception, due to a desire for a conservative analytic approach. Again, the point was to find definitive evidence of the theme in the text to show either indisputable, or lack of, evidence for this theme.[7]

### A Preemptive Foreign Policy

Also examined was whether and how the president emphasized freedom and liberty in two communications that were crucial in presenting and justifying the administration's preemptive foreign policy doctrine. This analysis provides insight into the link between the administration's universalist conceptions of freedom and liberty, and the policy that undergirded the war with Iraq. The president spoke publicly for the first time about a policy of preemption in his commencement address at the U.S. Military Academy in West Point, New York, on June 1, 2002,[8] and in September 2002, the administration issued a *National Security Strategy* document that discussed foreign policy generally, including the preemption doctrine.[9]

## A UNIVERSAL GOSPEL OF FREEDOM AND LIBERTY: THE EVIDENCE

Language about freedom and liberty in the president's national addresses and corresponding newspaper editorials is presented first in this section, followed by analysis of the same emphases in the president's West Point address and the *National Security Strategy* document.

### Presidential Addresses and News Editorials

President Bush more than doubled his emphasis upon freedom or liberty in national addresses after the terrorist attacks, and the press closely paralleled this discursive shift. Data in Figure 4.1 show that 9 percent of the president's paragraphs prior to September 11 contained "freedom" or "liberty" language, compared with 19 percent of paragraphs after the attacks. A similar doubling occurred in newspaper editorials: 15 percent prior to September 11 contained "freedom" or "liberty" language, compared with 30 percent after the attacks.[10] Notably, 84 percent of the president's references to these values emphasized "freedom" (these data are not shown).

Analysis of the use of "freedom" and "liberty" language over time revealed a modest address-by-address synchronicity between the president's language and that of editorials.[11] These data are arrayed in Figure 4.2. Close analysis of the trend lines shows that the newspaper editorials largely shadowed the president's discourse for 10 of the 14 post-terrorist attack addresses, with the exceptions being three in 2002—the State of the Union, Homeland Security in June, and the September 11 anniversary—and the president's calling of an end to "major combat" in Iraq in May 2003. In the first and last of these instances, newspaper editorials still contained substantial "freedom" and "liberty" discussion.

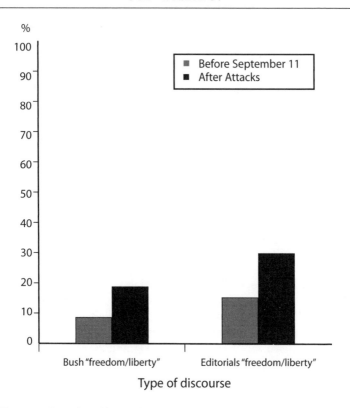

**Figure 4.1** "Freedom/liberty" discourse in Bush addresses by paragraph and in newspaper editorials in the two days following addresses

The evidence also indicates that President Bush and newspaper editorials were more likely to emphasize freedom or liberty as universal norms following the terrorist attacks. Data in Figure 4.3 show that 6 percent of presidential address paragraphs prior to September 11 presented freedom or liberty as universal norms, compared with 12 percent after the attacks. A similar pattern was present in the newspaper editorials: 7 percent prior to September 11 presented freedom or liberty as universal norms, compared with 15 percent after the attacks.[12] Patterns in Figures 4.1 and 4.3, then, reveal that the president's addresses and newspaper editorials following these addresses were significantly more likely after September 11 to emphasize freedom and liberty *and* to present these values as universal norms transcending cultures, context, and history. In addition, consideration

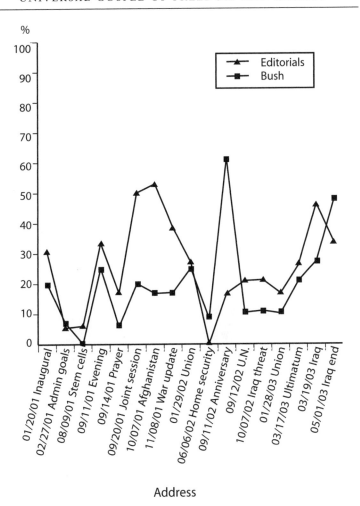

**Figure 4.2** "Freedom/liberty" discourse in Bush addresses by paragraph and in newspaper editorials in the two days following addresses

of these results together indicates that after September 11 fully two-thirds of the paragraphs about freedom and liberty in the president's national addresses positioned these values as universal norms, while exactly half of analyzed newspaper editorials did the same.

Interestingly, though, there was a negligible address-by-address synchronicity over time between the president's emphasis on

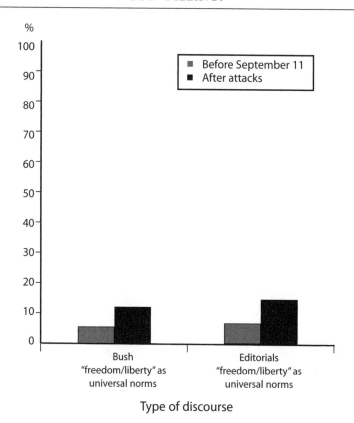

**Figure 4.3** Claims of freedom/liberty as universal norms in Bush addresses by paragraph and in newspaper editorials in the two days following addresses

freedom and liberty as universal norms and the presence of this discourse in editorials.[13] These data are arrayed in Figure 4.4. This figure does indicate two periods after September 11 of fairly parallel emphasis on freedom and liberty as universal norms in presidential addresses and newspaper editorials: first, the period immediately after the terrorist attacks and during initial U.S. military action in Afghanistan in late 2001, and second, the build-up to war in Iraq, beginning in autumn 2002 and carrying through to spring 2003. These results, in combination with the data in Figure 4.2, indicate that the press most closely followed the president's discourse about core U.S. values in periods of war or military action.

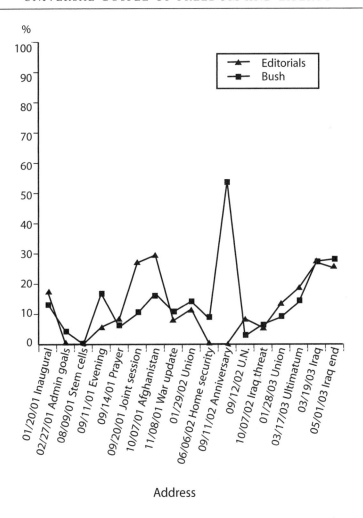

**Figure 4.4** Claims of freedom/liberty as universal norms in Bush addresses by paragraph and in newspaper editorials in the two days following addresses

Such a "war-time relationship" is important because the president and respective newspaper editorials were particularly likely to emphasize freedom or liberty, both generally and as universalist norms specifically, in the period immediately surrounding military action in Iraq in 2003. The president roughly doubled his emphasis on freedom and liberty, both generally and as universal norms specifically, in his March 17 ultimatum to Saddam Hussein, the March 19 announcement of U.S. military operations, and the May 1 "victory" address. Data in Figure 4.5 show that during these "Iraq war" addresses, 32 percent of presidential paragraphs contained "freedom" or "liberty" language, compared with 17 percent in Bush's other post-attacks addresses; similarly, claims that these values represented universal norms were present in 22 percent of paragraphs in the president's "Iraq war" addresses, compared with 11 percent in other post-attacks addresses.[14] Corresponding newspaper editorials paralleled these shifts, particularly for the universal norms discourse. During the "Iraq war" period, 35 percent of analyzed editorials contained "freedom" or "liberty" language, compared with 28 percent of other post-attacks editorials. More markedly, claims that these values represented universal norms were present in 23 percent of "Iraq war" editorials, compared with 12 percent of other post-attacks editorials.[15] These values, then, were particularly emphasized in this war context by the president and in news discourse. Later in this chapter we will see that these values were similarly emphasized in the president's presentation and justification of the preemptive foreign policy doctrine that was crucial in providing rationale in the months leading up to the Iraq war.

Excerpts (a) from the president's addresses provide insight into these strategic emphases (including the interchangeable usage of freedom and liberty) and (b) from newspaper editorials are indicative of the press's echoing of this language and ideas.

On the evening of September 11, the president said, "America was targeted for attack because we're the brightest beacon for freedom and opportunity in the world" (Bush, 2001a). Similarly, at the National Cathedral memorial service three days later, the president said, "In every generation, the world has produced enemies of human freedom. They have attacked America because we are freedom's home and defender" (Bush, 2001c). A week later in his September 20 address before Congress, the president declared:

> I know there are struggles ahead and dangers to face. But this country will define our times, not be defined by them. As long as the United States of America is determined and strong, this will not be an age of terror; this will be an age of liberty, here and across the world.
>
> (Bush, 2001e)

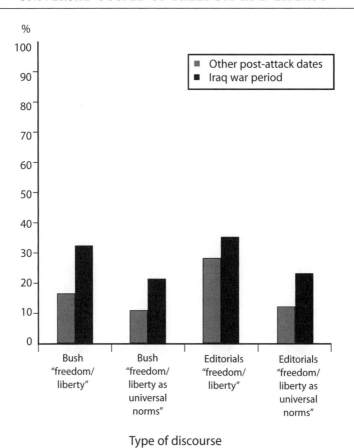

**Figure 4.5** "Freedom/liberty" discourse and claims of freedom/liberty as universal norms in Bush addresses by paragraph and in newspaper editorials in the two days following addresses

A few words later he added: "Freedom and fear are at war. The advance of human freedom, the great achievement of our time and the great hope of every time, now depends on us." On October 7, in announcing military operations in Afghanistan, Bush said: "The name of today's military operation is Enduring Freedom. We defend not only our precious freedoms but also the freedom of people every-where to live and raise their children free from fear" (Bush, 2001h). In his State of the Union address in 2002, the president declared,

"America will lead by defending liberty and justice because they are right and true and unchanging for all people everywhere," and then in a series of concluding paragraphs said:

> In a single instant, we realized that this will be a decisive decade in the history of liberty, that we've been called to a unique role in human events. Rarely has the world faced a choice more clear or consequential.
>
> Our enemies send other people's children on missions of suicide and murder. They embrace tyranny and death as a cause and a creed. We stand for a different choice, made long ago on the day of our founding. We affirm it again today. We choose freedom and the dignity of every life.
>
> Steadfast in our purpose, we now press on. We have known freedom's price. We have shown freedom's power. And in this great conflict, my fellow Americans, we will see freedom's victory.
>
> (Bush, 2002a)

In the September 11 anniversary address, delivered from the base of the Statue of Liberty on Ellis Island, freedom and liberty were emphasized in fully 61 percent of the president's paragraphs. He said:

> There is a line in our time and in every time between those who believe that all men are created equal and those who believe that some men and women and children are expendable in the pursuit of power. There is a line in our time and in every time between the defenders of human liberty and those who seek to master the minds and souls of others. Our generation has now heard history's call, and we will answer it.
>
> (Bush, 2002h)

He later added: "We respect the faith of Islam, even as we fight those whose actions defile that faith. We fight not to impose our will but to defend ourselves and extend the blessings of freedom." The next day at the United Nations, Bush's focus turned but his discourse did not: "Liberty for the Iraqi people is a great moral cause and a great strategic goal. The people of Iraq deserve it; the security of all nations requires it" (Bush, 2002i). In his State of the Union address in 2003, the president said, "We exercise power without conquest, and we sacrifice for the liberty of strangers. Americans are a free people, who know that freedom is the right of every person and the future of every nation" (Bush, 2003a). And in his ultimatum to Saddam Hussein on March 17, Bush said, "The power and appeal of human liberty is felt in every life and every land. And the greatest power of freedom is to overcome hatred and violence and turn the creative gifts of men and women to the pursuits of peace" (Bush, 2003c).

The final presidential address analyzed, in which the president called an end to "major combat" in Iraq, was delivered on the U.S.S. *Abraham Lincoln* aircraft carrier (Bush, 2003e). Freedom or liberty was emphasized in nearly half (48 percent) of the paragraphs. Early in the address the president said: "In this battle, we have fought for the cause of liberty and for the peace of the world." Shortly thereafter, he declared the universality of the values:

> In the images of celebrating Iraqis, we have also seen the ageless appeal of human freedom. Decades of lies and intimidation could not make the Iraqi people love their oppressors or desire their own enslavement. Men and women in every culture need liberty like they need food and water and air. Everywhere that freedom arrives, humanity rejoices, and everywhere that freedom stirs, let tyrants fear.

And then, near the end of the address, he linked the administration's war with Iraq, the first of a preemptive nature in U.S. history, with significant national moments and leaders:

> Our commitment to liberty is America's tradition, declared at our founding, affirmed in Franklin Roosevelt's Four Freedoms, asserted in the Truman Doctrine and in Ronald Reagan's challenge to an evil empire. We are committed to freedom in Afghanistan, in Iraq, and in a peaceful Palestine. The advance of freedom is the surest strategy to undermine the appeal of terror in the world.

He added, "Where freedom takes hold, hatred gives way to hope. When freedom takes hold, men and women turn to the peaceful pursuit of a better life. American values and American interests lead in the same direction: We stand for human liberty."

Similar language was present in newspaper editorials. On September 12, 2001, the *Tampa Tribune* said, "As the free world mourns losses that far exceed the death toll at Pearl Harbor, we Americans are reminded that freedom is not forever won. Every generation seems destined to have to reclaim it at enormous cost." Following the president's address to a joint house of Congress, the *New Orleans Times-Picayune* said:

> "Great harm has been done to us," President Bush declared. "We have suffered great loss, and in our grief and anger we have found our mission and our moment. Freedom and fear are at war." We have no choice. A wide-ranging effort to shut down terrorist activity can prevent future attacks on the United States, and it would be a service to the civilized world.
>
> (*New Orleans Times-Picayune*, September 21)

The next day, the *Omaha World-Herald* compared Bush with Winston Churchill, noting that:

> Churchill wrote his own speeches. Bush, for the most part, does not. Does that really matter? No. Thursday night, Bush made those words and that vision fully his own, and ensconced them firmly in the hearts and minds of freedom-loving people everywhere.
>
> (*Omaha World-Herald*, September 22)

Following the commencement of U.S. military action in Afghanistan, the *Cleveland Plain-Dealer* said:

> Our goal is to eliminate or render powerless those who would threaten our safety and deprive us of the liberties that perhaps we had come to take for granted. With those liberties at risk — perhaps as never before — yesterday began the long and righteous campaign to show the world we will not surrender them without a fight.
>
> (*Cleveland Plain-Dealer*, October 8)

On the same day, the *St. Louis Post-Dispatch* declared: "Like their ancestors on the Lexington green, the pilots over Afghanistan have fired a shot heard around the world. It is once again a shot fired for freedom, this time on behalf of civilization's war to be free from the fact and the fear of terrorism." And following the 2002 State of the Union, the *Minneapolis Star Tribune* directly picked up the president's discourse:

> Bush gets high marks from the American people for his overall conduct of the war. He deserves those high marks, and he deserves the support of the American people as he continues to press the campaign. The president put it well: "We have known freedom's price. We have shown freedom's power. And in this great conflict, my fellow Americans, we will see freedom's victory."
>
> (*Minneapolis Star Tribune*, January 30)

Newspaper editorials followed the president's turning of focus to Iraq beginning in autumn 2002. On September 13, following the president's address at the United Nations, the *Chicago Sun-Times* said, "The free world, whether it likes to admit it or not—whether it becomes actively involved in its own self-defense or not—depends on our efforts." On October 8 following the president's national address on Iraq, the *Portland Oregonian* said that Bush's address "held out an American commitment to a freer, economically stable future for Iraq and the Iraqi people," while the next day the *New Orleans Times-Picayune* opined that "Saddam Hussein and al Qaida clearly share a hatred of the United States and a disdain for the basic features of a free society." In January 2003, following the president's State of the Union address, the *Seattle Times* said that "at its best, this speech touched on America's call to all people living under tyrants and despots. When Bush said America is prepared to offer liberty to strangers, he recalled the best of what this country has done around the world." On the same day, the *Houston Chronicle* said, "Few would quarrel with Bush's conclusion: 'We exercise power without conquest, and sacrifice for the liberty of strangers.'" In response to the initiation of military action in Iraq, the New York *Daily News* said:

> America is not out to enslave the Iraqi people. It is not on a crusade against Islam. It is doing what it has always done: standing up for liberty and the rights of humankind to live unencumbered by the chains of beastly brutality. We are now at

war. May it be sure but swift. May God protect our troops and bring them all safely home. And may Iraq awake some morning soon to something it has not seen in generations: a new dawn of freedom.

(New York *Daily News*, March 20)

The same day, the *St. Louis Post-Dispatch* declared, "freedom is something for which all human beings deeply yearn." And following the president's address calling an end to major combat in Iraq, the *Tampa Tribune* concluded on May 3 that "War is hell, but fortunately for the strong and free, it works." And the same day the *Cleveland Plain-Dealer* said, "it's hard to argue against the core American idea of human liberty. And it's hard to deny the president the joy of his singular afternoon at sea among those who have made the latest payments toward freedom's cost." In sum, an emphasis on freedom and liberty, including claims that these values were universal norms for all peoples, consistently was present in the president's addresses and consistently was echoed in newspaper editorials between September 2001 and spring 2003.

One additional noteworthy form of discourse about freedom and liberty also was present in the president's national addresses after September 11—explicit claims about providential desires. A presidential declaration regarding the wishes of God would be rhetorically notable; as a result, any such claims were unlikely to occur often. A focus on the number of presidential addresses (rather than the percentage of paragraphs in addresses) indicates that claims about divine wishes regarding freedom and liberty were present in 4 of 14 presidential addresses (29 percent) between September 2001 and the end of the Iraq conflict in spring 2003, whereas they were nonexistent beforehand. Whether or not the explicit presence of God-speak was a personal choice of the president or a strategic choice by his advisors is difficult to determine. The use of this overtly Christian language does suggest, though, that the administration was confident that it could benefit by explicitly linking religious language with freedom and liberty, values at the core of U.S. national identity. Newspaper editorials, in contrast, almost never emphasized such linkages: only one analyzed editorial tied a divine plan to freedom and liberty, and it was following Bush's inauguration. This editorial, in the *St. Louis Post-Dispatch* on January 21, 2001, extrapolated from the president's claims that freedom and liberty were foundational to the nation's birth to note that in "calling for freedom and equality [the president] stressed the Founders' view that these are God-given rights." This editorial, however, was an anomaly—and an unremarkable one at that; otherwise the press stuck to its more secular, objectivity-based roots.

Nevertheless, Bush's overtly conservative Christian rhetoric was powerful, noticeably stepping over the once-solid line separating church from state. The president actually made five declarations of God's wishes regarding freedom and liberty after September 11; two were in one address. His first claim came in the address before Congress on September 20, 2001, in which he said: "The course of this conflict is not known, yet its outcome is certain. Freedom and fear, justice and cruelty have always been at war, and we know that God is not neutral between them" (Bush, 2001e). The initial words of the second sentence—a binary construction that set up a false opposition—became widely echoed in news discourse; the latter half of the sentence was every bit as central to the administration's political fundamentalism.

The next claims of this manner were present in the September 11 anniversary address in 2002, when the president twice explicitly placed providential desires within the context of national identity. He said:

> The attack on our nation was also attack on the ideals that make us a nation. Our deepest national conviction is that every life is precious, because every life is the gift of a Creator who intended us to live in liberty and equality. More than anything else, this separates us from the enemy we fight. We value every life. Our enemies value none, not even the innocent, not even their own. And we seek the freedom and opportunity that give meaning and value to life.
>
> (Bush, 2002h)

And a few paragraphs later, he said:

> We cannot know all that lies ahead. Yet, we do know that God has placed us together in this moment, to grieve together, to stand together, to serve each other and our country. And the duty we have been given, defending America and our freedom, is also a privilege we share. We're prepared for this journey.

And our prayer tonight is that God will see us through and keep us worthy.

In the 2003 State of the Union, as the conflict with Iraq loomed—28 of 80 paragraphs in this address (35 percent) were devoted solely to Iraq or Saddam Hussein—the president again explicitly declared divine desires regarding freedom and liberty: "Americans are a free people, who know that freedom is the right of every person and the future of every nation. The liberty we prize is not America's gift to the world, it is God's gift to humanity." He then added, "Americans have faith in ourselves, but not in ourselves alone. We do not know—we do not claim to know all the ways of providence, yet we can trust in them, placing our confidence in the loving God behind all of life and all of history" (Bush, 2003a). And in his address calling an end of "major combat" in Iraq on May 1, 2003 the president placed freedom, liberty, and U.S. actions on behalf of these values squarely within a Judeo-Christian heritage:

> Every name, every life, is a loss to our military, to our nation, and to the loved ones who grieve. There's no homecoming for these families. Yet we pray, in God's time, their reunion will come.
>
> Those we lost were last seen on duty. Their final act on this earth was to fight a great evil and bring liberty to others. All of you—all in this generation of our military have taken up the highest calling of history. You're defending your country and protecting the innocent from harm. And wherever you go, you carry a message of hope, a message that is ancient and ever new. In the words of the prophet Isaiah, "To the captives, 'come out,' and to those in darkness, 'be free.'"
>
> (Bush, 2003e)

Following the September 11 attacks, then, the president in four addresses made claims about providential desires regarding freedom and liberty—and about the role of the United States in promoting and defending these values. These claims were not all pervasive in his rhetoric; nonetheless direct references to God's will playing a part in U.S. politics occurred often enough to suggest a pattern.

## A Preemptive Foreign Policy

Freedom and liberty were also emphasized in the administration's justification of a preemptive foreign policy. As a reminder, data in Figure 4.5 indicated that freedom and liberty, both generally and as universal norms specifically, were particularly emphasized by the president (and echoed by newspaper editorials) in addresses immediately surrounding military action in Iraq. However, even prior to these addresses in the buildup to war was the administration's development of a preemptive foreign policy. This doctrine was unveiled publicly for the first time in the president's commencement address at West Point on June 1, 2002, and was subsequently elaborated in the administration's *National Security Strategy* document, issued in September 2002. In both texts, freedom and liberty were central.

Following introductory comments in the West Point address (Bush, 2002b), the president turned to an extended discussion of the administration's campaign against terrorism. He began, "Our war on terror is only begun, but in Afghanistan it was begun well. I am proud of the men and women who have fought on my orders. America is profoundly grateful for all who serve the cause of freedom, and for all who have given their lives in its defense." Soon thereafter, he said:

> This war will take many turns we cannot predict. Yet I am certain of this: Wherever we carry it, the American flag will stand not only for our power, but for freedom. Our nation's cause has always been larger than our nation's defense. We fight, as we always fight, for a just peace—a peace that favors human liberty. We will defend the peace against threats from terrorists and tyrants. We will preserve the peace by building good relations among the great powers. And we will extend the peace by encouraging free and open societies on every continent.
>
> Building this just peace is America's opportunity, and America's duty. From this day forward, it is your challenge, as well, and we will meet this challenge together. You will wear the uniform of a great and unique country. America has no empire to extend or utopia to establish. We wish for others only what we wish for ourselves—safety from violence, the rewards of liberty, and the hope for a better life.

[ 111 ]

The president then turned to the need for a new foreign policy approach, declaring that terrorism and "tyrants" necessitated that the United States "confront the worst threats before they emerge." In particular, he said, "[O]ur security will require all Americans to be forward-looking and resolute, to be ready for preemptive action when necessary to defend our liberty and to defend our lives." This marked the president's first public mention of a preemption policy and the only specific usage of this term in the address. That freedom and liberty were central to his justification of this policy is evident.

A few paragraphs later, the president placed this doctrine within the tradition of iconic U.S. leaders and accomplishments. In so doing, he made explicit his outlook regarding the universality of norms and values:

> Because the war on terror will require resolve and patience, it will also require firm moral purpose. In this way our struggle is similar to the Cold War. Now, as then, our enemies are totalitarians, holding a creed of power with no place for human dignity. Now, as then, they seek to impose a joyless conformity, to control every life and all of life.
>
> America confronted imperial communism in many different ways—diplomatic, economic, and military. Yet moral clarity was essential to our victory in the Cold War. When leaders like John F. Kennedy and Ronald Reagan refused to gloss over the brutality of tyrants, they gave hope to prisoners and dissidents and exiles, and rallied free nations to a great cause.
>
> Some worry that it is somehow undiplomatic or impolite to speak the language of right and wrong. I disagree. Different circumstances require different methods, but not different moralities. Moral truth is the same in every culture, in every time, and in every place.

The president then devoted several paragraphs to discussion of U.S. relations with other world leaders, which included his claim, "The United States, Japan and our Pacific friends, and now all of Europe, share a deep commitment to human freedom, embodied in strong alliances such as NATO. And the tide of liberty is rising in many other nations." Shortly thereafter, the president said: "Even in China, leaders are discovering that economic freedom is the only lasting source of national wealth. In time, they will find that social and political freedom is the only true source of national greatness. " The universality of these values remained an emphasis for the president, who eventually turned his focus beyond Europe and Asia: "When it comes to the common rights and needs of men and women, there is no clash of civilizations. The requirements of freedom apply fully to Africa and Latin America and the entire Islamic world. The peoples of the Islamic nations want and deserve the same freedoms and opportunities as people in every nation." He added, "And their governments should listen to their hopes."

A significant emphasis on freedom and liberty was also present in the administration's *National Security Strategy* document, issued three months later. A substantial prefatory statement by the president began the document, offering the political vision that undergirded the policy applications subsequently discussed. The preemptive doctrine was not discussed by name in the president's statement; rather, he offered a worldview that supported the need for U.S. action against "emerging threats before they are fully formed." Central to this justification were the values of freedom and liberty; indeed, the president's statement is replete with language about these values. The first paragraph is presented here in its entirety, with italicization of places emphasizing the values:

The great struggles of the twentieth century between *liberty* and totalitarianism ended with a decisive victory for the *forces of freedom*—and a single sustainable model for national success: *freedom*, democracy, and *free* enterprise. In the twenty-first century, only nations that share a commitment to protecting basic human rights and guaranteeing political and economic *freedom* will be able to unleash the potential of their people and assure their future prosperity. People everywhere want to be able to speak *freely*; choose who will govern them; worship as they please; educate their children—male and female; own property; and enjoy the benefits of their labor. These values of *freedom* are right and true for every person, in every society—and the duty of protecting these values against their enemies is the common calling of *freedom-loving people* across the globe and across the ages.

(National Security Council, 2002)

This paragraph contained eight references to "freedom" or "liberty," several of which suggested that these values are universal norms for all peoples. In addition, a number of other phrases in the paragraph clearly referred to the meaning of freedom and liberty without using these terms.

Similar language and emphasis on these values were present throughout the statement. For example, the president said that the United States had as a goal "to create a balance of power that favors human freedom: conditions in which all nations and all societies can choose for themselves the rewards and challenges of political and economic liberty." Later in the document, the president said:

> The United States will stand beside any nation determined to build a better future by seeking the rewards of liberty for its people. Free trade and free markets have proven their ability to lift whole societies out of poverty—so the United States will work with individual nations, entire regions, and the entire global trading community to build a world that trades in freedom and therefore grows in prosperity.

Soon thereafter, the president said: "In building a balance of power that favors freedom, the United States is guided by the conviction that all nations have important responsibilities. Nations that enjoy freedom must actively fight terror." A few sentences later he added that because "no nation can build a safer, better world alone," the United States would work in alliances with other "freedom-loving nations." And in the final paragraph, the president declared:

> Freedom is the non-negotiable demand of human dignity; the birthright of every person—in every civilization. Throughout history, freedom has been threatened by war and terror; it has been challenged by the clashing wills of powerful states and the evil designs of tyrants; and it has been tested by widespread poverty and disease. Today, humanity holds in its hands the opportunity to further freedom's triumph over all these foes. The United States welcomes our responsibility to lead in this great mission.

The evidence shows, then, that the administration's justification of its preemptive doctrine substantially emphasized freedom and liberty, often presenting these values as universal norms for all of humanity.

## FREEDOM AND LIBERTY, RHETORIC VERSUS REALITY

U.S. national identity was ripe for challenge, transformation, and reconstruction between September 2001 and spring 2003, a period bookended by historic challenges to the nation's self-conception. The terrorist attacks of September 11 led many people in the United States to wonder, in the words of an October 15 *Newsweek* magazine cover, "Why do others hate us?," while the war in Iraq that commenced in March 2003 was the first to begin with preemptive military action by the United States. During these months, President Bush in his national addresses consistently heralded freedom and liberty as defining moral qualities of the United States, presenting and affirming these attributes as central characteristics of the national ethos. Such emphasis had great strategic importance for the administration, and followed in the discursive footsteps of previous political leaders who turned to these values in pivotal moments to spur national cohesion and to mobilize public opinion. What made this particular presidency distinct, however, is that such rhetoric was in direct contradiction to the federal government's treatment of many residents of the United States during the same months. The profiling and detainment of hundreds of people of Arab or South Asian descent in the months after September 11, the push for deep and wide-ranging infringements on citizens' civil liberties that were enacted in the U.S.A. Patriot Act, and the deportations of countless immigrants on unrelated-to-terrorism matters all were in contradiction to the president's language of freedom and liberty.[16] The picture of the world suggested by the president's rhetoric was not matched by the experiences of a significant number of people in the United States, but it was the words of the president, not those of these politically invisible individuals, that controlled public discourse and the political agenda.

The temptation may exist to view the discourses identified in this chapter as solely political in origin and outcome. That would be a mistake. Freedom and liberty are deeply ensconced in a religious fundamentalist worldview, crucially intertwined with goals regarding the protection and spread of the faith.[17] Consistent claims by the president that these values had global appeal and benefits reflected a fundamentalist certainty that they offered universal norms crossing cultural and historical contexts. At the same time, the omnipresent sense of crisis provided a discursive space in which the administration

[ 115 ]

had the confidence to make explicit claims about providential wishes regarding freedom and liberty. The Bush administration, therefore, offered a dangerous combination: the president claimed to know God's wishes *and* presided over a global landscape in which the United States could act upon such beliefs without compunction. Indeed, the administration's decision for war in Iraq is wholly congruent with religious fundamentalists' willingness, in the words of Perkin (2000, p. 79), to impose "what they take to be God's will upon other people" because others are viewed as certain to benefit.[18] This military action in Iraq was undertaken even though a significant number of traditional international allies rejected the administration's views. In these early years of the twenty-first century, however, the will of the United Nations was meaningless to a U.S. president seemingly certain of the will of God.

The president's discourse, then, seamlessly converged the administration's religious fundamentalist worldview with the politics of the period. The freedom and liberty emphases offered a remedy for the national disequilibria engendered by the terrorist attacks, and when in 2002 the United States entered morally uncharted terrain with the creation and application of a preemptive doctrine, presidential declarations of the universal, divine nature of these values shut down potential opposition. The president cast freedom and liberty as central to the preemptive policy—so central that in his first public mention of this doctrine, at West Point, the president said that people in the United States needed "to be ready for preemptive action when necessary to defend our liberty and to defend our lives." Months later, when this doctrine was applied in the conflict in Iraq, the president in national addresses surrounding this war employed "freedom" and "liberty" language in one of every three paragraphs, a remarkable emphasis that could not have been missed by the U.S. public. This discourse included the president's linkage, on May 1, 2003, of the administration's "commitment to liberty" with the nation's founding and the leadership of Franklin Roosevelt, Harry Truman, and Ronald Reagan—a set of associations that attempted to lend further credibility to the nation's war in Iraq.

In essence, the administration now was saying that to question the preemptive doctrine and Iraq war meant to disagree with not only providential design, but also the nation's founders, FDR, Truman, and Reagan. Such an overt convergence of religion and politics is indicative of the heights of self-assuredness that had emerged for the president and his advisors by spring 2003.

This public confidence reflected and encouraged the response of newspaper editorials, which, with the exception of explicit claims about God's desires regarding freedom and liberty, consistently echoed the president's discourse about these values. "Freedom" and "liberty" language and emphasis on these values as universal norms significantly increased in analyzed newspaper editorials after September 11; these shifts over time paralleled the patterns of the president's communications. Roughly 30 percent of editorials in these U.S. newspapers contained "freedom" and "liberty" language after September 11, a doubling from editorials prior to the terrorist attacks. Further, half of editorials discussing freedom and liberty emphasized these values as universal norms after September 11, also a doubling from beforehand. These numbers peaked during the Iraq war context in spring 2003. These findings are consistent with the claims by Hutcheson et al. (2004) that there exists an "inexorable intertwining of political leaders and mass media, particularly *news* media, in the construction, articulation, and dissemination of national identity" (p. 47, their emphasis).[19]

At the same time, this echoing in newspaper editorials was much less likely to occur on an address-by-address basis than what was found in analysis of the president's binary discourse in Chapter 2, perhaps because the language of freedom and liberty was much less unusual (and thus, less newsworthy). With this in mind, one potential explanation is that once these values had been discursively re-established by the president and an echoing press in the immediate aftermath of the terrorist attacks—a process that began with Bush's public statement at Barksdale Air Force Base *a few hours* after the attacks—journalists may have felt less of an inclination consistently to follow the lead of each presidential address. Regardless, this lack of address-by-address synchronicity does not obscure the larger finding that news discourse paralleled the general patterns of presidential emphasis on the gospel of freedom and liberty over time, particularly during the periods of U.S. military action in 2001 and 2003. In short, the echoing continued.

# 5
# Unity, or else

In the days and weeks following the terrorist attacks, the U.S. Congress and public demonstrated historic levels of support for a presidential administration. Republicans and Democrats in Congress submitted to the administration's push for imminent action on anti-terrorism legislation, eventually passing the U.S.A. Patriot Act so quickly that prior to one vote most House of Representative members had only three hours to read an overhauled version of a 342-page law which amended 15 federal statutes.[1] Public opinion about President Bush's performance surged from just above 50 percent, where it had hovered for the eight-plus months of his presidency, to nearly 90 percent approval.[2] And leading news media, including the editorial pages of the *New York Times* and *Washington Post* as we saw in Chapter 3, climbed on board with the administration's plans for a "war on terrorism." The White House had publicly preached a philosophy of political civility and bipartisanism during the initial months of its tenure in Washington D.C.,[3] and now the administration suddenly had unified support across much of the political and media spectrum. But it was not enough, as Bill Maher learned.

Maher was host of an ABC late-night television program, *Politically Incorrect*, in which he and guests offered controversial opinions about issues of the day. On September 17, 2001, Maher addressed a claim by the president that the suicide bombers of September 11 were cowards. Maher referenced the Clinton administration's responses to previous terrorism against U.S. embassies overseas, and said: "We have been the cowards lobbing cruise missiles from 2,000 miles away. That's cowardly. Staying in the airplane when it hits the building, say what you want about it, it's not cowardly" (reported in McDaniel, 2001). The response was swift: Several companies withdrew advertising from *Politically Incorrect* and a number of local television stations suspended broadcasts of the show, prompting Maher to issue an apology.[4] On September 26, White House press secretary Ari Fleischer, when asked about Maher's comments, said:

It's a terrible thing to say, and it [is] unfortunate. And that's why—there was an earlier question about has the President said anything to people in his own party—they're reminders to all Americans that they need to watch what they say, watch what they do. This is not a time for remarks like that; there never is.

(Fleischer, 2001)

From the White House the message was clear: unprecedented public and political support was not enough. Any visible disagreement with the administration would not be kindly tolerated in the aftermath of September 11, and perhaps, as Fleischer suggested, not ever.

The argument in this chapter is that the discursive dynamic undergirding Fleischer's comments and the perspective he offered were often repeated in subsequent months as the administration responded to September 11, undertook the campaign against terrorism, and guided the nation through two wars. To be specific, the administration consistently demonstrated *intolerance for dissent* by adroitly pairing a consistent emphasis upon political civility and unity as central virtues of representative government with harsh rebukes when this norm was not met—that is, when other political actors challenged the administration. This pairing facilitated the administration's control over public discourse by making it politically painful for others to publicly disagree. Maher's comments and Fleischer's response in September 2001 fit this dynamic: a foundational discourse of unity was widely present, which provided the administration a platform to claim that any dissenting Americans needed "to watch what they say, watch what they do." This chapter argues that a fixation on unity over dissent is rooted in religious fundamentalism while offering great political value in times of crisis. Evidence is then presented both of dissent-chilling emphases in the Bush administration's discourse across several domains of policy, and of the role of news media in disseminating these communications.

## FUNDAMENTALISM, DISSENT, AND STRATEGIC COMMUNICATION

Considerable scholarship has linked religious fundamentalism with authoritarian decision-making and behavior.[5] That is, religious fundamentalists conceive of the world in a hierarchical manner in which wisdom and decisions are seen as emanating from sources of

[ 119 ]

perceived authority—particularly sacred texts, traditions, and selected leaders. These sources are not to be challenged. In the words of Lawrence (1989), "Fundamentalism is the affirmation of religious authority as holistic and absolute, admitting of neither criticism or reduction" (p. 27). While the greatest weight is given to religious texts, a belief that leadership in general is beyond challenge infuses a fundamentalist worldview, for leaders are considered conduits for God and as such are believed to be touched by divinity. This "holier than the populace" conception of authority prompts both a continual *emphasis upon unity* as a foundational normative expectation (to break from the herd is to go against divine wishes), and regular attempts by those in power, in the words of Garvey (1993), "to stamp out all forms of dissent" (p. 24). One way in which this latter characteristic becomes manifest is through the imposition of a significant *cost for dissent*. Infliction of a penalty may not squelch a particular instance of disagreement and may even provoke further criticism at the time, but such an action has a greater long-term benefit—it sends a message to others that deviation from the norm of unity carries a considerable price. The Bush administration between September 2001 and spring 2003 manifested both of these characteristics in its urge to control public discourse on its terms.

During these months the communication discipline of the Bush administration, as discussed in Chapter 1 and demonstrated in the previous three chapters (and later in this one), consistently produced a unified public message. Such unity among administration voices was not fortuitous, but rather political fundamentalism in practice; that is, it was orchestrated by expectations of unity and an omnipresent threat of a cost for any who deviated. Individuals in the administration who publicly clashed with the president risked receiving what Suskind (2003) calls the "Rove Treatment"—that is, criticism and belittlement by administration strategist Karl Rove, whose close ties to the Bush family date to the early 1970s and former President George H. W. Bush.[6]

Inside the administration, it was be with the president or be gone, a not-coincidentally parallel reality to the administration's "war on terrorism" treatment of other nations. As a result, rarely did a key administration member after September 11 publicly offer an opinion counter to or divergent from the president's.[7] This strategic approach was crucial in the administration's ability to dominate public discourse. Maltese (1994, p. 1) has argued, for example, that "any appearance of disunity among the president's ranks will be seized by the media as an opportunity for a story," thereby distracting from the administration's goals. Indeed, Entman (2003, p. 422) has noted, "strategically maladroit administrations, such as the Carter and Clinton White Houses, often found news frames spinning out of their control." Not so for the Bush administration.

In addition to exhibiting unity in their communications, the president and other administration members emphasized this principle in their public communications. The president arrived in Washington D.C. in January 2001 calling for a political environment marked by "civility." Following the terrorist attacks, this discourse was transformed into an emphasis upon unity, an idea that has historically resonated with the American public and had particular rhetorical power in this crisis context. While Beasley (2001) notes that an emphasis upon unity within diversity long has been a staple of U.S. presidential language, in the aftermath of the terrorist attacks such an emphasis provided an opportunity for the White House to characterize any strong disagreement as unpatriotic and hazardous. In the context of this nation-challenging crisis, therefore, the administration's calls for unity essentially meant that other political actors *should stand with the administration in pursuing the administration's goals.* When this did not occur, the administration in several instances declared a morally unambiguous cost for those who publicly disagreed: such dissenters were presented as a threat to American (and global) security.

In combination, then, an emphasis upon unity and harsh rebukes of dissenters allowed the Bush administration between September 11 and the Iraq war to do what Nagata (2001) has contended that fundamentalists always desire: to "close off the ideological marketplace" (p. 494) in a manner that benefits them. For this administration this meant not only shutting down the democratic ideal of free and open public debate, but also demeaning some who disagreed.

This chapter examines these emphases within discourse by the administration and in news coverage—newspaper articles, editorials, and television news to be specific—about three distinct "war on terrorism" goals: the U.S.A. Patriot Act, proposed and enacted in autumn 2001; Department of Homeland Security legislation, proposed and enacted in 2002; and two resolutions regarding the status of Iraq, one passed by Congress in October

2002 and one passed by the United Nations in November 2002. A range of administration voices were examined: the president for each policy goal, Attorney General John Ashcroft for the U.S.A. Patriot Act, and Secretary of Defense Donald Rumsfeld and Secretary of State Colin Powell for both Iraq resolutions.

Evidence presented later in the chapter shows that an emphasis upon unity and a willingness to impose a cost upon political actors who challenged the administration were widely present in the administration's public communications. At the same time, analysis of the administration's messages in conjunction with press coverage offers rich insight into why, in times of national crisis when citizens are far more likely to adopt a posture of support for a president, what is most important for an administration is whether the press consistently echoes its messages— even if coverage is critical at times.

It was a near certainty, for example, that the administration's attempts to squelch dissent would draw press criticism, for at least two reasons. First, the administration's emphasis upon unity implicitly challenged the well-known preference among mainstream journalists for stories that involve conflict between two or more people, sides or parties, thus decreasing the likelihood that news media would favorably highlight calls for unity.[8] Further, outright declarations by an administration of a penalty for dissent were almost guaranteed to raise the ire of journalists, for whom employment is predicated upon freedom of speech and press. Thus, if an administration had as its central goal that it be treated positively in press coverage, then attempts—or at least public attempts—to silence dissent would be avoided. And, certainly, an administration would not continue any such communications if it became apparent that press criticism would follow. In contrast, if an administration had a central goal of controlling public discourse, regardless of press treatment, there was great political value in pairing an emphasis on unity with harsh critiques when this norm was not met—because the former constrained political opponents in the crisis context, and the latter was likely to trigger media coverage that widely disseminated a message suggesting that the administration was to be supported, or else. Such an approach would be the one expected from a political fundamentalism interested in controlling public discourse with little regard for democratic debate, and it is the one revealed in this analysis.

## ANALYSIS OF DISCOURSE

Administration communications and news discourse were examined across three key administration policies and goals after September 11: (1) the U.S.A. Patriot Act legislation, proposed by the administration within weeks of the terrorist attacks and passed by Congress in late October 2001; (2) the proposal for a new Cabinet-level Department of Homeland Security, proposed by the administration in June 2002 and passed by Congress in November 2002; and (3) the proposal of two Iraq-focused resolutions, one to authorize U.S. military force that was formulated in September 2002 and passed by Congress in early October, and one to reopen Iraqi facilities to weapons inspectors that was initially discussed in September 2002 and passed by the United Nations Security Council in early November. Data are explained in this section according to the type of evidence: (a) emphasis in the discourse upon the importance of political unity with the administration, and (b) instances in which a cost was assigned to the speech or actions of political actors who challenged the administration.

### Political Unity

Administration discourse was collected in several steps. Communications by (a) Bush and Ashcroft regarding the U.S.A. Patriot Act, and (b) Bush regarding the Department of Homeland Security legislation were the same as those analyzed in Chapter 3. These procedures (discussed in Chapter 3) yielded 18 relevant texts for Bush and 13 for Ashcroft for the U.S.A. Patriot Act, and 121 texts for Bush regarding the Homeland Security Department. For discourse about Iraq, the National Archives and Records Administration's *Weekly Compilation of Presidential Documents* database was searched using the string of "Bush and Iraq" from September 12, 2002, when the president delivered a U.N. address about Iraq that symbolically marked the opening of the administration's push for the two resolutions, through November 7, the day prior to the U.N. Security Council's adoption of Resolution 1441. These dates incorporated debate in Congress, which passed an Iraq resolution on October 11. This procedure yielded 81 texts for Bush, a number of which also contained discussion of the Department of Homeland Security. These in-common texts were included in both the Homeland Security

Department and Iraq analyses, since they contributed to each discourse. The public communications of Powell and Rumsfeld also were analyzed for discussion of Iraq; the former was the primary "point person" for the administration in U.N. discussions, while the latter often spoke about Iraq due to military implications. Their communications were collected from the State and Defense department websites, which provides public communications by the secretaries. All communications between the dates of analysis were read, yielding 40 relevant texts for Powell and 26 for Rumsfeld.

To identify news coverage, newspapers and television news transcripts were searched in the Nexis database for the same dates as administration communications. Coverage of the U.S.A. Patriot Act was the same as that analyzed in Chapter 3: 209 articles and editorials across 15 geographically diverse newspapers, and 21 television news stories from the daily evening newscasts of ABC, CBS, and NBC networks. Coverage of the Department of Homeland Security legislation was also the same as that analyzed in Chapter 3: 81 editorials across 20 geographically diverse newspapers, and 51 television news stories from the evening newscasts of ABC, CBS, and NBC. News coverage about the Iraq debate was gathered via Nexis from the same media outlets as for the Homeland Security Department analysis. Editorials were collected using the string of "Iraq and (Bush or White House or administration or Congress) and editorial." This search yielded 1,437 texts, of which 181 were relevant. Television news transcripts again were collected from the evening newscasts of CBS, ABC, and NBC, using the same search string (minus "editorial"). This search yielded 327 texts, of which 165 were relevant. Editorials and television news transcripts were eliminated if they did not address the resolutions, potential for military combat or "Iraq threat" in general. The vast majority of eliminated texts were newspaper news stories (not editorials), "teasers" promoting other coverage, general news about Iraq, or content that mentioned the proposed resolutions in passing.

Administration communications about these policies were first analyzed, with a theme of "political unity" becoming apparent. Analysis focused on each specific communication (a) by the president, attorney general, or secretaries (for example, an address, testimony before Congress, press conference), or (b) in news coverage (for instance, news story or editorial). The theme was evaluated as absent or present, and was defined as follows:

*Political unity*: This theme was considered present if a reference was made to political unity in relation to administration goals or policies—unity either among U.S. leaders or more broadly among world nations. This reference did not have to be explicitly attached to the policies of focus (which, by definition, were discussed in the communications) because any reference to unity in the same communications was seen as comprising at least an implicit link. Examples included "bipartisan cooperation," "work with me/us," "strong support from the Council," "a strong consensus," "international coalition," and "largest coalition in the history of humankind."[9]

## Imposition of a Cost for Dissent

A series of public beratings—instances in which the administration overtly criticized other political actors for speech or actions that challenged the administration—was also analyzed. These instances were chosen for three reasons: (1) they corresponded to policies for which an emphasis upon unity by the administration also was examined; (2) a range of key administration actors were centrally involved in the instances; and (3) they occurred over time, rather than in one specific context or policy discourse. For these instances, both the administration's communications and news coverage on television networks ABC, CBS, and NBC, and in the *New York Times* and *Washington Post* were collected (op-ed pieces were excluded because the newspapers rarely have much say over their content). Analysis focused on three components of the discourse. First, what was alleged to have been placed at risk by dissenters' words or actions? Second, were the administration's messages emphasized in these media outlets? And third, how were the administration's messages treated in news coverage? As elaborated above, any hint of support in news coverage would have been a "bonus" for the administration, since dissent-squelching behavior was likely to be condemned in the press.

The first selected instance began with Attorney General Ashcroft's testimony before the U.S. Senate Judiciary Committee on December 6, 2001. This testimony, which commenced with a statement by Ashcroft and then followed with a number of questions from committee members, focused on the administration's domestic anti-terrorism efforts and the Department of Justice's role in these.[10]

The second instance began with the president's public address in Trenton, New Jersey, on September 23, 2002. In this address, a standard campaign speech for the most part, the president discussed a number of topics; what gained attention were his comments about the U.S. Senate and matters of U.S. security.[11]

The third instance began with public comments by Democratic Senator Tom Daschle, minority leader of the Senate, about the diplomatic efforts of the administration regarding Iraq. These comments were delivered to a convention of American Federation of State, County, and Municipal Employees on March 17, 2003—the same day that the United States broke off negotiations with the United Nations and just hours before President Bush issued a 48-hour ultimatum to Saddam Hussein to depart Iraq or face military attack.

## AN INTOLERANCE FOR DISSENT: THE EVIDENCE

Emphasis upon the importance of political unity in both the administration's discourse and news coverage is presented first, followed by analysis of the three instances in which the administration declared a cost for the speech or actions of political actors who challenged the administration.

### Political Unity

All three policies of focus in this analysis were proposed by the Bush administration. The U.S.A. Patriot Act was developed in the days after September 11 under the guidance of Attorney General Ashcroft, was introduced into Congress in early October, and was passed on October 25, 2001. The cabinet-level Department of Homeland Security was proposed in a national address by the president on June 6, 2002, and was introduced into Congress later that month, but had not been passed by the November elections, when Republican Party gains assured Congressional passage. The Iraq resolutions symbolically commenced with the president's address to the United Nations General Assembly on September 12, 2002, in which he declared that Iraq presented a collection of "dangers in their most lethal and aggressive forms, exactly the kind of aggressive threat the United Nations was born to confront" (Bush, 2002i). Following this address, the administration began negotiations on Iraq-related resolutions with the U.S. Congress and U.N. Security Council. Congress passed a resolution authorizing U.S. military force against Iraq on October 11, and the U.N. Security Council on November 8 passed Resolution 1441, which declared that Iraq needed to provide unfettered access to weapons inspectors and implied that military action would follow if this did not occur.

Analysis of the administration's communications show that considerable emphasis was placed upon "political unity." In particular, data in Figure 5.1 show three patterns.[12] First, language about the importance of political unity was consistently present across the administration's leading officials, indicating that they spoke with a common voice in emphasizing this principle. Second, the president was remarkably consistent in his discourse over time, with an emphasis on unity in roughly 90 percent of his communications across the policy goals of the U.S.A. Patriot Act, Homeland Security Department, and Iraq. Third, the president was more likely than Ashcroft, Powell, and Rumsfeld to emphasize political unity, particularly in discourse about Iraq; the president's greater emphasis helped to establish contexts in which these Cabinet members applied specific pressures via negotiations and conversations with other political actors. Each of these patterns is suggestive of the strategic nature of the Bush administration's communications.

Some excerpts provide insight into how an emphasis on the importance of political unity was made manifest in the administration's communications. In talking about the Patriot Act in autumn 2001, the president, following a meeting with congressional leaders at the White House on September 19, said:

> I want to welcome the members of the leadership of the Congress here, and I want the nation to know how proud I am of how they have helped unite our country. Senator [Tom] Daschle and the Speaker and Senator [Trent] Lott and Representative [Richard] Gephardt have really showed that in times of emergency and crisis, that our government can function in a way that is just exemplary.
>
> (Bush, 2001d)

The president often suggested that nationalism had come to supersede partisanship; in an address to airline employees in Chicago on September 27, Bush said, "Traveling with me today were Republicans and Democrats, but make no mistake about it, they're first and foremost patriotic Americans" (Bush, 2001g). He later added, "We are united in bringing justice to those folks who did the evil deed on September 11."

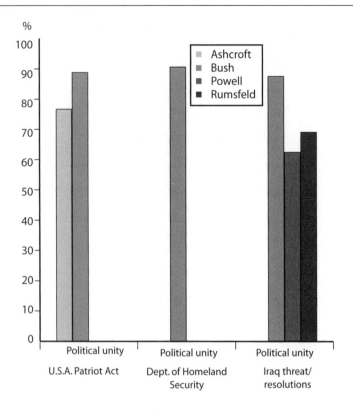

**Figure 5.1** Emphasis on "political unity" by administration leaders in public communications about administration policy goals

Ashcroft, as the administration's "point person" on the Patriot Act, often explicitly linked political unity with the anti-terrorism legislation. On September 17, he noted that he had met with Senate and House leadership the previous day:

The meetings we had were very productive. And I'm optimistic that we will be able to act quickly to provide law enforcement with the additional tools that are necessary to fight terrorism. I was encouraged by the members' support and their pledge to work as members of the Congress with the Department of

Justice to move this agenda of anti-terrorism legislation forward.

(Ashcroft, 2001a)

On October 4, Ashcroft said that Congress had shown an "extraordinary commitment to the cause of our nation's security" in his discussions with them about anti-terrorism legislation. He added, "I'm gratified for the progress that has been made and I believe that there are a number of areas in which we can continue to work cooperatively together to strengthen this legislation and bring it to final passage" (Ashcroft, 2001b). And when adoption of the law began to appear near on October 18, Ashcroft said he was "extremely gratified by the expeditious, bipartisan, bicameral attention that this anti-terrorism legislation has received" (Ashcroft, 2001f).

These emphases continued more than eight months later in the president's communications about the Department of Homeland Security. On July 26, 2002, the president said that he looked forward to working with Congress "to get the bill right, to make sure that when we look back at what we've done, we will have left behind a legacy, a legacy that will allow future Senators and future members of the House and a future president to say, 'I can better protect the homeland thanks to what was done in the year 2002.'" He added, "I'm confident we will respond in a way that will make America proud—America proud of our efforts to come together" (Bush, 2002d). On August 7, after the bill had been passed by the House of Representatives, the president said, "This isn't a Republican issue, folks. This isn't a Democrat issue. This is an American issue" (Bush, 2002f). On September 2, Bush said:

I've asked the Congress to join me in creating a new Homeland Security Department. And the reason I did is because I wanted to be able to come and, when I see the people, say, "Our most important priority is to protect America, and therefore, I want all agencies involved with protecting America under one umbrella."

(Bush, 2002g)

By mid-autumn, however, Senate Democrats were refusing to yield to the administration's desire to not allow federal employees in the new Homeland Security Department to unionize; as a result, the president sharpened his emphasis on unity. On October 18, he said: "The House passed a good homeland security bill. The House heard my call to have a bipartisan approach to protecting the homeland. The House heard the call to put aside politics and not let interests—be interested in special interests but to focus on the American people, not only today but down the road. And the House passed a bill." Not so for the Senate, Bush said: "They're stuck in the Senate. The Senate can't get it done right now. It's stuck" (Bush, 2002q).

This emphasis upon political unity became nearly omnipresent in autumn 2002 when Bush, Powell, and Rumsfeld turned their focus to Iraq. On September 18, following a meeting with congressional leaders, the president said:

> We talked about a resolution out of Congress and how it was important for us to work with Congress to pass a strong resolution. I told the members that within the next couple of days this administration will develop language as—that we think is necessary. And we look forward to working with both Republicans and Democrats to get a resolution passed. I want to thank the leadership for its commitment to get a resolution done before members go home for the election break. I think it's an important signal. It's an important signal for the country, but as importantly, it's an important signal for the world to see that this country is united in our resolve to deal with threats that we face.
> (Bush, 2002j)

On September 26, the president said about the Iraq resolution before the Congress, "This is not a partisan issue, folks. This is an issue that is important for America. This is an American issue, a uniquely American issue." Bush added that, regarding Saddam Hussein, "there's no doubt his hatred is mainly directed at us. There's no doubt he can't stand us. After all, this is a guy that tried to kill my dad at one time" (Bush, 2002l). After Congress passed the resolution, the president on October 12 said, "Our country and our Congress are now united in purpose. America is speaking with one voice" (Bush, 2002o). The president then turned his attention to the United Nations. On October 14, he said: "The United Nations needs to make a choice, whether it will be the League of Nations or the United Nations, whether it will be an empty debating society or a group of countries who have got the capacity and the will and the backbone to help keep the peace." He added that "if need be, the United States will lead a strong coalition of freedom-loving nations and disarm Saddam Hussein" (Bush, 2002p). And on October 18 he said:

> We call upon the United Nations to show us whether or not this is a body that can effectively keep the peace, or it's like one [of] its predecessors, the League of Nations. We call upon people to come together to disarm this man before he harms the United States or our friends and allies.
>
> (Bush, 2002q)

This emphasis upon the importance of unity in dealings with Iraq ran consistently through the communications of administration leaders. Secretary of Defense Rumsfeld, speaking to the House of Representatives Armed Services Committee on September 18, urged Congress to pass a resolution so that "a clear signal" could be sent "to the world community and to the Iraqi regime that our country is united in purpose and prepared to act" (Rumsfeld, 2002a). Three days later in an interview with the *Sunday Times* of London, Rumsfeld highlighted international support for U.S. actions against terrorism generally, and in regard to Iraq specifically:

> We have a coalition in the global war on terrorism of over 90 countries, something like half of all nations in the world. It is without question the largest coalition in human history.... It's a breathtakingly broad and deep coalition. It is a current, visible manifestation of the fact that the United States recognizes the value of cooperating with other countries.... The United States government has been talking to dozens and dozens of countries all over the world [about Iraq] and any number have agreed to help in one way or another.
>
> (Rumsfeld, 2002b)

And in a Department of Defense press briefing on October 7, Rumsfeld opined about deliberations in Congress that "everyone seems to think that there will be a resolution, and it'll pass overwhelmingly by the Congress" (Rumsfeld, 2002c).

Secretary of State Powell was the central administration figure in negotiations among U.N. Security Council members. On September 13, the day after the president's address to the U.N. General Assembly,

Powell emphasized the importance of both domestic and international support for the administration's goals. He noted that he and Rumsfeld would testify before Congress in the next few weeks, adding "I am confident after we make the case we will get the support that the president will need" (Powell, 2002a). In another communication the same day, Powell said his goal was "to achieve consensus within the Security Council on what we should do about [Iraq]," later adding that it was important for the United Nations "to come together to deal with this crisis" (Powell, 2002b). On September 19, in testimony before the House of Representatives Committee on International Relations, Powell said:

> I ask that the Congress consider [this matter] carefully and quickly, and I ask for immediate action on such a resolution to show the world that the United States is united in this effort. To help the United Nations understand the seriousness of this issue, it would be important for all of us to speak as a nation, as a country.
>
> (Powell, 2002c)

On October 9, on the *Larry King Live* program on CNN, Powell declared: "We have to be firm at this moment in history. We have to be united as a Cabinet, as a nation, and I think we are. And we also should be united as an international community, the United Nations coming together" (Powell, 2002d). And on October 28, in a round-table with European journalists, Powell said, "It would be much better for all concerned if we could find a way that the Council is united and worked together as a council on these elements that I've just discussed. And that's what we're trying to achieve" (Powell, 2002e). A week later, on November 4, Powell in interviews with news media from U.N. Security Council member nations, said: "I think we are all united behind the need for a strong resolution," later adding:

> I think what we are now seeing is a coalition is forming, not necessarily a coalition for war, but a coalition for peace, a coalition that understands that peace will only come in this part of the world if Iraq is disarmed, and a coalition that is saying to Iraq that you have violated your obligations and it cannot be tolerated.
>
> (Powell, 2002f)

Finally, on November 7, as the Security Council vote was imminent, Powell said, "We took this time to talk to our friends and allies to make the case....They had their principles and red lines and we had ours, and we found a way to converge. And I think the convergence is near complete" (Powell, 2002g). Indeed it was: The Security Council voted 15–0 the next day.

Turning to analysis of news coverage about these policies, two patterns emerged in the data in Figure 5.2. First, political unity received considerably less emphasis in news coverage than it did in administration communications, present in roughly 10 to 20 percent of most news coverage across these policies. In an "apples to apples" comparison, the administration's time-fixated calls for imminent action (analyzed in Chapter 3) were present in a quarter to more than half of the analyzed news discourse. Both were extensively emphasized by the administration, but the emphasis on urgent action accorded seamlessly with predominant journalistic conceptions of what qualifies as news, whereas the emphasis on unity challenged traditional news norms. This point will be returned to later in this chapter. Even at the lesser emphasis, though, political unity was a visible component of news discourse on these matters. A second point is that political unity did receive considerable emphasis in analyzed newspaper editorials about Iraq, of which 61 percent highlighted the importance of political unity.

Some excerpts provide insight into the ways in which an emphasis on political unity became manifest in news coverage. In autumn 2001, a *Washington Post* article on September 20 reported "the Bush administration yesterday presented Congress with its proposed antiterrorism package as lawmakers vowed to continue their bipartisan push for a swift response to last week's air assaults on New York and Washington." A *St. Louis Post-Dispatch* article the same day quoted Vermont Senator Patrick Leahy, chair of the Senate Judiciary Committee: "'There are far more things that unite us than divide us,' Leahy said, with Ashcroft at his side. 'We all have the same Constitution.'" The article later added, "[E]ven those most likely to raise concerns about civil liberties stressed the desire to work in unity as they moved forward on the package." A CBS news story on October 2 reported, "Congress is coming together on a wide-ranging plan to strengthen the anti-terrorism laws." A *San Francisco Chronicle* story on the same day said, "In a swift show of bipartisan unity, lawmakers on the House Judiciary Committee reached a compromise on

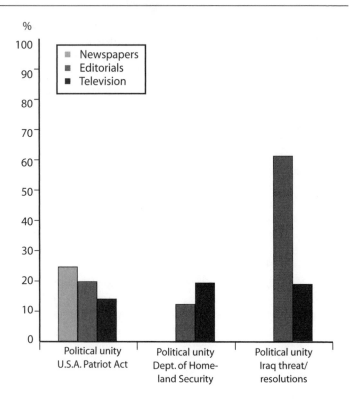

Figure 5.2 Emphasis on "political unity" in news coverage about administration policy goals

anti-terrorism legislation yesterday that would make it easier for law enforcement to wiretap phones, track e-mail messages and seize the assets of those suspected of terrorism." And a *Washington Post* editorial on October 3 noted, "[T]he process in both houses has been impressively bipartisan, with only a couple exceptions. The emerging compromise is not yet where it ought to be, but is headed in the right direction."

For the Department of Homeland Security, greater emphasis upon political unity appeared in television newscasts than in editorials. An NBC news story on June 6, the evening of the president's address to the nation, reported that "Congressional reaction [is] almost universally positive," adding, "Republicans and Democrats agree the framework here is sound." A CBS news story on July 16 said that "both parties want to pass legislation to create the department in time for the September 11 anniversary and say it's in everyone's interest that they work together," then presented this quote from Democrat representative Jane Harman: "I constantly make the point that the terrorists won't check our party registration before they blow us up." When the political debate became a bit heated, a *New York Times* editorial on August 2 said: "Lawmakers on Capitol Hill and Bush administration officials should use the recess that begins this week-end to cool their rhetoric and find common ground on which this department can be created. It shouldn't be that hard: All sides claim to be committed to the same national goals." A *New York Daily News* editorial said:

> We have met the enemy, and it is Al Qaeda. And Saddam Hussein. And any country that supports the terrorism that spawned the evil that tore our world apart a year ago.... Moving slowly, risking little, letting our anxieties and other frightened nations stoke our doubts, divert our attention and sap our resolve ... this is the stuff of defeatism. We declare to ourselves—with pomp and ceremonies—how united and resolute we are. It would be all the more reassuring if we acted on it.
>
> (*New York Daily News*, September 15)

And on September 26, an NBC news story said, "Look for both sides to try to hammer out a compromise. They don't want to go home this fall to an election, saying, 'We couldn't come together on a homeland security bill.'" Of course, this is exactly what did happen—ultimately to the electoral benefit of the Republican Party.

For the debate about Iraq, an emphasis on unity was particularly present in newspaper editorials, perhaps because editorial boards, as opinion leaders in ways that traditional reporting is not, felt a need to emphasize the importance of unity and to assess whether the administration was achieving it in pressing toward Iraq. At the same time, noticeable echoing was present in television news coverage. On September 15, three days after the president's address to the United Nations, ABC news reported that "the administration now wants Congress to pass a resolution supporting the president before its

October recess," then quoted Condaleezza Rice, the administration's National Security Adviser: "[The president] wants the will of the American people to have been expressed by the Congress, to show the world, and indeed, to show Saddam Hussein, that you have a unified American view, that it is time to deal with this threat." Similarly, a *Denver Post* editorial on September 19 said: "The administration wants a congressional resolution before the U.N. acts, showing the world the United States is, well, united. We think our representatives should act too, but only after they've done their due diligence." The *Seattle Times* editorial board opined:

> The president said Iraq would have to disarm itself and destroy its capacity to produce weapons of mass destruction. International arms inspectors must be allowed unfettered access to the entire country. Otherwise, the president pledged the United States would lead a coalition force against Iraq. No talk of going alone.
>
> (*Seattle Times*, October 8)

On October 12, the day after passage of a congressional resolution authorizing the president to use military force against Iraq, a CBS news story declared that the administration had "seized the moment" in previous days by inviting "a bipartisan crowd" of key congressional leaders to the White House. The story continued, "By today, even Senate Democratic Leader Tom Daschle said he was with the president," then quoted Daschle: "'And because I believe it is important for America to speak with one voice at this critical moment, I will give—I will vote to give the president the authority he needs.'" The *Minneapolis Star Tribune* on October 20 suggested that the administration had "made the right distinctions" in dealing differently with Iraq and North Korea, but emphasized that the two foreign policy foci shared "a common element: the need to work constructively with others. Every day the world proves again how unpredictable it is. Dealing with that unpredictability requires a community effort." And on October 23, as the administration neared a formal first draft of a resolution for the U.N. Security Council about mechanisms to guarantee Iraqi disarmament, the *Washington Post* editorialized: "In effect, President Bush has risked the indefinite delay or evisceration of his campaign to eliminate the Iraqi threat in order to build a broad international coalition and preserve the authority of the United Nations. We believe the risk was worth taking."

In sum, an emphasis upon the importance of political unity was widely present across Bush administration members' public communications about the U.S.A. Patriot Act in 2001 and Department of Homeland Security and Iraq in 2002. In turn, this emphasis upon unity was visible but not predominant in news discourse about these matters, with one important exception—newspaper editorials about congressional and United Nations resolutions targeting Iraq.

## Imposition of a Cost for Dissent

As a second component of the analysis, three instances were examined in which the administration imposed a cost for the speech or actions of political actors who challenged the administration. The first instance was the testimony of Attorney General Ashcroft before the Senate Judiciary Committee on December 6, 2001. This testimony provided an opportunity for senators to question Ashcroft about the administration's response to terrorism. Of particular interest to the Senate was (a) the administration's decision to establish military tribunals as appropriate legal forums to try some people arrested in the "war on terrorism"; and (b) the Department of Justice's treatment of civil liberties under the far-reaching oversight provisions of the U.S.A. Patriot Act, which Ashcroft had spearheaded and Congress had passed in late October. Notably, the lone dissenter in the Senate's 98–1 vote in favor of the Patriot Act, Democrat Russell Feingold of Wisconsin, was a member of the Judiciary Committee and was present to question Ashcroft. Also relevant is that Ashcroft had served in the Senate 1994–2000, which included time as a member of the Judiciary Committee.

In his opening statement, Ashcroft began by recalling the events of September 11, noting the number of lives lost and the administration's subsequent mobilization against terrorism. Ashcroft said, "Since those first terrible hours of September the 11th, America has faced a choice that is as stark as the images that linger of that morning. One option is to call September 11th a fluke, to believe it could never happen again, and to live in a dream world that requires us to do nothing differently." The other option, he said in a binary form of communication, was the one chosen by the administration—"to fight back, to summon all our strength and all our resources and devote ourselves to better ways to identify, disrupt, and dismantle terrorist networks." Soon thereafter, he suggested that American civil liberties posed a threat to national security:

> Terrorist operatives infiltrate our communities, plotting, planning, waiting to kill again. They enjoy the benefits of our free society, even as they commit themselves to our destruction. They exploit our openness—not randomly or haphazardly—but by deliberate, premeditated design.
>
> (Ashcroft, 2001g)

He then listed a number of actions undertaken by the Department of Justice to protect national security, which led to these remarks:

> In all these ways and more, the Department of Justice has sought to prevent terrorism with reason, careful balance, and excruciating attention to detail. Some of our critics, I regret to say, have shown less affection for detail. Their bold declarations of so-called fact have quickly dissolved, upon inspection, into vague conjecture. Charges of "kangaroo courts" and "shredding the Constitution" give new meaning to the term, "the fog of war." Since lives and liberties depend upon clarity, not obfuscation, and reason, not hyperbole, let me take this opportunity today to be clear: Each action taken by the Department of Justice, as well as the war crimes commissions considered by the President and the Department of Defense, is carefully drawn to target a narrow class of individuals—terrorists. Our legal powers are targeted at terrorists. Our investigation is focused on terrorists. Our prevention strategy targets the terrorist threat.
>
> Since 1983, the United States government has defined terrorists as those who perpetrate premeditated, politically motivated violence against noncombatant targets. My message to America this morning, then, is this: If you fit this definition of a terrorist, fear the United States, for you will lose your liberty.
>
> We need honest, reasoned debate; not fearmongering. To those who pit Americans against immigrants, and citizens against non-citizens; to those who scare peace-loving people with phantoms of lost liberty; my message is this: Your tactics

only aid terrorists—for they erode our national unity and diminish our resolve. They give ammunition to America's enemies, and pause to America's friends. They encourage people of good will to remain silent in the face of evil.

Ashcroft concluded shortly thereafter, noting that "not long ago I had the privilege of sitting where you now sit" and that he had "the greatest reverence and respect for the constitutional responsibilities you shoulder." However, "In accordance with over 200 years of historical and legal precedent, the executive branch is now exercising its core constitutional powers in the interest of saving the lives of Americans." Having made clear that dissent threatened such lives, he added:

I trust that Congress will respect the proper limits of executive-branch consultation that I am duty-bound to uphold. I trust, as well, that Congress will respect this president's authority to wage war on terrorism and defend our nation and its citizens with all the power vested in him by the Constitution and entrusted to him by the American people.

The response by Ashcroft to criticisms of the Department of Justice and his claims of the dangers of dissent from administration goals received considerable emphasis in news media. The evening newscasts and Sunday talk shows of CBS, ABC, and NBC were searched in the Nexis database (search string of "Ashcroft or Senate") from Thursday, December 6, through Sunday, December 9 (*Nightline* also was included for ABC). Seven programs included coverage of Ashcroft's testimony, and *all of them* emphasized some portion of his quote that "to those who scare peace-loving people with phantoms of lost liberty; my message is this: Your tactics only aid terrorists—for they erode our national unity and diminish our resolve. They give ammunition to America's enemies, and pause to America's friends." In several instances, these words were the only point of emphasis from Ashcroft's testimony. Further, while some expressed disagreement with Ashcroft or the perspective in his comments, overt criticism was rare in television coverage. A CBS news story concluded "for now anyway, senators seem ready to give the administration the benefit of the doubt when it comes to tactics for dealing with the terrorists." Vice-president Dick Cheney (on NBC's *Meet the Press*) and Republican Senator John McCain (on CBS's *Face the Nation*) were given opportunities to defend and explain Ashcroft's statements, which they did while also arguing on behalf of administration goals generally. On ABC's *Nightline*, Ted Koppel displayed Ashcroft's words and then added that the attorney general and senators mostly "underplayed their parts. The Democrats called for greater oversight and more details but pledged their support." And ABC reporter Antonia Mora noted, "Committee Democrats emphasize that their concerns about civil rights did not mean that they want to protect terrorists."

Thirteen pieces in the *New York Times* and *Washington Post* (search string of "Ashcroft" in Nexis) included coverage of his testimony during the same dates. All of this coverage either directly quoted his words about dissent or referred to the perspective suggested in them; indeed, this was the focus of lead paragraphs in front-page stories in both newspapers on the day after the testimony. The *Times* story began, "In forceful and unyielding testimony, Attorney General John Ashcroft today defended the administration's array of anti-terrorism proposals and accused some of the program's critics of aiding terrorists by providing 'ammunition to America's enemies.'" More of his words about dissent followed in the next paragraph. Similarly, the *Post* story began, "Attorney General John D. Ashcroft resolutely defended the Justice Department's anti-terrorism tactics yesterday, telling a Senate committee the measures are necessary to prevent future attacks and suggesting that criticism of them aids the terrorist cause." Ashcroft's specific words about dissent came two paragraphs later. In addition, the *Times* included unedited excerpts from the attorney general's discussion with senators, and selected Ashcroft's comment, "To those who scare peace-loving people with phantoms of lost liberty; my message is this: Your tactics only aid terrorists" as the newspaper's Quotation of the Day on December 7. Harsh criticism of Ashcroft's words was leveled in the newspapers' editorials, with headlines of "John Ashcroft misses the point" (*Times*), "The Ashcroft smear" (*Post*), and "An oversight by the Senate" (*Post*). Even in these, however, the administration's underlying and more important message was echoed by the press: there was a cost for challenging the administration.

The second instance analyzed in which the administration imposed a cost for dissent occurred in late September 2002. The political environment had become contested: Democrats in the Senate were refusing to pass the president's version of the Department of Homeland Security legislation and the administration was pushing Congress to pass a resolution authorizing the use of military force against Iraq. On September 23, on the same day that former Vice-president Al Gore in a public address criticized the president for a "do-it-alone, cowboy-type reaction to foreign affairs" (quoted in Marinucci and Wildermuth, 2002), the president spoke publicly in Trenton, New Jersey. Many times previously the president had criticized the Senate for not acting on his Homeland Security Department legislation. In this address, however, the president slightly altered his wording to say that while the House of Representatives had passed his bill, "the Senate is more interested in special interests in Washington and not interested in the security of the American people." A *Washington Post* story brought the statement to the attention of leading Democrats, who interpreted the allegation to be related to both the Iraq resolution and Homeland Security legislation. Democrat Senate leader Tom Daschle harshly responded:

> You tell those who fought in Vietnam and in World War II they're not interested in the security of the American people. That is outrageous. He [the president] ought to apologize to the American people. That is wrong. We ought not politicize this war.
>
> (Daschle, 2002)

The president's original statement, that disagreement with the administration endangered U.S. security, in combination with Daschle's response triggered a storm of media coverage. News coverage on the evening newscasts and Sunday talk shows of CBS, ABC (*Nightline* also analyzed), and NBC were searched in the Nexis database (search string of "(Bush or president) and (Daschle or Senate)") from Monday, September 23, through Sunday, September 29. These programs had 10 stories about Bush's comments or subsequent responses. Several, including all three of the network's lead stories on the matter, included the president's original statement. A number of stories also included quotes from Daschle and, in counter-response, from the administration or from Republican leaders. On September 25, ABC included a quote from Republican Senate leader Trent Lott: "who is the enemy here? The president of the United States or Saddam Hussein?" CBS included a response from the president that "my job is to protect the American people. It's my most important job, most important assignment I have, and I will continue to do that, regardless of the season." And NBC quoted both the president's statement that "You may try to politicize it. I—I view it as my main obligation. That is to protect the American people," and a comment from White House press secretary Ari Fleischer: "The president is stating the fact. Unless and until this passes, the Senate will not have acted in the interest of the security of the American people." The coverage continued in similar form across *Nightline* and the Sunday talk shows: the president's statement served as a starting point, a critical response followed, and then a counterpoint from the administration or another Republican leader was offered. This news cycle worked to the administration's advantage, keeping the story alive and amplifying the dissent-squelching message.

A search of Nexis using the same search string found 12 pieces in the *New York Times* and *Washington Post*. The president's words were either directly quoted or referenced in all of this coverage, including the lead paragraphs both of the *Post* story that triggered the Democratic response and in the front-page stories in both newspapers on the day following Daschle's comments in the Senate.[13] The *Post* story on September 26 began, "Senate Majority Leader Thomas A. Daschle (D–S.D.) blasted President Bush yesterday for 'politicizing' debate over national security and demanded he apologize for contending that the Democratic-controlled Senate is 'not interested in the security of the American people.'" Similarly, the *Times* story that day began, "Pent-up partisan rancor over domestic security legislation and Iraq policy erupted today when Senator Tom Daschle, the majority leader, demanded an apology from President Bush for saying the Senate was 'not interested in the security of the American people.'" Thus, the administration's infliction of a political price on Democratic leader Daschle was given substantial billing in these newspapers. Further, the *Times*, in its fashion, included stand-alone excerpts of the words of Bush and Daschle, thereby giving the administration's imposition of a cost for dissent further visibility. Finally, editorials in each paper criticized, albeit in a restrained manner, the Bush and Daschle comments as partisan politics, with headlines of "The healthy politics of Iraq" (*Times*) and "Spinning on Iraq" (*Post*). All of this news discourse, even that which reported or expressed criticism of the president's words, disseminated the message that criticism of or disagreement with the administration carried a price.

The third analyzed instance in which a penalty was imposed for dissent occurred in mid-March 2003 as war in Iraq became imminent. On March 17, the administration discontinued its efforts to convince the U.N. Security Council to act upon a resolution authorizing military force against Iraq, following up on Resolution 1441 passed five months earlier. The same day, Senate Democrat leader Daschle again challenged the administration, as he had in September 2002. He said, "I'm saddened, saddened that this president failed so miserably at diplomacy that we are now forced to go to war. Saddened that we have to give up one life because this president couldn't create the kind of diplomatic effort that was so critical for our country" (quoted in Kunhenn, 2003). Six hours later, the president addressed the nation to issue a 48-hour ultimatum for Saddam Hussein to leave Iraq or face U.S. military attack. With war looming and in the context of previous large national and international protests against the war, the president and top administration officials did not publicly respond to Daschle's comments. However, in the White House press briefing the next day, press secretary Ari Fleischer said:

> Of course, members of Congress, including Senator Daschle, are well within their rights to express their opinions. If you take a look at what Senator Daschle has said about the inevitability of using force in 1998, and if you take a look at what Senator Daschle said about the importance of raising the rhetoric to a higher level and not politicizing the rhetoric [in September 2002], I find his statement to be inconsistent. But perhaps he has a better explanation. ... It just strikes me as inconsistent with previous things he has said.
>
> (Fleischer, 2003)

Several questions and notable Fleischer responses followed in the briefing. Asked later about what he meant in suggesting inconsistencies by Daschle, Fleischer said he was referring to "statements made on February 12, 1998, in the Congressional Record; statements made on February 5, 1998, as reported in *The Chicago Tribune*—that all deals with the inevitability of the use of force against Saddam Hussein—as well as statement on September 25, 2002, in the

Congressional Record about not politicizing the rhetoric and rising to a higher level." Asked subsequently if he expected Democrats to limit criticism during the war, Fleischer said: "I think these are judgments that constituencies need to make. Every member of Congress represents a constituency and they have to make their own judgments about what to say and leave it to their constituents to judge." Asked then if potential Democrat decisions to "tone down the rhetoric" would be "encouraging," Fleischer added:

> All I can say is, on this topic, there are obviously deep splits within the Democratic Party. And there are a number of Democrats who support the President; there are a number of Democrats who don't and won't. They are both within their rights. The Republican Party is rather unified on this measure; the Democrat Party is not. And that's a reflection of the reality of the two parties.

The White House message was understated, as it had to be, but nonetheless clear: criticism of the president *by* Democrats would be met with prepared, documented, politically focused criticism by the administration *of* Democrats.

Supported by this White House reaction, a harsher rebuke of Daschle swiftly emerged from Republican congressional leaders—and was emphasized in news discourse. News coverage on the evening newscasts and Sunday talk shows of CBS, ABC (*Nightline* also analyzed), and NBC was searched in the Nexis database (search string of "(Bush or president) and (Daschle or Senate)") from Monday, March 17, through Sunday, March 23. These programs had six stories about Daschle's comments or subsequent responses. Much of the coverage emphasized *reactions to* Daschle's comments. ABC anchor Peter Jennings began his network's coverage: "In Washington, war has become a very hot political item. Today, Republican members of Congress were going after the Senate minority leader, Democrat Tom Daschle, for criticizing President Bush's war plans." Reporter Linda Douglass next said, "With war now just hours away, Republicans suggested today that members of Congress who criticized President Bush are less than patriotic." Daschle's statement was then presented, followed by a quote from Republican speaker of the House Dennis Hastert: "Those comments may not undermine the president as he leads us into war and they may not give comfort to our adversaries. But they come mighty close."

In a similar news narrative, anchor Tom Brokaw began NBC's coverage, "At the White House today, there were lots of harsh words directed at Democrats on Capitol Hill, Senate Minority leader Tom Daschle in particular." Reporter Campbell Brown next said, "Tom, accusations today from the White House and Republicans that Democrats are being unpatriotic for criticizing a president about to take the country to war." Daschle's comments were then presented, followed by a quote from Hastert, "Senator Daschle has spent more time criticizing the leadership of President Bush than he has spent criticizing the tyranny of Saddam Hussein," and one from Republican senator Rick Santorum: "I think Senator Daschle clearly articulated the French position." In contrast to the other two networks, CBS mentioned Daschle's comments in two stories but they were not the sole point of focus in either.

Coverage in the *New York Times* and *Washington Post*, as with television, was more muted than for the previous two analyzed instances in which the administration imposed a cost for dissent. A search of Nexis using the same search string found six pieces in these newspapers. Neither newspaper devoted a front-page story to the matter, and coverage was similar in presentation to television content—it often emphasized reactions to Daschle's words. The primary *Post* article had a headline of "GOP to hammer Democratic war critics," and began, "Congressional Republicans are implicitly challenging the patriotism of some Democrats who have criticized President Bush's war plans, a sign that the divisive politics marking the 108th Congress are unlikely to cease during wartime." The article continued, "While many foreign leaders and tens of millions of Americans oppose war with Iraq, Bush and GOP congressional leaders are reacting with vitriol" to the criticisms of the president by Daschle. The primary *Times* article had a headline of "Republicans scold Daschle for criticism," and began, "Senator Tom Daschle, the Democratic leader, called President Bush's diplomatic efforts in the Iraq crisis a miserable failure on Monday, in a speech that drew strong criticism today from the White House and Congressional Republicans." Daschle's words came next in the article, followed by quotes and perspectives from Hastert, Fleischer, Republican Senator Bill Frist, and Republican Senator James M. Inhofe, who said Daschle should apologize to the president. Only the *Post* had an editorial on the matter, arguing on behalf of free speech and against Republican Party rhetoric—of which it provided examples from Hastert, Frist, and House of Representatives leader Tom DeLay. The latter had responded to Daschle with a press release headlined, "Fermez La Bouche, Monsieur Daschle"—that is, "shut your mouth."

From attorney general admonitions to congressional tongue lashings, the administration between September 2001 and spring 2003 declared that dissent was unpatriotic and threatened U.S. goals, and made clear that such behavior would carry a significant political price. In turn, at least in the three analyzed instances, this message resounded through leading news coverage, even—particularly?—critical coverage.

## DISSENT, AUTHORITARIANISM, AND THE NEWS ECHO

Previous chapters offered insight into how the conservative religious grounding of the administration engendered a political fundamentalism that, after September 11, emphasized a binary conception of reality, manifested an obsession with time in regard to administration policies, and decreed that freedom and liberty were universal norms for all peoples. The evidence in this chapter suggests that these fundamentalist characteristics were joined and supported by an intolerance for dissent, which became apparent through two discursive strategies: a consistent emphasis upon political unity and periodic public rebukes for those who did not meet this expected norm. These administration communications significantly constrained U.S. public debate during months of historic decision-making as the nation undertook two wars and enacted sweeping anti-terrorism legislation that remade the relationship between the federal government and citizens. In seeking these changes, a more inclusive presidency might have sought out ideas from others and encouraged political discussion about the "war on terrorism." The Bush administration, however, welcomed such discourse if and only if support was offered for administration decisions. Indeed, it is ironic and seemingly self-damning that at the same time the administration claimed it was extending individual freedoms and democracy by confronting terrorists in Afghanistan and Saddam in Iraq, it was actively attempting to squelch dissent within the American political context. Apparently liberty was not universal after all.

It also is noteworthy that the administration exhibited rigorous internal harmony in its public communications. An emphasis upon unity and impositions of a cost for dissent were present in the communications of several administration leaders over time, across policy goals, and in interactions with a range of domestic and international officials.[14] These integrated behaviors were indicative of a fundamentalist philosophy in which support for leadership is "absolute and unquestioned" (Marty and Appleby, 1992, p. 26) and therefore requires, in the words of van der Vyver (1996), "ruthless condemnation of, and intolerance toward, all competing forces" (p. 22). When other political actors did not meet the administration's prescription of political unity after September 11, the president and other administration leaders did not follow their own mantra of civility. Rather, they responded with the imposition of a significant cost—what Perkin (2000) refers to as "punishing them for their disbelief" (p. 79)— making clear that political actors who chose not to stand with the administration would pay a price. In short, this communications approach worked hard to close off potential avenues of dissenting thought and action, exactly the outcome that authoritarian-minded fundamentalists desire. The concluding words of Ashcroft in testimony before the U.S. Senate three months after the terrorist attacks were instructive: "I trust, as well, that Congress will respect this president's *authority* to wage war on terrorism and defend our nation and its citizens with all the *power* vested in him by the Constitution and entrusted to him by the American people" (emphasis added).

The administration's desire was not the enactment of political unity per se, therefore, but rather unity *in support of the administration's goals*. What was espoused as national oneness for the good of the people was really a front for "You better all do what we say." Those who did not submit were publicly derided as unpatriotic. In December 2001, Ashcroft said that criticisms of the administration "only aid terrorists—for they erode our national unity and diminish our resolve. They give ammunition to America's enemies, and pause to America's friends." In September 2002, the president declared that Democrats in the Senate were "not interested in the security of the American people." And in March 2003, White House press secretary Ari Fleischer systematically outlined political costs for criticizing the president, while Republican leaders in Congress dressed down Democrat Senator Daschle—even characterizing him as French in the ultimate political slap of the moment. In a similar manner, though not a point of analysis here, Secretary of Defense Rumsfeld dismissed France and Germany as "old Europe" in January 2003 when these nations refused to support another U.N. Security Council resolution against Iraq.[15] In all cases, the administration dictated that dissent from its goals not only carried a sizable political price, but also threatened U.S. (and global) security. In so doing, the administration consistently returned to the moral power of the events of September 11, in the process priming public fears about more terrorism and reminding Americans that the nation was in crisis mode, thereby encouraging continued support for the president. In sum, the administration's dissent-squelching behavior had great political benefits.

Analysis of news coverage, however, indicated that the administration's emphasis on unity was far from overwhelmingly echoed by the mainstream press, perhaps because this discourse implicitly challenged the dominant news norm of conflict, which drives the overriding emphasis in political news coverage upon strategy and the horse race competition of electoral politics. An environment in which political unity was emphasized countered the desires of journalism, which in particular relies upon conflict between the executive and legislative branches of government to provide a sense of journalistic objectivity in its coverage of government.[16] As a result, that the administration's emphasis upon political unity had less of a presence in news coverage than the discourses analyzed in preceding chapters was not overly surprising. Support for this interpretation is offered by the one instance in which the administration's emphasis on unity did have a significant presence in news coverage—editorial discourse about Iraq. The mild conflict between the administration and Congress about Iraq, and the much larger conflict between the United States and the U.N. Security Council nations, provided an environment in which the administration's requests for political unity became of great interest *and* of pivotal strategic importance as the possibility of war loomed, a potentiality which distinguished this discourse from the other two examined. More so than television news coverage, newspaper editorial boards perhaps felt a responsibility as the institutional voices of the American press to emphasize the importance of unity and to assess whether the administration was attaining it. Notably, though, while an emphasis on political unity was relatively less echoed in the press than discourses examined in earlier chapters, it nonetheless still had a visible presence across the differing forms of news coverage within each of the policy domains examined.

At the same time, the administration's public criticisms of dissenting political actors perfectly fit news norms. In each of the three instances analyzed, the rebukes of individuals who challenged the administration triggered substantial news discourse distinguished by the similarity of narratives in news coverage by the television networks and in the *New York Times* and *Washington Post*. To be specific, coverage contained two notable characteristics: first, great emphasis was placed upon the administration's words and perspectives, which often were given greater prominence than contrasting viewpoints; second, criticisms of the administration's comments were commonplace, but such critiques nonetheless continued to amplify the messages of the administration. The periodic public rebukes of dissenting political actors, then, were suggestive that the administration viewed news media treatment of its messages to be less important than whether the messages simply were echoed in press coverage. Had the administration been primarily concerned about generating manifestly favorable news coverage, the response to Ashcroft's comments in 2001 would have made clear that imposition of a cost for dissent was the wrong political pathway. For an administration profoundly strategic in its communications, harsh public criticisms of dissenters would not have emerged again, and certainly not when the administration was pursuing Iraq resolutions or about to initiate military action in Iraq. That public rebukes of dissenters did again and again emerge was suggestive that the administration willingly accepted press criticisms in exchange for wide dissemination of its message that the administration was to be supported, or else.

Finally, these discourses not only worked to the political advantage of the administration, they contributed to a broader environment in which dissent from the president was equated with anti-Americanism, and societal actors—including news media—adjusted their conduct and communications accordingly. In autumn 2001, U.S. news media agreed to a request by National Security Adviser Condaleezza Rice to limit public release of videotapes of Osama bin Laden,[17] and CNN executives issued a reportorial directive that coverage of Afghanistan civilian deaths due to U.S. military action should be balanced by an emphasis upon the loss of lives on September 11.[18]

In the same period, the American Council of Trustees and Alumni organization issued a November 2001 report identifying

117 statements or behaviors by U.S. academic faculty and public officials that it described as "blaming America first" and "giving comfort to America's enemies" (American Council of Trustees and Alumni, 2001). In 2003 in the context of the Iraq conflict, CBS News anchor Dan Rather was strongly criticized for granting an interview, and thus audience, to Saddam Hussein,[19] and NBC fired news correspondent Peter Arnett after he criticized the U.S. war effort in an interview with Iraq's state-run television network.[20] Shortly thereafter, actor Tim Robbins, an outspoken anti-war critic, was disinvited from a public appearance at the Baseball Hall of Fame.[21]

To be clear, the effects of the administration's political fundamentalism were not merely detrimental to these mentioned individuals (losing a public speaking engagement is hardly a tragedy). What these examples show is how pervasive and institutionalized the climate of intolerance had become. The administration's ideology encouraged restrictions in free speech and engendered a meaningful shift in how some news organizations and social institutions thought about free speech. As a result, the American public sphere was losing voices while one perspective kept gaining volume.

# 6
# Political fundamentalism, the press, and Democrats

In September 2000, the conservative think tank Project for the New American Century (PNAC) produced a white paper outlining its vision for a conservatively minded, U.S.-led world order. In this document, titled *Rebuilding America's defenses: Strategy, forces and resources for a new century*, the organization presented a plan to counter what it saw as a threat to American global dominance. In the document the PNAC proclaimed that America was the top empire, but also warned that its absolute power was at risk:

> The United States is the world's only superpower, combining preeminent military power, global technological leadership, and the world's largest economy. Moreover, America stands at the head of a system of alliances that includes the world's leading democratic powers. At present the United States faces no global rival. America's grand strategy should aim to preserve and extend this advantageous position as far into the future as possible. There are, however, potentially powerful states dissatisfied with the current situation and eager to change it, if they can.
>
> (Kagan, Schmitt, and Donnelly, 2000, p. i)

The PNAC stated that it was concerned with the balance of power in Europe, East Asia, and the Middle East (more specifically, the oil-producing region around it—that is, the Persian Gulf), as well as the threat of terrorism, organized crime, and the actions of other "non-state" individuals and entities. In order to preserve world peace, the PNAC proposed "four essential missions" to be carried out by the U.S. military:

- defend the American homeland
- upgrade military power so that the nation might fight and decisively win multiple, simultaneous major theater wars
- perform the "constabulary" duties associated with shaping the security environment in critical regions
- transform U.S. forces to exploit the "revolution in military affairs."

Homeland defense was the top priority. The PNAC declared that with the end of the Cold War, the singular, Soviet-motivated, nuclear war threat had ended, but in its place had risen multiple adversaries with growing arsenals. Hence, the United States "must counteract the effects of the proliferation of ballistic missiles and weapons of mass destruction that may soon allow lesser states to deter U.S. military action by threatening U.S. allies and the American homeland itself" (p. 6). Two years earlier, in a letter to President Clinton, the PNAC had singled-out Saddam Hussein as one of these dangers to world peace and stability:

[W]e are convinced that current American policy toward Iraq is not succeeding, and that we may soon face a threat in the Middle East more serious than any we have known since the end of the Cold War. In your upcoming State of the Union Address, you have an opportunity to chart a clear and determined course for meeting this threat. We urge you to seize that opportunity, and to enunciate a new strategy that would secure the interests of the U.S. and our friends and allies around the world. That strategy should aim, above all, at the removal of Saddam Hussein's regime from power. We stand ready to offer our full support in this difficult but necessary endeavor.

The policy of "containment" of Saddam Hussein has been steadily eroding over the past several months. As recent events have demonstrated, we can no longer depend on our partners in the Gulf War coalition to continue to uphold the sanctions or to punish Saddam when he blocks or evades UN inspections. Our ability to ensure that Saddam Hussein is not producing weapons of mass destruction, therefore, has substantially diminished.

... [I]f Saddam does acquire the capability to deliver weapons of mass destruction, as he is almost certain to do if we continue along the present course, the safety of American troops in the region, of our friends and allies like Israel and the moderate Arab states, and a significant portion of the world's supply of oil will all be put at hazard. As you have rightly declared, Mr. President, the security of the world in the first part of the 21st century will be determined largely by how we handle this threat.

(Letter to President Clinton on Iraq, 1998)

Many of the PNAC's words and strategies resounded in the aftermath of September 11. In the days and months that followed, the group of policy intellectuals known as "neo-conservatives" began to hold sway in the Bush administration, formulating the rationale and much of the actual components of the "war on terrorism" policies. These individuals included founding PNAC members Vice-President Dick Cheney, Defense Secretary Donald Rumsfeld, Deputy Secretary of Defense Paul Wolfowitz, and former Defense Policy Board Chairman Richard Perle.

These conservative political machinations prompted an uncompli-cated story told by many liberals in subsequent days: in the aftermath of the terrorist attacks of September 11, neo-conservatives in Wash-ington D.C. capitalized by moving a conservative president, guided by strategist Karl Rove, toward a hard-line foreign policy approach. In turn, the U.S. public went along with the president because they always do in times of crisis. This story, however, is incomplete. Miss-ing is an understanding of how seamlessly neo-conservatives' ideas blended with the administration's religious fundamentalist world-view, which provided a ready-made apocalyptic prism for interpret-ing the political landscape following September 11. To neglect this religious piece—which is a common error among liberals, a point argued later in this chapter—is to fail to recognize how the adminis-tration rhetorically made these policies attractive or at least palatable to a large segment of the American public *and* silenced the voices of dissenting political actors. Liberals, political moderates, and others ignore the power of the convergence of politics and religion at their own risk, because the historic political successes of the administration can be explained by the conceptual model offered in Chapter 1, which argues that political fundamentalism is likely to (re)emerge, gain a wide public presentation, and receive a favorable hearing in the United States when four characteristics are present:

- a nation-challenging crisis occurs
- national political leaders are religiously conservative
- the same political leadership is skilled in strategic communications
- the news media give substantial emphasis to leaders' communications.

All four factors were important contributors to the Bush administration's political predominance in the aftermath of September 11. The factors, however, were not equally integral to the emergence and dissemination of the administration's political fundamentalism. Strategic communications, in particular, were the fulcrum force; that is, the administration's choices about language and specific communication approaches were the crucial mechanisms that gave voice to and shaped the meaning of the other three components. At the same time, the administration's communications were widely echoed by the mainstream U.S. news media and rarely ardently challenged by leading members of the Democratic Party. These processes and relations and their implications are the focus of this chapter.

## THE STRATEGIC COMMUNICATIONS OF THE BUSH ADMINISTRATION

The Bush administration was ideally positioned for the questions about morality and nation that were triggered by September 11. Language and ideas about these matters were close at hand in an administration known for a devout Christian president, daily Bible studies, faith-based initiatives, and close ties with conservative religious leaders.[1] Still, transforming these religious groundings into a *political* fundamentalism required careful, strategic communication. This rhetorical work gained its foundational footing with the administration's strongly moral response to September 11. The president declared the day's events to be an act of "war" and indicative of a struggle between good and evil in which the United States' freedom and liberty were under attack. This response, Entman (2003) has argued, conveyed "an unambiguous and emotionally compelling frame" that helped to spur congressional, news media, and public support for at least the initial stages of U.S. reaction (p. 416). Indeed, the combination of the public's propensity to rally behind the president in times of crisis and the administration's rhetoric engendered levels of support that were historically remarkable and unthinkable only a week earlier.

The administration's moral language is evidence of the claim by Lakoff (1996) that conservatives, particularly religiously grounded ones, recognize that politics is not only about policies, issues, and interest groups, but also about "family and morality, about myth and metaphor and emotional identification" (p. 19). Claiming the moral high ground within hours of the terrorist attacks gave the administration a perch from which it subsequently controlled public discourse and the political agenda at least through the Iraq war.

The discursive responses of the president and administration to the September 11 attacks, then, were as important as the events themselves in the administration's subsequent predominance. Bush's binary conceptions and claims about the universality of freedom and liberty in national addresses soon intertwined with the administration's persistent requests-cum-demands for urgent action and political unity on "war on terrorism" policies. The political fundamentalism of the president and administration infused these discourses with a moral vigor that went far in closing off opportunities for others, including leaders of the Democratic Party, to voice or demonstrate concerns or opposition. To not acquiesce to the administration's policy desires or to not act with political unity meant more than disagreement with the president; it meant a rupture in the religiously grounded, politically focused "structure of feeling" (Williams, 1977) that the administration consistently put forward and the press consistently echoed.

Further, when public criticism from the political mainstream did emerge, the administration periodically made clear that such dissent carried a high price—specifically, claims that administration critics "aid terrorists" and "give ammunition to America's enemies" (Ashcroft in 2001), were "not interested in the security of the American people" (Bush in 2002), and "come mighty close" to undermining the president and giving comfort to adversaries (House of Representatives Speaker Dennis Hastert in 2003). To publicly challenge the administration between September 11 and the Iraq war was to risk much, too much for many political leaders and the mainstream press. The loser in all of this was the American public, who desperately needed a robust conversation about September 11 and "war on terrorism" policies, but did not receive the opportunity.

A second reason that the administration dominated the political agenda during these months is that it was able to extend the crisis from September 11 to Saddam Hussein. This process began publicly in January 2002 with the president's declaration that Iraq, Iran, and North Korea constituted an "axis of evil," and was sustained by consistent emphasis on Saddam and the potential for another September 11. The introduction of Iraq into the campaign against terrorism marked a convergence of the administration's fundamentalist fixations on the struggle of good versus evil, security versus peril, and the merit of preemptive action; the president's hatred for Saddam because he tried to assassinate Bush's father; and the potential electoral capital involved.[2] The administration never explicitly linked Saddam or Iraq to the events of September 11, but insertion of them into the "war on terrorism" discourse nonetheless tied the two in many citizens' minds. In September 2002, 51 percent of U.S. adults said that Saddam was "personally involved" in the September 11 attacks, a number that remained at 52 percent in May 2003.[3] In turn, the administration's focus on Iraq was timed perfectly for the 2002 elections: The president spoke at the United Nations on September 12, Congress passed a resolution supporting military force on October 11, and U.N. Security Council negotiations about a resolution lasted until November 8, three days after the election.

In short, extension of a crisis context well beyond September 11 and its immediate aftermath worked to the administration's electoral advantage—but did so in a manner that prolonged the fear, anxiety, and uncertainty engendered by the terrorist attacks. Indeed, the administration effectively institutionalized these outcomes with the Department of Homeland Security. Since its creation, the department has helped perpetuate an atmosphere of paranoia with its fluctuating color-coded terror alerts—government-declared warnings that offer the public no facts or specifics. The U.S. electorate and international community deserved better.

A third reason that the administration dominated public discourse is that it built closely upon the language and communication approaches of the Reagan administration, thereby offering a time-tested, religiously conservative political discourse that was certain to resonate with at least a significant minority of the American populace. In his inaugural in 1981, Reagan said:

As for the enemies of freedom, those who are potential adversaries, they will be reminded that peace is the highest aspiration of the American people. We will negotiate for it, sacrifice for it; we will not surrender for it now or ever.

(Reagan, 1981)

In parallel language, Bush on September 20, 2001, said: "On September 11th, enemies of freedom committed an act of war against our country." Similarly, consider this binary-rich passage from Reagan's 1984 State of the Union address:

I've never felt more strongly that America's best days and democracy's best days lie ahead. We're a powerful force for good. With faith and courage, we can perform great deeds and take freedom's next step. And we will. We will carry on the tradition of a good and worthy people who have brought light where there was darkness, warmth where there was cold, medicine where there was disease, food where there was hunger, and peace where there was only bloodshed.

(Reagan, 1984)

And a passage in Reagan's State of the Union address the following year paralleled the universal gospel of freedom and liberty that Bush would emphasize after September 11:

Harry Truman once said that, ultimately, our security and the world's hopes for peace and human progress "lie not in measures of defense or in the control of weapons, but in the growth and expansion of freedom and self-government."

And tonight, we declare anew to our fellow citizens of the world: Freedom is not the sole prerogative of a chosen few; it is the universal right of all God's children. Look to where peace and prosperity flourish today. It is in homes that freedom built. Victories against poverty are greatest and peace most secure where people live by laws that ensure free press, free speech, and freedom to worship, vote, and create wealth.

(Reagan, 1985)

The similarity of language between Bush and Reagan underscores the convergence of religion and politics that manifested in these two administrations. Altogether different, however, were the contexts for this convergence: the United States is now the world's sole super-power, so a binary conception of reality and a certainty about the universality of freedom and liberty, U.S.-style, can be acted upon by Bush in ways not feasible for Reagan. The consequences after September 2001 were grave for domestic and international debate and for nations who did not choose to be "with the United States" in its campaign against terrorism.

Fourth, the president delivered televised national addresses at an unprecedented pace—15, including the Columbia eulogy, in the 20 months between the September 11 attacks and the calling of an end to "major combat operations" in Iraq on May 1, 2003. The president's speech before Congress and 82 million Americans on September 20, 2001, gave him a bully pulpit upon which the administration capitalized. The president used these addresses to bypass Congress in attempting to build support for policies and goals, a strategy that scholars have termed "going public" (Canes-Wrone, 2001; Kernell, 1997). In particular, in several addresses the president discussed some of the administration's most significant matters:

- September 20, 2001: formal declaration of a "war on terrorism."
- October 7, 2001: announcement of military action in Afghanistan.
- January 29, 2002: State of the Union, containing declaration of an "axis of evil."
- June 6, 2002: announcement of Department of Homeland Security proposal.
- September 12, 2002: address at United Nations about Iraq.
- January 28, 2003: State of the Union, of which more than one-third focused on Iraq.
- March 17, 2003: declaration of ultimatum to Saddam and Iraq.
- March 19, 2003: announcement of military action in Iraq.
- May 1, 2003: declaration of end to major combat operations in Iraq.

These addresses, in combination with the administration's omnipresent calls for new action and political unity, consistently put Congress on the defensive and manufactured positive news coverage for the administration. To be clear, the goal of these presidential addresses was not to spur political debate, but rather to declare what the administration had done, was doing, or intended to do. That is, the president delivered essentially more than a dozen State of the Union-like addresses over 20 months, a display of presidential discursive power that was antithetical to the checks and balances that U.S. citizens expect of their federal government. With the help of the press, the administration rendered Congress and the public superfluous.

Finally, the administration benefited from a U.S. news media that gave it the benefit of the doubt in a manner rarely afforded to presidents and administrations. To be specific, the typically jaded stance among journalists toward government was dropped—at least for a period of time. CBS News anchor Dan Rather made this shift in journalistic sensibilities explicit in a September 22, 2001, interview on *CNN Tonight*, in which he said:

> I want to fulfill my role as a decent human member of the community and a decent and patriotic American. And, therefore, I am willing to give the government, the president and the military the benefit of any doubt here in the beginning. I'm going to fulfill my role as a journalist, and that is ask the questions, when necessary ask the tough questions. But I have no excuse for, particularly when there is a national crisis such as this, as saying—you know, the president says do your job, whatever you are and whomever you are, Mr. and Mrs. America. I'm going to do my job as a journalist, but at the same time I will give them the benefit of the doubt, whenever possible in this kind of crisis, emergency situation.
>
> (in Blitzer and Kurtz, 2001)

This modification of journalistic posture toward government, combined with the news media's willingness to let down the guard of objectivity in covering the terrorist attacks and national mourning, engendered a news discourse of public empathy and support for national leadership in the immediate aftermath of September 11.[4] Such a reaction by the mainstream press in the immediate aftermath of September 11 pleased significant segments of the public.[5] What pleases the public is not always what is best for democracy, however. Indeed, this shift in journalistic perspective laid the foundation for the widespread press echoing of the administration's message that occurred for months on end—an echoing that left the U.S. public without a critical eye on the administration from outside the walls of government between autumn 2001 and spring

2003. Notably, the role of the press will be taken up again later in this chapter.

The particularly key attribute in the Bush administration's political successes in the aftermath of September 11, then, was the ability to craft a strategic communications approach grounded in a conservative religious worldview that controlled public discourse. It is important to acknowledge, though, that other explanations might be offered for the underlying motivations of the administration discourses identified here. An attempt to gain insight into the foundational worldview of an individual, let alone that of a presidential administration, is difficult. Rarely can "smoking gun" evidence be offered that definitively rules out an explanation. In particular, two other potential arguments merit mention. First, some might suggest that the president and administration crafted a political discourse in which religious language was adopted for solely strategic reasons—that is, to signal that this administration was friendly to religious conservatives and, therefore, merited their support. A second counter-argument might be that the president offered a benign variant of the "civil religion" which traditionally has been part of politics in the United States.[6] To adopt these interpretations, however, is to be mistakenly cynical (the former argument) or naive (the latter) about the nature of the faith of the president and others in the administration. Further, both conclusions dismiss the need for systematic scrutiny of the administration's religious groundings. Such analysis, offered in earlier chapters and expanded in the following paragraphs, strongly suggests that a fundamentalist worldview served as a centrifugal force, rather than merely in a strategic or civil role, for the president and this administration in the aftermath of September 11.

The argument that a conservative religious conception of the world offers a unifying explanation for the Bush administration's discourses between autumn 2001 and spring 2003 fared well when "tested" through examination of a large number of communications by the president and other administration leaders. Across hundreds of communications—about differing policies, at differing times, and among differing administration leaders—the evidence suggests that in the aftermath of September 11 the president and administration exhibited a political fundamentalism that strategically integrated a conservative religious understanding of the world with a political language. Sometimes the religious language was explicit and thus served as a signal to religious conservatives. Much more often the language was not ostensibly religious—and therefore seemed "merely" political—but nonetheless promulgated a religious fundamentalist worldview. Consistent and substantial emphases on a binary conception of reality, an obsession with time, a universal gospel of freedom and liberty, and intolerance for dissent, in combination, were indicative of a coherent, religiously conservative understanding of the world given voice in political terms. If this president and administration were not religiously conservative, then they faked it with astonishing skill between autumn 2001 and spring 2003. With this in mind, perhaps the best test of the authenticity of the worldview manifested by the president and administration is the perception of religious conservatives themselves.

Their position has been unequivocal: They embraced George W. Bush as one of their own in a manner unmatched by previous presidents—a reaction far beyond mere support and almost certainly available only for a true believer. Consider the perspective of Richard Land, president and CEO of the Ethics and Religious Liberty Commission of the Southern Baptist Convention, the nation's predominant religious fundamentalist organization with 16 million members, more than 42,000 churches and considerable political influence.[7] Land, a graduate of Princeton and Oxford and an advisor to the White House on the intersection of religion and politics, was quoted in Lawson (2003):

> "George Bush is an evangelical Christian, there is no doubt about that," Land told [Lawson]. "The president's evangelicalism means he believes in the truth of the Bible, with a capital $T$: the virgin birth, the death of Christ on the cross for our sins, the physical resurrection, and, most important, a personal relationship with Jesus." Land said he trusted the younger Bush even more than he trusted Ronald Reagan. "Bush is traditional and religious, and now there is no 'Nancy factor'—no need to go through a Nancy Reagan-type figure to get to the president." He said that the president didn't change after September 11 but that the world changed: "The president believes America has a purpose in the world, and that purpose is to fan the flame and light the candle of freedom. I believe that he believes—as do I and

many evangelicals—that we have a responsibility to help people experience the freedom that is their God-given right."

(p. 396, emphasis in original)

The confidence of religious conservatives about the faith of the president is so high that he came to be viewed as the de facto leader of the Christian Right with Pat Robertson's resignation as head of the Christian Coalition in December 2001. In the words of conservative religious leader Gary Bauer, former head of the Family Research Council, "I think Robertson stepped down because the position has already been filled," adding that Bush "is that leader right now. There was already a great deal of identification with the president before 9–11 in the world of the Christian right, and the nature of this war is such that it's heightened the sense that a man of God is in the White House."[8] In sum, a wide collection of evidence is suggestive that the Bush administration's communications and policies had a grounding in a conservative religious worldview.

## AN ECHOING PRESS

U.S. news media substantially echoed the public communications of the Bush administration in the period between September 11 and the Iraq war in spring 2003. Across the wide range of administration communications examined, the news media consistently gave voice to the words and ideas of the president and other administration leaders. To be clear, news media sometimes disagreed with the administration and occasionally were strongly critical, as we saw in the response to the administration's dissent-squelching. Some press criticism was willingly tolerated by the administration, because the consistent echoing of the president's and administration's language disseminated and encouraged a certain conception of the world—a conception grounded in a conservative religious worldview that enacted a particular political agenda. Following the terrorist attacks, news coverage—and, in turn, public opinion—about U.S. politics was constructed, described, delimited, and circumscribed by the Bush administration, particularly the president. The administration's strategic language choices and communication approaches were the key factors in prompting this outcome. However, certain normative and structural characteristics of the U.S. news media system also were of importance in facilitating the press's echoing of administration communications. In particular, two central features of the American news media, one regarding the routines and practices of journalism and one regarding ownership, were crucially important.

A consistent finding in studies of news content is that mainstream journalists rely overwhelmingly on governmental officials as authoritative sources.[9] In the words of Bennett:

> Mass media news professionals, from the boardroom to the beat, tend to "index" the range of voices and viewpoints in both news and editorials according to the range of views expressed in mainstream government debate about a given topic.
>
> (Bennett, 1990, p. 106)

In a representative form of government, journalists' reliance on elite sources, particularly government authorities, is predicated upon the view that citizens elected a significant number of these individuals, so the press should emphasize their perspectives. This reliance nonetheless carries an important implication: while most U.S. media outlets are *economically free* from government control, they nonetheless are *journalistically dependent* upon political leadership for information and opinion statements. This reliance on government officials is further heightened in times of crisis, when news media look to the presidential administration for perspective and leadership.[10] In so doing, journalists depend heavily upon perspectives emanating from Congress and other sectors of Washington D.C. to provide a sense of balance.[11] When these other actors support the administration, or at least are unwilling to publicly voice criticisms, news coverage will inevitably favor the president and his policies. As a result, the support of other political actors for the administration in autumn 2001 and a subsequent unwillingness or inability to substantially challenge the administration's discourse about political unity significantly encouraged the press to give emphasis to the administration's communications. This outcome was made all the more likely by the reality that most journalists at U.S. news media are U.S. citizens, who inevitably cover events and ideas through the lens of their cultural values, and therefore also likely looked to the president for perspective and leadership.[12] Their unconscious ethnocentrism limited their ability to see past the White House's rhetoric.

The presence of these news routines means that presidential administrations always will have opportunity for political profit when crises arise. However, the mainstream press's reliance on the voices of government leaders is particularly ripe for exploitation by an ideology of political fundamentalism, for several reasons. First, fundamentalism has much to gain from the development or extension of crisis contexts. The larger the crisis and the more widely it is experienced in U.S. culture, the greater the likelihood that a conservative religious worldview will have appeal to citizens. The salve of "getting the faith" can easily spread over the masses during a national trauma and tragedy, offering comfort and simple, ready-made answers for the unfathomable. Of course, this is not to say that conservatives wish harm on their fellow citizens. However, the sudden onset of a soul-searching anxiety and reflection about one's priorities does work to the advantage of fundamentalism.

In turn, the press thrives on coverage of crisis due to its perceived importance, the magnitude of the actors involved and the large audiences who pay attention. As a result, journalists are more than happy to echo political leaders' claims that something is a crisis. With September 11 and the "war on terrorism" now established as the looming presence in U.S. politics, news media have an administration-manufactured crisis narrative, dominated by the president, in which to frame coverage. This narrative well fits what Kovach and Rosenstiel (1999) term the "blockbuster mentality" of news organizations—that is, the desire for mega-stories, such as O. J. Simpson, the Clinton–Lewinsky scandal, and the 2000 presidential cliffhanger. News media, then, can be counted on to emphasize and extend crises, a proclivity that political fundamentalism leverages.

The ultimate loser in this relationship is democracy. When political leadership and the press both stand to benefit from the framing of an event or set of ideas as a crisis, political leaders easily ignore any dissonant voices among the public. Indeed, this is what happened during the buildup to the war in Iraq, when hundreds of thousands of Americans protested publicly in February 2003, the largest public demonstrations since the Vietnam War era. The press covered these protests, to be sure. But when the president dismissed these demonstrations (claiming that he welcomed their right to protest, but that their views were wrong) and made clear that the administration would not veer from its impending conflict with Iraq, the press returned to echoing the administration's messages—and not the dissonant public outcry. The implication is substantial: Opinions of the public, inevitably lacking the authority inherent in the voices of government officials, have little realistic chance to challenge a governmental narrative in news discourse. In particular, news coverage in crisis contexts will almost always be supportive of the government; only after the crisis diminishes will the press exert independent authority to examine governmental claims and actions, as indeed occurred in summer and autumn 2003 when the U.S. mainstream press began to inspect the administration's claims regarding Iraq and alleged weapons of mass destruction. While such press scrutiny is still useful even at the later date, it comes far too late for military members committed to the field and for individuals or nations who are on the receiving end of an administration's actions. An echoing press therefore, is far from a neutral press.

Second, journalists' desire for conflict, drama, and rhetorical flourishes makes them an easily breached conduit for strong moral language, which is something at which political conservatives, particularly religious ones, excel. Conflict between competing forces is inherently suggested by moral discourse (particularly when presented in binary form). MacDougall (1982) suggests that there is "no single other element of reader interest that is present more frequently" in news coverage than conflict (p. 119). Similarly, according to Price and Tewksbury (1997), "A major tendency of news reporting is to look for good fights and to let readers know who is fighting whom" (p. 178).[13] Journalists also seek news that incorporates dramatic elements commonly found in popular entertainment, such as suspense, risk or danger, downfall and redemption, and compelling characters. A morally charged discourse —such as good versus evil, security versus peril, or the need for an enduring commitment against terrorism, to name a few Bush administration examples—taps into familiar themes and provides pithy sound bites in a manner that news media are happy to use to capture public attention. In several ways, then, news media are inclined to prefer the moral language of political fundamentalism— it is compelling, dramatic, and intertwined with culturally familiar narratives. It also tends to demean and marginalize differing viewpoints, of course. But mainstream journalists operating under the value-free expectation of objectivity comfortably ignore such an outcome. As a result, an "objective" press is always open to exploitation by rhetorically sophisticated political actors.

Third, U.S. journalists' dependence on the White House for political news means that mainstream news media inevitably will echo any themes that *consistently* emerge from an administration, offering yet another newsgathering reality that works to the advantage of political fundamentalism, with its remarkably unified public discourse among administration leaders. Indeed, in only one instance between September 2001 and the Iraq war in spring 2003 was a public presentation of a unified Bush administration challenged—in late summer 2002, when disagreements about how to approach Iraq were publicly aired for a short time and some Republican leaders, including House majority leader Dick Armey, publicly spoke against taking on Iraq.[14] A *Newsweek* cover on September 16, which hit the newsstands a week earlier, trumpeted "The war over war" in the administration between Secretary of State Powell and Secretary of Defense Rumsfeld. However, when the administration symbolically launched its push toward Iraq beginning with the president's address at the United Nations on September 12, these public disagreements were gone. When asked on CNN's *Larry King Live* on October 9 about differences of administration opinion, Powell responded:

> We are knitted together as a Cabinet team, as a national security team, on this issue, under the leadership of the president. He has given us clear guidance. He has given us clear instructions and he's given us a vision of what we have to accomplish. And we know what we have to do. We have to be firm at this moment in history. We have to be united as a Cabinet, as a nation, and I think we are. And we also should be united as an international community, the United Nations coming together.
> (Powell, 2002d)

In times of political normalcy, journalists might respond to a unified administration by turning to other topics, particularly when there is little public challenge from other elites. Nothing new from the administration would be viewed as no news, period. In a time of crisis, however, journalists see a consistent emphasis upon administration voices to be an appropriate function of the press, even if those voices continue to say the same thing over time. The result is that news media are far more likely to echo the desired messages of a *unified* administration—an outcome that is substantially encouraged by an ideology of political fundamentalism.

These normative characteristics of the U.S. press, then, operate to the advantage of a conservative presidential administration functioning at the nexus of politics and religion. So too do the economic realities of the U.S. media system. As noted, most U.S. media outlets are economically free from government control. A commercial media system must draw financial support from somewhere, though, and in America that support is provided primarily by social and cultural institutions that purchase advertising time to reach consumer audiences. As a result, a commercial press is always economically dependent on its ability to attract readers, viewers, and listeners. For such media outlets to challenge national leadership runs the risk of loss of financial support—because significant numbers of the public may choose not to buy or tune in to the media outlet, thereby driving down advertising rates; or because advertisers, who often have sizable investments in existing social and political structures, may not want to be associated with a particular media outlet or program. This is the "normal" situation; in times of crisis, when nationalism runs higher and wider, a commercial media system simply *cannot* engage in substantial governmental criticism without potential dire economic consequences—a point exemplified in the experiences of Bill Maher and ABC in September 2001. This is an economic dynamic to the U.S. media system that works to the benefit of any presidential administration in office when a crisis develops. However, the rise of Fox News Channel over the past decade has created a clear economic tilt among media organizations toward appeasing conservatives.

Like all cable television outlets, Fox News Channel is watched by a much smaller percentage of Americans than those who watch the evening newscasts of over-the-air networks ABC, CBS, and NBC. Unlike the broadcast networks and cable competitors CNN and MSNBC, though, Fox has created a market niche that openly appeals to political conservatives. Launched in 1996, Fox trumpets itself as a "fair and balanced" alternative to its competitors, a none too subtle dig at the alleged liberal biases that a decent number of Americans perceive in mainstream news coverage.[15] Fox was viewed as no more than an irritant to other media outlets until conservatives used it as a vehicle to disseminate their views during the Clinton–Lewinsky scandal and subsequent push for impeachment. In the aftermath of September 11 and during the early stages of U.S. military action in Afghanistan in autumn 2001, Fox offered a picture of the United States and the campaign against terrorism that, in the words of

Rutenberg (2001), became "a sort of headquarters for viewers who want their news served up with extra patriotic fervor." With this message and with continuing increases in its distribution among cable systems, Fox saw its audience numbers surge. This climb continued in subsequent months: Fox ended 2002 ahead of CNN in the ratings competition and received the highest ratings in its history during the Iraq war in spring 2003.[16]

Fox's successes caught the attention of its competitors. In response, MSNBC moved sharply to the right and CNN attempted a number of strategies to regroup. In February 2003, MSNBC fired liberal talk show host Phil Donahue because, according to an internal memo, Donahue presented "a difficult public face for NBC in time of war" when "our competitors are waving the flag at every opportunity" since he "seems to delight in presenting guests who are anti-war, anti-Bush, and skeptical of the administration's motives" (quoted in Kurtz, 2003). MSNBC subsequently hired former Republican congressman Joe Scarborough and ardently conservative radio host Michael Savage (who lasted only a few months), and in late March in the early days of the Iraq war, MSNBC terminated its contract with correspondent Peter Arnett after Arnett gave an interview with Iraqi television in which he was critical of the Bush administration's war planning.

CNN in September 2001 hired well-known personality Paula Zahn away from Fox News and then added Connie Chung in June 2002 in order to chart a course of creating distinctive programs centered on individual personalities—the exact formula that propelled Fox into cable dominance and a sea change from CNN's traditional "news is the star" dictum.[17] CNN's political news reporters also felt the ideological heat from Fox, according to CNN reporter Christiane Amanpour, who said in September 2003:

> I think the press was muzzled and I think the press self-muzzled. I'm sorry to say but certainly television and, perhaps, to a certain extent, my station was intimidated by the administration and its foot soldiers at Fox News. And it did, in fact, put a climate of fear and self-censorship, in my view, in terms of—of the kind of broadcast work we did.
>
> (in Brown, 2003).

The rise of Fox and the aforementioned developments among its cable competitors has resounding implications for the U.S. political system: conservative, "patriotic" news, particularly if presented in a consumer-friendly manner, has a viable mass audience. In a commercial media environment, news outlets must respond or face financial peril—as the actions of MSNBC and CNN indicate. These economic realities of the U.S. press, then, operate to the advantage of political conservatives, who essentially now have a popular national television platform to join with a conservative national newspaper, the *Wall Street Journal*, and the significant collection of talk radio hosts who amplify the conservative message.[18] The addition of Fox to this growing media constellation is no small matter, because these 24-hour television outlets increasingly have become the primary news source for Americans since September 11—fully half of the public said cable TV news was its primary source for news in the initial months of 2003, up from 35 percent in mid-2001—and often drive news and political discourse in America.[19] Liberals, of course, do not have a clearly left-leaning television outlet, an explicitly liberal mainstream newspaper, or a network of talk radio hosts.[20] Both the normative routines and the economic base of U.S. news media, therefore, are favorably situated for conservatives, particularly those operating at the nexus of religion and politics. The loser, again, is democracy. When political ideology trumps news, debate and decision-making always suffer. Further, it is this relation between conservative politics and media that makes the continued dominance of political fundamentalism a real possibility in a world in which the next fear-inducing crisis is only a terrorist attack away.

## THE DEMOCRATS' LANGUAGE

For the president, his strategic adviser Karl Rove, and political conservatives in general, the post-September 11 ascendancy of political fundamentalism was a momentous period in U.S. history. According to a White House aide, quoted in a *USA Today* article on March 17, 2003, the day that Bush issued his ultimatum to Saddam Hussein, "the president sees himself as redefining the U.S. role at a moment the 'tectonic plates' of the world order are shifting—as they did in 1776 and 1914 and at other big moments in history" (Page, 2003). In the words of Lemann, in his analysis of the relationship between President Bush and strategist Rove, the goals are indeed sizable:

The real prize is creating a Republican majority that would be as solid as, say, the Democratic coalition that Franklin Roosevelt created—a majority that would last for a generation and that, as it played itself out over time, would end up profoundly changing the relationship between citizen and state in this country.

(Lemann, 2003, p. 75)

For the president, the two dominant U.S. political parties, and all Americans, the stakes are considerable. After September 11 and under George W. Bush, the Republican Party became the dominant force in U.S. politics, holding the presidency, both houses of Congress, a majority of state legislators for the first time in half a century, and an increasing party allegiance among the American public. An effective response by the Democratic Party and its leaders will require new thinking on their part and, above all, a new understanding of the power of language and strategic communication. The Bush administration between autumn 2001 and spring 2003 offers some instructive insights.

A successful integration of politics, language, and morality, particularly a conservative religious morality, propelled the rise of political fundamentalism in the United States in the late 1970s, sustained it as a presence for more than two decades, and made it ascendant in the aftermath of September 11. This strategic convergence is a direct byproduct of the recognition among conservatives, largely lost upon liberals, that language is not a neutral means of talking about and representing reality. In the words of Lakoff:

> [L]iberalism itself has a view of discourse that puts it at a disadvantage. Liberalism comes from an Enlightenment tradition of supposedly literal, rational, issue-oriented discourse, a tradition of debate using "neutral" conceptual resources. Most liberals assume that metaphors are just matters of words and rhetoric, or that they cloud the issues, or that metaphors are the stuff of Orwellian language. If liberals are to create an adequate moral discourse to counter conservatives, they must get over their view that all thought is literal and that straightforward rational literal debate on an issue is always possible. That idea is false—empirically false—and if liberals stick to it they will

[ 170 ]

have little hope of constructing a discourse that is a strong moral response to conservative discourse.

(Lakoff, 1996, p. 387)

Political conservatives over recent decades have developed a coherent, resonant discourse—rooted for some in a religious fundamentalism—that defends and promotes their values; liberals in the Democratic Party by and large have not. The beginning step for political liberals is to realize that their survival as a viable political entity in the United States depends upon their ability to develop a new *language*, more so than their ability to craft new policies. Choices about and emphases in communication suggest and highlight particular ways of understanding reality that enact cultural change every bit as powerfully as choices about policy goals. The intertwined communication strategies and policies of the Bush administration infused this understanding—that language choices represent *and* constitute political realities—among administration members and throughout their public discourse. Language always reflects and contributes in some manner to particular cultural understandings, power relations, and moral frameworks. Equipped with such an understanding, political liberals would be newly prepared to undertake a number of strategies that would help them to construct a resonant moral discourse of their own.

First, Democrats have to develop a consensus about their values and the relative ordering of those values. In the civil rights movement days of the 1960s, U.S. political liberals had a clear "value hierarchy" in which civil rights for all was placed on the highest moral ground in their language and policies.[21] In the decades since, Democrats, as a group, have inadequately updated this value hierarchy to reflect new or evolving public concerns; a successful challenge to political fundamentalism in the post-September 11 period requires both an update and a consensus. This will not be easy for liberals. An analysis of rhetoric across several Congresses since the Second World War indicated liberals were more "integratively complex" in their political reasoning.[22] This is not a backhanded way of saying conservatives were simple-minded. Rather, in evaluations of political issues and ideas, liberals (and centrists) were more likely to perceive conflicting values in policy debates to be of *similar importance*, such as "social equality *and* economic freedom, economic growth *and* environmental protection, crime control *and* civil liberties," and so on (Tetlock,

[ 171 ]

1989, p. 141, emphasis added). As a result, liberals are much more likely than conservatives to experience a kind of mental paralysis that hinders a willingness and ability to argue persuasively about the moral value of a particular policy position. An example is the matter of hate speech. Some U.S. liberals side with the First Amendment and unfettered speech, while others side with the Fourteenth Amendment's guarantees of "life, liberty, and property" and "equal protection of the laws," which they see as mandating citizenry protection from a climate of racist, sexist, or similarly hateful discourse. Whichever side liberals choose, their empathy for the other position hinders their ability to speak with moral rectitude.

Political conservatives do not suffer such paralyses. There is a certainty and consensus among U.S. political conservatives about a hierarchy of values that simply is not present—or at least not on public display—among liberals. This confidence about the moral order is rooted in a conservative religious worldview for many U.S. political conservatives,[23] including several key members of the Bush administration. Such individuals, as a result, tend to exhibit an "absolute and overweening certainty" that their conception of reality is the right one (Barr, 1977, p. 338), an outlook that undergirds their political decisions and discourse. Consider the words of President Bush in his commencement address at West Point in June 2002: "Some worry that it is somehow undiplomatic or impolite to speak the language of right and wrong. I disagree. Different circumstances require different methods, but not different moralities. Moral truth is the same in every culture, in every time, and in every place."

Among Democrats, the lack of a collective certainty about the relative hierarchy of their beliefs inevitably engenders what might be termed a *moral fatigue* in the pursuit of political matters—that is, some inevitably tire, some become willing to compromise, and some turn to pursuit of other policies thought to be no less important. The Democrats' resolute, "take no prisoners" discourse about abortion is the exception that reveals the rule. In contrast, health care was the moral issue *du jour* of the Democratic Party in the early 1990s, but then was sporadically emphasized for nearly a decade. Gay and lesbian rights were the focus of the Clinton administration's first act in office, but were rarely mentioned again. Education? The environment? Affirmative action? All are issues for which the lack of a clear value hierarchy and consensus about that ranking has impaired Democrats' ability to speak with moral suasion about their agenda. This outcome will not change until they change, collectively.

Second, Democrats might find and exhibit this sense of a value hierarchy by drawing upon and tapping into a religious tradition of their own: the long history of a liberal religious conscience in the American psyche, rooted in the ideas and language of grace, mercy, justice, love, and humility. Antebellum abolitionists, women suffragists, "Social Gospel" activists, anti-monopoly muckrakers, civil rights and liberties advocates, inner-city, rural, and overseas aid workers—many of the individuals who participate(d) in these activities have been motivated by a religiously based understanding of the world. However, discursive evidence that religion can play a positive role in U.S. life is often non-existent among leading Democrats. Consider the words of Al From, chairman of the Democratic Leadership Council, a centrist Democrat group: "We went for years in the Democratic Party without recognizing God and we pay a high price for that" (in Swarns and Cardwell, 2003). Political liberals' ceding of the languages of religion and faith to Republicans has been noticed and interpreted in less than favorable terms for liberals. In summer 2003, 51 percent of U.S. adults said conservatives were "friendly" toward religion, 25 percent said they were "neutral," and 10 percent said they were "unfriendly." In contrast, only 26 percent of U.S. adults said that liberals were friendly toward religion, 33 percent said they were neutral, and a full 27 percent said liberals were unfriendly to religion.[24]

In a nation in which overwhelming numbers of Americans claim to believe in God, the Democrats' largely faith-free discourse has created an unnecessary hurdle. It is no coincidence that the only two Democrats to occupy the White House since the 1960s emerged from Southern conservative religious environments in which they developed an appreciation of faith as a positive force, an appreciation that helped them to develop a discourse, including a compelling moral language, with appeal beyond the base of the Democratic Party.

This is certainly not to say that an effective moral discourse must be built upon a religious foundation. Indeed, a third option for liberals would be to emphasize the moral power of a representative democracy and its norms of open and public debate—norms that were swept aside in the administration's creation and push for the U.S.A. Patriot Act, Department of Homeland Security, and preemptive war in Iraq. The president, for example, dismissed the substantial anti-war protests in early 2003—the nation's largest public demonstrations in three decades—as the equivalent of a "focus group" (quoted in Purdum, 2003). The highlighting of democratic norms has been successful before. Political communication scholar Dhavan Shah and colleagues (2002) note that liberals, in defending President Clinton during the Lewinsky scandal in the late 1990s, denounced Clinton's behavior but declared a responsibility to serve as "guardians of the Constitution who had no choice but to defend U.S. democratic processes in the face of conservatives' efforts to 'hijack the presidency'" (p. 344). These authors offer evidence that these arguments by liberals were a relatively small part of news coverage about the scandal and impeachment, yet were crucial in sustaining Clinton's favorable public approval.

In the post-September 11 era, a reservoir of public concern about the treatment of civil liberties by the Bush administration has developed. By March 2004, 260 communities and three states—Hawaii, Alaska, and Vermont—had passed resolutions condemning the U.S.A. Patriot Act or calling for its review.[25] And the American Civil Liberties Union experienced a 30 percent increase in membership between September 11 and June 2003—an increase far surpassing any in the organization's 83-year history, spurred in part by former Georgia conservative congressman Bob Barr's vocal allegiance with the ACLU.[26] These are opportunities for Democrats to capitalize by emphasizing the moral importance and centrality of *liberal*-democratic values for Americans.

Fourth, the loss of the international goodwill toward the United States that was widely present after September 11 offers a moment for U.S. liberals to build a moral discourse and policy framework that positions America as a strong but benevolent global leader. Bloom (1990) argues that public opinion in nation-states can be mobilized successfully by political leaders if at least one of two circumstances is present: the nation is threatened, or there is an opportunity of "enhancing" national identity (p. 79). Among Americans the terrorist attacks instigated a nation-challenging crisis that provided an opportunity for political fundamentalism; that is, the clear threat to U.S. self-identity opened a discursive space in which the Bush administration's convergence of conservative religion and politics capitalized. The opposition among traditional U.S. allies to the Iraq war, however, placed the United States in a far different position vis-à-vis international opinion—respected for its freedoms, but perceived by a sizable contingent of people to be a heavy-handed bully, at minimum, and an empire-building imperialist at worst. To be sure, U.S. military action in Iraq was supported and welcomed by some, but the erosion of favorable opinion toward the United States between autumn 2001 and spring 2004 was dramatic in many nations, including traditional western allies.[27] In this context, liberals have the potential to offer a *nation-enhancing* discourse that emphasizes the importance of U.S. policies demonstrating a morally benevolent global leadership, perhaps through humanitarian interventions in civil strife, famines or disease in Africa, or even a sustained commitment to nation-building in Afghanistan and Iraq.

Conservatives can also advocate policies that enhance the nation's identity, of course—and indeed, the Bush administration's self-moniker of "compassionate conservativism" and 2003 earmarking of funds to fight AIDS in Africa and dispatch of troops to help end civil war in Liberia are examples. What liberals can distinctly offer is a *coherent* political framework of moral humanitarianism in which domestic and foreign policies have been integrated over time. This framework has a twentieth-century legacy, beginning with the efforts of Woodrow Wilson in the First World War and continued in the Roosevelt administration's "New Deal" and Second World War leadership, the Truman administration's racial integration of the armed forces and rebuilding of Europe, the Democrats' civil rights and Great Society advocacy in the 1960s and 1970s, the Carter administration's Middle East peace accords, and the Clinton administration's welfare reform and interventions in Yugoslavia and Somalia.

In the aftermath of September 11, though, a nation-enhancing discourse alone is not likely to be sufficiently persuasive among a U.S. citizenry that remains concerned about potential terrorist attacks. With this in mind, liberals are far better positioned to pair an emphasis on security with an emphasis on the moral *responsibility* of Americans to live in a manner that is true to the values the nation seeks to defend. That is, there is rich potential to craft a compelling American "social myth" (Niebuhr, 1967) that emphasizes security and argues that security gains value if, and only if, people—both Americans and others—are able to live out the freedom, liberty, equality, justice, and opportunity that represent the U.S. ideals. Such a discourse would go far to countering the "security at whatever cost" perspective of the Bush administration and political conservatives.

The argument here, then, is that the short-term relevance and long-term viability of the Democratic Party are dependent upon the ability of its leaders to develop a language that conveys their moral concerns and does so in a strategic, compelling manner. In a mass media-dominated political environment, the current discourses of liberals—of uncertain and mixed mind about what values truly matter, unconnected to religious faith, with inadequate emphasis upon democratic norms, and unable to capitalize with a coherent moral humanitarianism—are simply less likely than those of conservatives to gain the upper hand in U.S. politics, receive an echoing by the mainstream press, or resonate with the American public. Failure by liberals to develop a new language has the potential consequence of moving Democrats to the role of a mere opposition party. Indeed, the prospect of a single-party-dominated U.S. political system—regardless of which party is dominant and whether that dominance lasts the 20 months analyzed here or extends for the generation or more that is the expressed hope of the president and conservative strategists—is an outcome that should concern all Americans.

The Bush administration's political fundamentalism in the aftermath of September 11 stamped out any chance of a desperately needed, multi-vocal public and international conversation regarding the appropriate values, policies, and responsibilities of the globe's sole superpower in a world of terrorism. Until and unless U.S. liberals recognize this challenge for what it is—a discursive one, in which the tools of competition are rhetorical—the Democrats will continue to suffer as a party. The damage, however, will certainly not end there.

# 7
# Renewing democracy

The evidence is clear: The Bush administration brought a political fundamentalism into the mainstream of American politics in the aftermath of September 11. The president and his team did so by strategically choosing language and communication approaches that were structurally grounded in a conservative Christian outlook, but were primarily political in manifest content. The U.S. public's surge of support for the president and the press's nationalistic response following the terrorist attacks provided the opening. It was a sizable and unexpected moment in history during which the administration's discourses were given a deferential and wide hearing. Bush's adept communications machinery took over from there. Whether the severity of this nation-challenging crisis meant that the public would have embraced nearly any form of competent leadership emanating from the White House is an unknown question. What *is* known is that this administration presented only one model of leadership after the terrorist attacks—one that was profoundly fundamentalist in its conception of reality, expectations and treatment of others, and pursuit of policy goals. The combination of this worldview with adroit strategy allowed the administration to grasp control of public discourse and the political agenda with such speed, certainty, and authority that news media, other political leaders, and the public were rendered mute. Had this lasted for weeks, even a few months, it would have been unfortunate but perhaps understandable given the nature of the September 11 attacks. However, it was not until *nearly two years later*, after the president had declared an end to major combat in Iraq in May 2003, that the administration relinquished its pressure sufficiently for other U.S. political leaders—most particularly, Democrats beginning their run for the White House—and the U.S. mainstream press to begin consistently asking tough questions.

While Christian conservatives and hard-line neo-conservatives may see the developments after September 11 in a positive light (after all, one might say that God and the United States have been given a larger piece of the planet to play with), all Americans should be leery of any government that merges religiosity into political ends. Noble ideals such as freedom and liberty are clearly worth pursuing, but the administration promoted these concepts with its left hand while using its right hand to treat others—including many U.S. citizens—in an authoritarian, dismissive manner. Further, the president's consistent rhetoric about the "war on terrorism" being a divinely ordained undertaking forced political opponents and the public into an undue position: they were either with the Bush administration or against God. Unfortunately, the Bush administration appears to be the latest entry in an American historical record which shows that beliefs and claims about divine leading are no guarantee that one will exercise power in a consistently liberating, egalitarian manner. With a more global view, social scientist Ernest Becker observed:

> Many religionists have lamented the great toll that the Hitlers and the Stalins have taken in order to give their followers the equivalent of religious expiation and immortality; it seemed that when man lost the frank religious dimension of experience, he became even more desperate and wild; when he tried to make the earth alone a pure paradise, he had to become more demonic and devilish. But when one looks at the toll of scapegoats that religious integrations have taken, one can [see] ... that religious mystifications have so far been as dangerous as any other.
> (Becker, 1975, p. 124)

Ultimately, whatever their underlying beliefs may be, what political leaders *do* is what matters most. In turn, the actions of American leaders take on particular magnitude because the global hegemony of the United States is unrivaled at the moment. How the power and wealth of the world's sole superpower are to be exercised is the defining question of the times. The answer from the Bush administration is that it intends to focus its might and a good chunk of the nation's resources in a campaign against terrorism, both at home and abroad. The president's 2004 State of the Union address reaffirmed his message that this *is* God's cause. He returned to the administration's universal gospel message with his declaration that "I believe that God has planted in every human heart the desire to live in freedom." And in closing his discussion of U.S. overseas actions, Bush said that "America is a nation with a mission," adding a few lines later,

"America acts in this cause with friends and allies at our side, yet we understand our special calling" (Bush, 2004). Such certainty about God's will, avowed implicitly and explicitly countless times since September 11, leaves little room for doubt—or democracy.

The ultimate irony (some would say hypocrisy) of the administration's leadership is that its political fundamentalism looks, sounds, and feels remarkably similar to that of the terrorists it is fighting. Both see the world through a binary lens of good versus evil, in which complex understandings of the "enemy" are rejected as inconceivable. Both are obsessed with time, in a couple of ways. First, one's temporal actions are thought to be directly related to one's eternal relationship with a supreme being. Second, sustenance is derived from the belief that providence is on their side in this struggle. Both also assert that they offer universal norms of human relationships and behavior that are divinely decreed for all peoples. In each case, *others* are perceived to have perverted, or chosen against, these mores. Finally, both worldviews demand unflinching support and exact a sizable cost from those who dissent.

The comparisons do not hold through all matters, of course, but the similarities are real. One is hard pressed to see how claims made by Osama bin Laden, that he and his followers are delivering God's wishes for the United States (and others who share western customs and policies), are much different from claims made by George W. Bush, that the United States is delivering God's wishes to the Taliban or Iraq. Clearly, flying airplanes into buildings in order to kill innocent people is an indefensible immoral activity. So too, some traditional allies told the Bush administration, is an unprovoked preemptive invasion of a sovereign nation. In both instances, the aggression manifested in a form that was available to the leaders. Fundamentalism in the White House is a difference in degree, not kind, from fundamentalism exercised in dark, damp caves.[1]

The governmental leaders of the world's sole superpower failed Americans and the world's citizens in the aftermath of September 11. At a minimum, during the 20 months analyzed here there should have been some willingness by the administration to consider differing conceptions of the global and political landscape; there should have been greater transparency and openness by the administration in its development of policies;[2] there should have been more of the humility toward other nations that Bush, when running for the presidency, said would emanate from his White House;[3] and there should have been a substantive assessment of whether or not a preemptive foreign policy was morally appropriate. None of this would have interfered with U.S. security, and the benefits for democracy, both in the United States and globally, would have been enormous. Each of these, however, would have required the president and administration to acknowledge that they might be wrong, that they perhaps did not have all the answers or could not do it alone, and that they might not have a direct pipeline to God. For an administration with a fundamentalist worldview, asking for help or being open to criticism is anathema. Once the door is opened to questions or doubt, the battle is perceived to have been lost. Better to die on the hill of certainty, without considering alternatives, than to countenance a more complex understanding of faith, politics, or human relations.

Indeed, whether an administration with a worldview rooted in religious fundamentalism can engage in reasoned, open, and public deliberation is doubtful. Requesting the *support* of others is easily accomplished, because the authority of the administration is safely maintained. Altogether different is *treating others as co-equals*, because this approach comes dangerously close to suggesting that the administration's leadership and perspectives are insufficient. For a fundamentalist administration, any criticisms, questioning, or disagreements from other political leaders are likely to be perceived as a substantial affront, an attempt to impugn the administration's religious-cum-political vision. Such an outlook starts at the top in the Bush administration, which is headed by a president whose communications show a resistance to nuance, a certainty of the rightness of his perspectives, a belief that the administration is on a divine mission, and an expectation that his decisions should not be publicly challenged or crossed.[4] This is a perilous combination. The administration's message from September 11 through the Iraq war was that the United States could and would go it alone. Harvard professor and former Defense Department assistant secretary Joseph Nye has persuasively argued, however, that the United States *cannot* go it alone if it hopes to achieve peace and stability. His view is that American hegemony is most positively employed on the nation's and world's behalf when U.S. military might is accompanied by a substantial emphasis upon U.S. "soft power":

A country may obtain the outcomes it wants in world politics because other countries want to follow it, admiring its values, emulating its example, aspiring to its level of prosperity and openness. In this sense, it is just as important to set the agenda in world politics and attract others, as it is to force them to change through the threat or use of military or economic weapons. This aspect of power—getting others to want what you want—I call soft power.

(Nye, 2002, pp. 8–9)

Nye adds, "Soft power arises in large part from our values. These values are expressed in our culture, in the policies we follow inside our country, and in the way we handle ourselves internationally." This is a perspective that is lost on the Bush administration, and that must be reclaimed by the United States.[5] To not do so is to court disaster for all peoples.

The ability of Americans to renew democracy at home and respect abroad will require courage to break the bondage of fear, which since September 11 has been the dominant national emotion. Fear was introduced by the terrorist attacks, of course, but within hours it was built into the administration's discourses of good versus evil and security versus peril. This was not happenstance.[6] Fear was instrumental in convincing the public that the administration's vision of simplicity, familiarity, and "security at whatever cost"—the latter perspective institutionalized in the Department of Homeland Security—was right or at least palatable.

The administration capitalized upon fear in several other ways, too. It issued occasional terror alerts while telling the public little more than to watch for anything suspicious, and it consistently declared that its anti-terrorism policies required imminent passage, lest more harm occur. Its squelching of dissent relied upon a standing threat that the administration would exact a price from any who publicly challenged it, a behavioral pattern that reached a nadir in summer 2003. In response to former government employee Joseph Wilson's criticisms of claims in the president's 2003 State of the Union address regarding attempts to purchase uranium by Iraq, a high administration source allegedly fed news media the name of Wilson's wife, a CIA operative.[7] This leak violated federal law and placed Wilson's wife and her contacts in danger—all the "better" for an administration that desires to stifle dissent and instill fear in political adversaries. Finally, the preemptive foreign policy provides a new hammer that the administration can use to coerce other members of the international community to adopt, or at least accept, the administration's perspective. In short, the administration's political fundamentalism has trafficked in fear since September 11.

This must change, because fear, more so than any other human emotion, is the enemy of democracy. Fear paralyzes people, engendering a sense of impotence in which any form of apparent strength gains appeal. Survival becomes the dominant concern. There is no simple cure for fear, but perhaps the most important place to start is to find a renewed vision of hope. When people have hope that things can get better, they become open to thinking expansively and creatively, to caring for others beyond their own existence. The presidencies of Franklin Roosevelt, John Kennedy, Ronald Reagan, and Bill Clinton in the twentieth century stand apart because they offered a vision of hope for the United States that captured the imagination of sizable segments of the American electorate. In this regard Reagan's political fundamentalism differed significantly from Bush's: Reagan's 1984 re-election effort, for example, famously declared in a campaign commercial that it was "Morning again in America."[8]

A political leader with a realistic yet positive vision of democratic possibilities (at home and abroad) would go far in helping the United States return as an admired leader to the global stage, but an enlightened president only would be one important step. The participation of other so-inclined cultural actors also is crucial: humanitarian and religious groups, arts and music communities, educational institutions and associations, health and medical industries, and others have to become more critically aware of and engaged in the political arena. Blind faith in U.S. governmental leadership to act with integrity and on behalf of the *mass* public does not work, has never worked. The lessons of McCarthyism in the 1950s, the Vietnam War in the 1960s, Watergate in the 1970s, and Iran-Contra in the 1980s are being learned anew in the United States.

Two institutions, in particular, abdicated their responsibilities in the aftermath of September 11 and must re-establish their democratic gravitas. The first is the U.S. Congress, which significantly facilitated the Bush administration's steamrolling actions. Republicans in the House of Representatives, with a comfortable majority, rubber-stamped the administration's policies from the moment of the terrorist attacks. This occurred most egregiously in the case of the U.S.A. Patriot Act, when House speaker Dennis Hastert scrapped a bill that had been unanimously passed by the Judiciary Committee, in favor of a far more aggressive version favored by Attorney General John Ashcroft, and then forced a House vote within hours.[9] The Senate performed marginally better. Only one senator of either party voted against this legislation, even though a number expressed acute reservations. Some Senate Democrats did argue against the administration's push for the Homeland Security Department and the Iraq resolution, both in autumn 2002, but the party was more than enough divided to seal its demise in national elections. Congress so pleased and appeased the administration that Bush may complete a full term in office without vetoing a bill—the first president to do so since John Quincy Adams in the 1820s.[10]

With a conservative Supreme Court unwilling to challenge the executive branch in this crisis period, the president governed more or less unilaterally—which is exactly what the administration desired. Left unchecked, the White House's political fundamentalism provided and enacted a worldview that reaped electoral rewards at the cost of democratic dialogue and the international goodwill that flowed to the United States after September 11. For the good of the nation and world, Congress must regain its footing as a viable branch of the federal government.

Finally, the news media must acknowledge the crucial role they play in the everyday process of shaping people's perceptions of reality. Located at the cultural intersection of social, political, legal, and economic arenas, news media present interpretations of the world that always reflect and contribute to individuals' experiences. The emphasis on fear emanating from the White House after September 11 was *welcomed* by U.S. media outlets, because fear spurs interest in news coverage as people attempt to gain a sense of control. Indeed, the U.S. public's "news interest" reached levels between September 2001 and spring 2003 that had not been attained for at least a decade (see Pew, 2001b, 2002b, 2003a).[11] The terrorist attacks provided a tragedy that seemed made for mass media, set in the nation's news capitals. Leading news outlets capitalized upon the crisis context with special, nationalistic newspaper sections and flag-waving television network logos.

Over subsequent months, U.S. military action in Afghanistan in autumn 2001, the president's "axis of evil" claims in the 2002 State of the Union, the periodic elevation of threat warnings, the push for the Homeland Security Department and Iraq resolutions in summer and autumn 2002, and finally the Iraq war in spring 2003 provided news media with administration-constructed opportunities to engage in "objective" news coverage that nonetheless contributed to a climate of fear.

Further, the press's echoing of the administration's binary, time-fixated, and dissent-squelching discourses did the same. Journalists' traditional defense is that they do not make the news, they just report it. However, all news is framed in certain ways that seek to maximize audience interest; emphases on evil, peril, and conflict were present in news coverage not solely because they were highlighted by administration sources, but also because journalists wanted to draw readers and viewers—and *had* to do so in the American commercial media system. The U.S. news media may not have created the environment of fear in September 2001, but they bear some substantial responsibility for sustaining it month after month thereafter.[12]

The news media's considerable power to influence public opinion is a viewpoint that news organizations trumpet when selling advertising time but deny when assessing blame for negative societal outcomes. The evidence clearly indicates, however, that the mainstream press was complicit in the Bush administration's ability to grasp and maintain control of public discourse and to act without political compunction for almost two years. Between early September 2001 and spring 2003 leading individuals and institutions of the U.S. news media resoundingly echoed the administration's worldview, thereby propping up the president and administration. All that the vast majority of Americans knew about international terrorism, beyond the attacks on New York and Washington D.C., was what they read or saw in news coverage. The administration's words and ideas dominated this coverage. It was not that mainstream U.S. journalists never challenged administration policies over these months; they did, particularly the approach to the Iraq war in early 2003. Rather, the chief failure of the press was that they too rarely questioned the administration's *discourses*—of good versus evil and security versus peril, time fixations, God-decreed universality of freedom and liberty, and emphasis on unity over dissent. Once these discourses became amplified consistently in leading press outlets, the administration had gained the rhetorical high ground and had gone far in determining policy decisions. The press contributed to these outcomes as surely as Karl Rove did.

For democracy to be renewed among the American populace, mainstream journalists have to recognize that the fate of the nation is intertwined with the fate of the press. Journalists and news organizations are more than just messengers. They must serve as the voices of the people—particularly when the people are ignored or silenced by political leaders, as is too often the case in modern nation-states and certainly was so in the United States between September 11 and the Iraq war. The news media should report on what the nation's elected and appointed leaders say and do, of course. But an obsequious posture by journalists toward political leadership benefits only those in power, particularly during crisis contexts but even so during "normal politics." Democracy is a fiction if a free press functions like one beholden to elites, because to dominate news discourse *is* to control public opinion.

The freedom of the press guaranteed by the First Amendment was put in place, and has been upheld by countless judicial decisions since the First World War, because news organizations are thought to offer an important safeguard against the corrosive tendencies of power and to serve as guardians of democratic practices. That is, the press is expected to provide a bulwark against governmental oppression, rather than a buttressing of it. Never is such a contribution of the press more necessary than in times of crisis, and yet the evidence after September 11 and throughout U.S. history suggests that these are the contexts in which the press becomes most likely to echo the perspectives of governmental leadership. This pattern must end. The democratic ideals of the nation will have the opportunity to be fully realized only when news media re-establish their positions as a consistent check on the absolute power of government—and sustain this role through the next nation-challenging crisis.

# Notes

## Chapter 1 Religion, politics, and the Bush administration

1.  For *Washington Post* coverage, see M. Allen, Comforting words as a matter of faith. *Washington Post*, 3 February 2003, retrieved from washingtonpost.com on 3 February 2003; D. Milbank, Bush links faith and agenda in speech to religious group. *Washington Post*, 10 February 2003, p. A-2; E. J. Dionne, Jr., When presidents talk of God. *Washington Post*, 14 February 2003, p. A-31, retrieved from washingtonpost.com on 26 August 2003.
2.  For *New York Times* coverage, see B. Keller, God and George W. Bush. *New York Times*, 17 May 2003, p. A-17, retrieved from Nexis database, 6 June 2003; N. D. Kristof, God, Satan, and the media. *New York Times*, 4 March 2003, p. A-25. The *Times* also included a longer essay from G. Wills, With God on his side. *New York Times*, 30 March 2003, retrieved from Nexis database, 6 June 2003.
3.  See C. Hitchens, God and man in the White House. *Vanity Fair*, August 2003, pp. 76–81.
4.  See G. Lawson, George W.'s personal Jesus. *Gentlemen's Quarterly*, September 2003, pp. 330–5, 394–6, 399.
5.  M. E. Marty, The sin of pride. *Newsweek*, 10 March 2003, pp. 32–3.
6.  For discussion of public perceptions as of spring 2003 of Bush's leadership, see D. S. Broder, Bush's leadership pinnacle. *Washington Post*, 27 April 2003, p. B-7.
7.  The "rally 'round the flag effect" is what political scientists call the public's tendency to respond to crises by extending strong support to the president and other political leaders. See, for example, W. D. Baker and J. R. Oneal, "Patriotism or opinion leadership: the nature and origins of the 'rally round the flag' effect," *Journal of Conflict Resolution* 45 (2001): 661–87; R. A. Brody, *Assessing the president* (Stanford, CA: Stanford University Press, 1991); J. E. Mueller, "Presidential popularity from Truman to Johnson," *American Political Science Review* 64 (1970): 18–33.
8.  On worldviews, see also C. Geertz, "Religion as a cultural system," in M. Banton (ed.), *Anthropological approaches to the study of religion*, pp. 1–46 (London: Tavistock, 1966); D. C. Leege and L. A. Kellstedt,

"Religious worldviews and political philosophies: capturing theory in the grand manner through empirical data," in D. C. Leege and L. A. Kellstedt, *Rediscovering the religious factor in American politics*, pp. 216–31 (Armonk, NY: M. E. Sharpe, 1993); D. K. Naugle, *Worldview: the history of a concept* (Grand Rapids, MI: W. B. Eerdmans, 2002); G. R. Peterson, "Religion as orienting worldview," *Zygon*, 36/1 (2001): 5–19.

9. On a religious fundamentalist worldview, see J. A. Carpenter, *Revive us again: the reawakening of American fundamentalism* (New York: Oxford University Press, 1997); L. Kaplan, "Introduction," in L. Kaplan (ed.), *Fundamentalism in comparative perspective*, pp. 3–14 (Amherst, MA: University of Massachusetts Press, 1992); B. Lawrence, *Defenders of God: the fundamentalist revolt against the modern age* (San Francisco, CA: Harper & Row, 1989); G. M. Marsden, *Fundamentalism and American culture* (New York: Oxford University Press, 1980); and N. T. Ammerman, "North American Protestant fundamentalism," in M. E. Marty and R. S. Appleby (eds), *Fundamentalisms observed*, pp. 1–65 (Chicago: University of Chicago Press, 1991). Another central component of a religious fundamentalist worldview is the belief that holy Scripture—in this case, the Bible—is accurate on all matters and has unchanging meaning for all times. This aspect of fundamentalism does not have a political application that can be manifestly identified in the same manner as the attributes of focus in this book, although some might suggest its presence can be seen in the administration's desire for strict Constitutionalist judges.

10. See also R. Bellah, *The broken covenant: American civil religion in time of trial* (Chicago: University of Chicago Press, 1992, 2nd ed.); M. Cristi, *From civil to political religion: the intersection of culture, religion and politics* (Waterloo, Ontario: Wilfrid Laurier University Press, 2001); R. V. Pierard, *Civil religion and the presidency* (Grand Rapids, MI: Academic Books, 1988); N. L. Rosenblum (ed.), *Obligations of citizenship and demands of faith: religious accommodation in pluralist democracies* (Princeton: Princeton University Press, 2000).

11. On the rise and influence of Christian conservatives in American politics, see J. Gallagher and C. Bull, *Perfect enemies: the religious right, the gay movement, and the politics of the 1990s* (New York: Crown Publishers, 1996); Kaplan, "Introduction"; M. Lienesch, *Redeeming America: piety and politics in the new Christian right* (Chapel Hill: University of North Carolina Press, 1993); J. Whittle, "All in the family: top Bush administration leaders, religious right lieutenants plot strategy in culture 'War,'" *Church & State* 55/5 (2002): 4–8; C. Wilcox, *Onward Christian soldiers? The religious right in American politics* (Boulder, CO: Westview Press, 2000).

12. The origins of Christian fundamentalism in the United States can be found in the late nineteenth and early twentieth centuries. A confluence of social, theological, and cultural influences prompted a group of Bible teachers and evangelists to publish a series of paperback volumes, titled *The fundamentals*, between 1910 and 1915. These works offered a broad defense of the Christian faith, including core matters of biblical authority and the doctrines of the Trinity, sin, and salvation, against the perceived encroachments of modern science and historical criticism. These volumes became the reference point for a broader movement and the coining of the term "fundamentalism." The degree of political involvement among fundamentalists since has waxed and waned over time. See Marsden, *Fundamentalism and American culture*, for an excellent treatment of the origins and influence of fundamentalism in the United States. The term "modern political fundamentalism" is used in this book to refer to the political engagement of Christian fundamentalists (and some evangelicals, a group often difficult to distinguish from fundamentalists) that emerged in response to the American cultural crises of the 1960s, has focused heavily on the "moral" issues of the times (abortion, family values, prayer in public schools, and the civil rights of gays and lesbians), has become increasingly sophisticated in its mechanisms of political influence and usage of modern mass media forms, and with the Bush administration gained the White House.

13. The words in quotes ("cultural mainstream") are drawn from M. E. Marty, *Religion and republic: the American circumstance* (Boston: Beacon Press, 1987). On the rise of fundamentalism in American culture in the 1960s and 1970s, see also A. J. Reichley, "The evangelical and fundamentalist revolt," in R. J. Neuhaus and M. Cromartie (eds), *Piety and politics: evangelicals and fundamentalists confront the world*, pp. 69–95 (Washington, D.C.: Ethics and Public Policy Center, 1987).

14. On the notion of America as a "chosen nation," see Lienesch, *Redeeming America*; E. L. Tuveson, *Redeemer nation: the idea of America's millennial role* (Chicago: University of Chicago Press, 1968).

15. See S. Bruce, "The Moral Majority: the politics of fundamentalism in secular society," in L. Caplan (ed.), *Studies in religious fundamentalism*, pp. 177–94 (London: Macmillan Press, 1987).

16. For detail on the network among religious conservatives during the 1980s, see S. Diamond, *Spiritual warfare: the politics of the Christian Right* (Boston: South End Press, 1989); Lienesch, *Redeeming America*.

17. For the role of Falwell and his arguments, see Ammerman, "North American Protestant fundamentalism," p. 46.

18. On the linkage of Ronald Reagan and Christian conservatives, see W. Edel, *Defenders of the faith: religion and politics from the pilgrim fathers*

*to Ronald Reagan* (New York: Praeger, 1987); Lienesch, *Redeeming America*; Reichley, "The evangelical and fundamentalist revolt."

19. On the appointment of religious conservatives by Reagan, see Diamond, *Spiritual warfare*; Reichley, "The evangelical and fundamentalist revolt."

20. Falwell quote drawn from M. Weiler and W. B. Pearce, "Ceremonial discourse: the rhetorical ecology of the Reagan administration," in M. Weiler and W. B. Pearce (eds), *Reagan and public discourse in America*, pp. 11–42 (Tuscaloosa, AL: University of Alabama Press, 1992), p. 27.

21. On the increased intertwining of religious conservatives with political conservatives, more broadly, see N. Easton, *Gang of five: leaders at the center of the conservative ascendancy* (New York: Simon & Schuster, 2000); Gallagher and Bull, *Perfect enemies*; Lienesch, *Redeeming America*.

22. On the wariness of Christian conservatives toward George H. W. Bush, see Easton, *Gang of five*.

23. On the shift from the Moral Majority to the Christian Coalition, see C. Wilcox, M. DeBell, and L. Sigelman, "The second coming of the new Christian right: patterns of popular support in 1984 and 1996," *Social Science Quarterly* 80/1 (1999): 181–93.

24. This claim about the electoral importance of the Christian Coalition is drawn from Gallagher and Bull, *Perfect enemies*, p. 229. See also L. Edwards, *The conservative revolution: the movement that remade America* (New York: Free Press, 1999).

25. On the role of the Christian Coalition in the impeachment process against Bill Clinton, see C. Berlet and M. N. Lyons, *Right-wing populism in America: too close for comfort* (New York: Guilford Press, 2000); Easton, *Gang of five*. On the conservative pursuit of Clinton more generally, see D. Brock, *Blinded by the right: the conscience of an ex-conservative* (New York: Crown Publishers, 2002).

26. On the predominance of Christian conservatives in the Republican Party, see J. C. Green, L. A. Kellstedt, C. E. Smidt, and J. L. Guth, "The soul of the south: religion and the new electoral order," in C. S. Bullock III and M. J. Rozell (eds), *The new politics of the Old South: an introduction to Southern politics*, pp. 261–76 (Lanham, MD: Rowman and Littlefield, 1998); C. Wilcox, *Onward Christian soldiers?*

27. On the point of George W. Bush being viewed as more ideologically in the mold of Ronald Reagan than Bush's father, see B. Keller, The radical presidency of George W. Bush. *New York Times*, 26 January 2003, retrieved from Nexis database, 6 July 2003.

28. On the work by Republicans at the grass roots level, see A. Clymer, Buoyed by resurgence, G.O.P. strives for an era of dominance. *New York Times*, 25 May 2003, p. A-1.

29. This claim about the party identification of Republicans vs. Democrats is drawn from Clymer, "Buoyed by resurgence, G.O.P. strives for an era of dominance."

30. Notably, this political trend in national politics toward the Republican Party in the months after September 11 is akin to Bush's rise to the governorship in Texas, when the state turned away from its Democrat past and went Republican, thanks in part to Bush's political strategist Karl Rove. During the 1994 campaign for Texas governor against incumbent Ann Richards, Bush was already said to be catering to fundamentalists. He had "learned from his dad the peril of ignoring the Christian right; he talked about faith-based social services and the right to life" (Dubose, Reid, and Cannon, 2003, pp. 72–3). And it was said that his political communication strategy of acting like a gentleman, staying consistent in his message and appealing to the morals of the public helped him win the election.

31. On the ability of presidential administrations to stay consistently focused on their desired messages, see R. M. Entman, "Cascading activation: contesting the White House's frame after 9/11," *Political Communication* 20 (2003): 415–32.

32. In fact, the shift from a partisan to a non-partisan U.S. news system came about not because of new, enlightened ideas about fairness in the society, but because of the emergence of modern capitalism. By making the newspaper affordable to everyone, the "penny press" of the 1830s heralded the supposed end of political bias in journalism. Over time, and particularly following the Civil War, newspaper publishers discovered that a neutral story, rather than one slanted with a clear Republican or Democrat take on events, garnered a larger audience. Including everyone into the news frame was profitable. For an analysis of these developments, see G. Baldasty, *The commercialization of news in the nineteenth century* (Madison, WI: University of Wisconsin Press, 1992).

33. The concept of "imagined community" is drawn from B. Anderson, *Imagined communities: reflections on the origin and spread of nationalism* (New York: Verso, 1991, rev. ed.).

34. On the ways in which national identity is disseminated, see W. Bloom, *Personal identity, national identity and international relations* (Cambridge: Cambridge University Press, 1990); J. Hutchinson, *Modern nationalism* (Glasgow: Harper Collins, 1994); R. Poole, *Nation and identity* (London: Routledge, 1999); K. Deutsch, *Nationalism and social communication* (Cambridge, MA: M.I.T. Press, 1953).

35. Public opinion data drawn from Pew Research Center, American psyche reeling from terror attacks, 19 September 2001, retrieved 22 May 2003, from http://people-press.org/reports

36. Public opinion data drawn from S. Pinkus, Poll analysis: psychological

effects of September 11. *Los Angeles Times*, 2001, retrieved 22 May 2003, from http://www.latimes.com/news/custom/ timespoll

37. Public opinion data drawn from CBS News, Poll: America, a changed country. CBS News/New York Times poll, 9 September 2002, retrieved 20 June 2003, from http://www.cbsnews.com/stories /2002/09/07/september11/main521173.shtml

38. For insight into the process of priming, see, for example, S. Iyengar and D. R. Kinder, *News that matters* (Chicago: University of Chicago Press, 1987); J. A. Krosnick and L. Brannon, "The media and the foundations of presidential support: George Bush and the Persian Gulf conflict," *Journal of Social Issues* 49 (1993): 167–82; Z. Pan and G. M. Kosicki, "Priming and media impact on the evaluation of the President's performance," *Communication Research* 24 (1997): 3–30.

39. Public opinion data drawn from Pew Research Center, U.S. needs more international backing, 20 February 2003, retrieved 11 June 2003, from http://people-press.org/reports

40. Public opinion data drawn from Pew Research Center, TV combat fatigue on the rise, 28 March 2003, retrieved 11 June 2003, from http://people-press.org/reports

41. Public opinion data drawn from Pew Research Center, Religion and politics: the ambivalent majority, 20 September 2000, retrieved 20 June 2003, from http://people-press.org/reports

42. This claim, for example, was made by Marty, "The sin of pride"; Wills, "With God on his side."

43. For insight into the religious groundings of Ashcroft, Evans, and Rice, see S. Brill, *After: how America confronted the September 12 era* (New York: Simon & Schuster, 2003), p. 502; J. Donnelly, Fighting terror/theologians. *Boston Globe*, 16 February 2003, p. A-20; B. D. Hawkins, Condaleezza Rice's secret weapon. ChristianityToday.com, September/October 2002, retrieved 22 May 2003, from http://www.christianitytoday.com/cr/2002/005/1.18.html; F. Kiefer, The private faith of a public man. *Christian Science Monitor*, 6 September 2002, p. 1.

44. This claim was made explicitly in H. Fineman, Bush and God. *Newsweek*, 10 March 2003, pp. 22–30.

45. On the president's casting of his entire agenda in spiritual terms, see Milbank, "Bush links faith and agenda in speech to religious group."

46. This anecdote is drawn from Fineman, "Bush and God."

47. On the response of the press, see, for example, M. Dowd, Playing the Jesus card. *New York Times*, 15 December 1999, p. A-23, retrieved from Nexis database on 6 August 2003; S. Grady, Jesus holds all the cards in 2000 campaign. *Milwaukee Journal Sentinel*, 29 December 1999, p. A-18, retrieved from Nexis database on 6 August 2003.

48. On the view that cynicism among the press about politicians' religious claims often is out of touch with Americans whose religious faith is important to them, see E. J. Dionne, Jr., Religion and politics. *Washington Post*, 28 December 1999, p. A-23, retrieved from Nexis database on 6 August 2003.

49. Robertson quote drawn from Names and Faces. *Washington Post*, 3 January 2004, p. C-3, retrieved from Nexis database on 3 January 2004.

50. In the judicial branch of government, this "ordained from God" moral stance was donned by Alabama's chief justice Roy S. Moore in 2003 when he remained steadfast to keep his 5,280-pound granite Ten Commandments monument in the lobby of the State Supreme Court. Even when admonished by his profession and suspended from the bench, the so-called "Ten Commandments Judge" remained certain that his way was the just and divine way, even if it was deemed unconstitutional by others: "I'd do it all the same all over again," Chief Justice Moore said. "I said it back then and I'll say it again now. God is the basis of our law and our government. I cannot and will not violate my conscience." See J. Gettleman, He'd do it again, says the "Ten Commandments Judge." *New York Times*, 13 November 2003, p. A-18.

51. For insight into the role of communication in constructing people's understandings of reality, see P. Berger and T. Luckmann, *The social construction of reality* (New York: Doubleday, 1966); N. Fairclough, *Discourse and social change* (Cambridge: Polity Press, 1992); J. Potter and M. Wetherell, *Discourse and social psychology* (London: Sage, 1987); G. Turner, *British cultural studies: an introduction* (New York: Routledge, 1992).

52. Quoted words are drawn from G. Kress, "Ideological structures in discourse," in T. van Dijk (ed.), *Handbook of discourse analysis, vol. 4*, pp. 27–42 (London: Academic Press, 1985).

53. See S. Hall, "Culture, the media and the 'ideological effect,'" in J. Curran, M. Gurevitch, and J. Woollacott (eds), *Mass communication and society*, pp. 315–48 (Beverly Hills: Sage, 1979); S. Hall, "The rediscovery of 'ideology': Return of the repressed in media studies," in M. Gurevitch, T. Bennett, J. Curran, and J. Woollacott (eds.), *Culture, society and the media*, pp. 56–90 (London: Methuen, 1982).

54. For information on U.S. adults' level of "news interest," see Pew Research Center, Terrorism transforms news interest, 18 December 2001, retrieved 8 June 2002, from http://www.people-press.org; Pew Research Center, Domestic concerns will vie with terrorism in fall, 27 June 2002, retrieved 22 May 2003, from http://people-press.org/reports; Pew Research Center, U.S. needs more international backing, 20 February 2003, retrieved 11 June 2003, from http://people-press.org/reports

55. See J. B. Manheim, *All of the people, all of the time: strategic communication and American politics* (Armonk: M. E. Sharpe, 1991); J. B. Manheim, "Strategic public diplomacy," in W. L. Bennett and D. L. Paletz (eds), *Taken by storm: the media, public opinion, and U.S. foreign policy in the Gulf War*, pp. 131–48 (Chicago: University of Chicago Press, 1994).

56. On the strategic communications of political leaders, see, for example, R. M. Entman, *Democracy without citizens: media and the decay of American politics* (New York: Oxford University Press, 1989); J. A. Maltese, *Spin control: the White House Office of Communication and the management of presidential news* (Chapel Hill: University of North Carolina Press, 1994, 2nd ed.); W. Riker, *The art of political manipulation* (New Haven: Yale University Press, 1986); J. Zaller, "Strategic politicians, public opinion, and the Gulf crisis," in W. L. Bennett and D. L. Paletz (eds), *Taken by storm: the media, public opinion and U.S. foreign policy in the Gulf War*, pp. 250–74 (Chicago: University of Chicago Press, 1994).

57. On the religious foundations of some political conservative ideology and discourse, see pp. 65–107 in G. Lakoff, *Moral politics: what conservatives know that liberals don't* (Chicago: University of Chicago Press, 1996).

58. On the influence within the White House of Karl Rove, see N. Lemann, The controller. *New Yorker*, 12 May 2003, pp. 68–83; R. Suskind, Why are these men laughing? *Esquire*, January 2003, pp. 96–105.

59. On public unity among administration officials, see J. M. Broder, A nation at war: the commander. *New York Times*, 23 March 2003, p. B-4; D. Horsey, Serving up the GOP agenda. *Seattle Post-Intelligencer*, 16 February 2003, p. G-1.

60. On the public unity among Reagan administration officials, see M. Hertsgaard, *On bended knee: the press and the Reagan presidency* (New York: Farrar Straus Giroux, 1988); Maltese, *Spin control*.

61. That the administration chose a metaphor—a "war on terrorism"—to frame its response to September 11 is a strategically rich decision, by itself. In the words of Stiver (1996), a philosopher interested in religious language, "Metaphor has long been recognized as a literary device that enables us to depict well-known things in striking and focused ways," so much so that, "Philosophically speaking, what is important about metaphor is that it can do more than embellish; it can direct us to what we have never seen before" (p. 117). In short, metaphors are powerful linguistic tools in the construction of reality.

62. On the lack of unity among Democrats, see D. Balz, Democrats in search of a leader. *Washington Post*, 17 November 2002, p. A-4; R. Brownstein, Centrists losing ground in Democratic tug of war. *Los Angeles Times*, 21 June 2003, p. A-16; A. Clymer, Democrats seek a

stronger focus, and money. *New York Times*, 26 May 2003, p. A-1; Keller, "The radical presidency of George W. Bush."

63. For press influence in times of "political normalcy," see D. P. Fan, *Predictions of public opinion from the mass media* (Westport, CT: Greenwood Press, 1988); J. Zaller, *The nature and origins of mass opinion* (Cambridge: Cambridge University Press, 1992); D. V. Shah, M. D. Watts, D. Domke, and D. P. Fan, "News framing and cueing of issue regimes: explaining Clinton's public approval in spite of scandal," *Public Opinion Quarterly* 66 (2002): 339–70.

64. In regard to news coverage being filtered through journalists' cultural values, see H. Gans, *Deciding what's news* (New York: Vintage Books, 1979); G. Gerbner, "Ideological perspectives and political tendencies in news reporting," *Journalism Quarterly* 41 (1964): 495–508; D. Hallin, "Hegemony: the American news media from Vietnam to El Salvador, a study of ideological change and its limits," in D. Paletz (ed.), *Political communication research*, pp. 3–25 (Norwood, NJ: Ablex, 1987); N. K. Rivenburgh, "Social identity and news portrayals of citizens involved in international affairs," *Media Psychology* 2 (2000): 303–29; G. Tuchman, *Making news: a study in the construction of reality* (New York: Free Press, 1978); A. Calabrese and B. Burke, "American identities: nationalism, the media and the public sphere," *Journal of Communication Inquiry* 16/2 (1992): 52–73.

65. On mainstream news media's reliance on government officials as sources, see Gans, *Deciding what's news*; S. D. Reese, A. Grant, and L. H. Danielian, "The structure of news sources television: a network analysis of 'CBS News,' 'Nightline,' 'MacNeil/Lehrer,' and 'This Week with David Brinkley,'" *Journal of Communication* 44/2 (1994): 84–107; L. V. Sigal, *Reporters and officials* (Lexington, MA: D. C. Heath, 1973).

66. On mainstream news media's heavy reliance on government officials as sources early in crises and in national security contexts, see D. C. Hallin, R. K. Manoff, and J. K. Weddle, "Sourcing patterns of national security reporters," *Journalism Quarterly* 70 (1993): 753–66; J. Hutcheson, D. Domke, M. A. Billeaudeaux, and P. Garland, "U.S. national identity, political elites, and a patriotic press following September 11," *Political Communication* 21 (2004): 27–51; J. Zaller and D. Chiu, "Government's little helper: U.S. press coverage of foreign policy crises, 1945–1991," *Political Communication* 13 (1996): 385–405.

67. On the vast conservative network, see Brock, *Blinded by the right*; Edwards, *The conservative revolution*; T. Ferguson and J. Rogers, *Right turn: the decline of the Democrats and the future of American politics* (New York: Hill and Wang, 1986). On the allegations by conservatives of "liberal media bias," see M. Watts, D. Domke,

D. Shah, and D. Fan, "Elite cues and media bias in presidential campaigns," *Communication Research* 26 (1999): 144–75; D. Domke, M. Watts, D. Shah, and D. Fan, "The politics of conservative elites and the liberal media argument," *Journal of Communication* 49/4 (1999): 35–58. On the predominance of conservatives in the talk radio industry, see D. A. Jones, "The polarizing effect of news media messages," *International Journal of Public Opinion Research* 14/2 (2002): 158–74; J. Leland, Why the right rules the radio waves. *New York Times*, 8 December 2002, retrieved 1 July 2003 from Nexis database.

68. For criticism of Fox, see, for example, J. Rutenberg, Fox portrays a war of good and evil, and many applaud. *New York Times*, 3 December 2001, retrieved 3 December 2001 from http://www.nytimes.com

69. On the ratings of Fox, see J. Getlin, Fox news' patriotic fervor sets it apart in ratings race. *Los Angeles Times*, 11 April 2003, p. A-16; B. Lowry, For cable networks, 2002 was solid year. *Los Angeles Times*, 1 January 2002, Part 5, p. 4.

70. On MSNBC's changes, see H. Kurtz, Protest letters to MSNBC draw Savage response. *Washington Post*, 5 March 2003, p. C-1. Some of these changes are discussed in Chapter 6.

71. Even when a media outlet remains politically moderate, the influence of the never-ending news cycle is substantial. It makes the press, particularly 24-hour cable television networks, and the public more vulnerable to exploitation, because journalists, in the words of Kovach and Rosenstiel, are:

> increasingly oriented toward ferrying allegations rather than ferreting out the truth ... [which] means the news is delivered less completely. This gives the reporting a more chaotic, unsettled, and even numbing quality. It can make tuning into the news seem inefficient. It also makes it more difficult to separate fact from spin, argument, or innuendo, and makes the culture significantly more susceptible to manipulation.
>
> (1999: p. 6)

72. On the tendency of mainstream news media to criticize the administration when other political leaders do so, see S. L. Althaus, J. A. Edy, R. M. Entman, and P. Phalen, "Revising the indexing hypothesis: officials, media, and the Libya crisis," *Political Communication* 13 (1996): 407–21; W. L. Bennett, "Toward a theory of press–state relations in the United States," *Journal of Communication* 36/2 (1990): 103–25; R. M. Entman and A. Rojecki, "Freezing out the public: elite and media framing of the U.S. anti-nuclear movement," *Political Communication* 10 (1993): 155–73.

73. This quote by Bush was reported in C. Crowley, President Bush vows to defend Taiwan if necessary. Cable News Network, *CNN Live Today* program, 25 April 2001.
74. On the emphasis upon unity within diversity by presidents, see V. Beasley, "The rhetoric of ideological consensus in the United States: American principles and American pose in presidential inaugurals," *Communication Monographs* 68/2 (2001): 169–83.

## Chapter 2 Marking boundaries

1. For audience information, see For ABC, a winning season, at least on paper. *Washington Post*, 27 September 2001, p. C-7; J. Harper, Bush's speech resonates with public, polls show. *Washington Times*, 30 January 2003, retrieved 11 April 2003 from http://www.washtimes.com/national
2. The words in quotes are taken from M. E. Marty and R. S. Appleby, "Introduction," in M. E. Marty and R. S. Appleby (eds), *Fundamentalisms and the state*, pp. 1–9 (Chicago: University of Chicago Press, 1993). Similar claims about fundamentalists are made by many authors; see, for example, L. Kirkpatrick, R. W. Hood, Jr., and G. Hartz, "Fundamentalist religion conceptualized in terms of Rokeach's theory of the open and closed mind: new perspectives on some old ideas," *Research in the Social Scientific Study of Religion* 3 (1991): 157–79.
3. This tendency to see and communicate about the world in either-or terms has been studied under a variety of headings, including binary (Altman and Nakayama, 1991; Derrida, 1972/1981), dichotomy (Prokhovnik, 1999), dualism (Cirksena and Cuklanz, 1992), dialectic (Burke, 1945/1969), and polarization (King and Anderson, 1971; Raum and Measell, 1974). The term "binary" is used in this book to refer to this general practice.
4. On this hostility toward these groups, see B. Altemeyer and B. Hunsberger, "Authoritarianism, religious fundamentalism, quest, and prejudice," *International Journal for the Psychology of Religion* 2 (1992): 113–33; B. Hunsberger, "Religious fundamentalism, right-wing authoritarianism, and hostility toward homosexuals in non-Christian religious groups," *International Journal for the Psychology of Religion* 6(1): 39–49.
5. Credit for this insight belongs with Robert Entman.
6. See also S. Dalby, *Creating the second Cold War: the discourse of politics* (London: Pinter, 1990).
7. The ability of binary constructions to marginalize or eliminate other ideas is discussed in J. M. Bing and V. L. Bergvall, "The question of questions: beyond binary thinking," in V. L. Bergvall, J. M. Bing, and

A. F. Freed (eds), *Rethinking language and gender research: theory and practice*, pp. 1–30 (New York: Longman, 1996); K. Cirksena and L. Cuklanz, "Male is to female as _____ is to _____: a guided tour of five feminist frameworks for communication studies," in L. F. Rakow (ed.), *Women making meaning: new feminist directions in communication*, pp. 18–44 (New York: Routledge, 1992); J. F. Perea, "The black/white binary paradigm of race: the 'normal science' of American racial thought," *California Law Review* 85/5 (1997): 1213–58; R. Prokhovnik, *Rational woman: a feminist critique of dichotomy* (New York: Routledge, 1999); L. M. Wyman and G. N. Dionisopoulos, "Transcending the virgin/whore dichotomy: telling Mina's story in Bram Stoker's Dracula," *Women's Studies in Communication* 23/2 (2000): 209–37.

8.   The tendency of journalists to emphasize conflict in news coverage is a widely documented phenomenon. See, for example, T. E. Patterson, *Out of order* (New York: Vintage, 1994); V. Price and D. Tewksbury, "News values and public opinion: a theoretical account of media priming and framing," in G. Barnett and F. J. Boster (eds), *Progress in Communication Sciences*, pp. 173–212 (Greenwich, CT: Ablex, 1997).

9.   On the importance of cultural resonance as a strategic communication approach, see W. A. Gamson, "The 1987 distinguished lecture: a constructionist approach to mass media and public opinion," *Symbolic Interaction* 11 (1988): 161–74.

10.  On the interpretive role of newspaper editorial boards, see T. N. Huckin, "Textual silence and the discourse of homelessness," *Discourse & Society* 13/3 (2002): 347–72; J. P. Vermeer, *The view from the states: national politics in local newspaper editorials* (Lanham, MD: Rowman & Littlefield, 2002).

11.  On the opinion leadership role of newspaper editorial boards, see P. J. Powlick, "The sources of public opinion for American foreign policy officials," *International Studies Quarterly* 39 (1995): 427–51; T. M. Schaefer, "Persuading the persuaders: presidential speeches and editorial opinion," *Political Communication* 14/1 (1997): 97–111.

12.  One person analyzed the presidential addresses and newspaper editorials. As a check of the accuracy of this analysis, a second person read approximately 10 percent of presidential paragraphs and 10 percent of editorials. Results from this self-check test showed that analysis of the documents was highly consistent and accurate. For presidential paragraphs, both the good/evil binary and the security/peril binary yielded an inter-coder agreement rate (that is, the extent of accuracy across textual analyses) of 100 percent. For editorials, the good/evil binary yielded an inter-coder agreement rate of 97 percent, which was 94 percent after controlling for agreement by chance (see Scott, 1955, for the formula to correct for chance), and the security/peril binary yielded an inter-coder

agreement rate of 93 percent, 86 percent after controlling for chance. Analysis of references to either sides of the binaries yielded an inter-coder agreement rate of 97 percent for presidential paragraphs, 94 percent after controlling for agreement by chance. For editorials, this analysis yielded an inter-coder agreement rate of 96 percent, 92 percent after controlling for agreement by chance. Inter-coder agreement was 100 percent for references to September 11 and 100 percent for any editorial criticism of the binary concepts.

13. Statistical tests indicated that the president's addresses were much more likely to include directly oppositional placements of "good" and "evil" after the terrorist attacks ($X^2$ = 3.1, d.f. = 1, $p<.10$).

14. Statistical tests indicated that newspaper editorials were significantly more likely to include directly oppositional placements of "good" and "evil" after the terrorist attacks ($X^2$ = 4.1, d.f. = 1, $p<.05$).

15. Statistical tests indicated that usage of "good" language before and after the terrorist attacks did not differ for the president ($X^2$ = .87, n.s.) or for newspaper editorials ($X^2$ = .36, n.s.).

16. Statistical tests indicated that usage of "evil" language increased significantly after the terrorist attacks by the president ($X^2$ = 9.3, d.f. = 1, $p<.05$) and in newspaper editorials ($X^2$ = 5.5, d.f. = 1, $p<.05$).

17. This correlation was .63 ($n$ = 17, $p<.05$).

18. The address-by-address correlation between the president and editorials for "evil" discourse was .63 ($n$ = 17, $p<.05$) and for "good" discourse was .19 ($n$ = 17, n.s.).

19. Emphasizing the negative is a common tactic used in political campaigns, which is one reason why "evil" might be the more heavily weighted concept for the Bush administration, especially given the history of Bush's key political advisor, Karl Rove. Moore and Slater (2003) note, "The practice of negative campaigning ... was something Rove not only practiced but taught at the University of Texas. Bill Israel was a teaching assistant with Rove one semester and recalls him instructing students how negative campaigning can turn voters quickly and decisively" (pp. 257–8). This style of strategic political communication helped Bush beat down John McCain in the 2000 presidential primary in South Carolina. Hence, Bush the president focusing more on "evil" language to discuss terrorism and "threatening nations" seems like a natural and preferred rhetorical tactic.

20. Statistical tests indicated that the president's addresses were much more likely to include directly oppositional placements of "security" and "peril" after the terrorist attacks ($X^2$ = 5.3, d.f. = 1, $p<.05$).

21. Statistical tests indicated that newspaper editorials were significantly more likely to include directly oppositional placements of "security" and "peril" after the terrorist attacks ($X^2$ = 9.0, d.f. = 1, $p<.05$).

22. Statistical tests indicated that after the terrorist attacks the president

significantly increased his usage of "security" language ($X^2$ = 20.9, d.f. = 1, $p$<.05) and "peril" language ($X^2$ = 19.2, d.f. = 1, $p$<.05).

23. Statistical tests indicated that after the terrorist attacks newspaper editorials were significantly more likely to include "security" language ($X^2$ = 18.3, d.f. = 1, $p$<.05) and "peril" language ($X^2$ = 38.9, d.f. = 1, $p$<.05).

24. This correlation was .65 ($n$ = 17, $p$<.05).

25. The address-by-address correlation between the president and editorials for "security" discourse was .64 ($n$ = 17, $p$<.05) and for "peril" discourse was .49 ($n$ = 17, $p$<.05).

26. Statistical tests indicated that "security" language was significantly more present in the president's addresses during the "homeland security" campaign period than in other post-attack addresses ($X^2$ = 11.1, d.f. = 1, $p$<.05).

27. Statistical tests indicated that "peril" language was significantly more present in the president's addresses during the "Iraq war" campaign period than in other post-attack addresses ($X^2$ = 15.5, d.f. = 1, $p$<.05).

28. On binaries and the cold war, see R. Ivie, "Metaphor and the rhetorical invention of cold war 'idealists,'" in M. Medhurst et al., *Cold war rhetoric: strategy, metaphor, and ideology*, pp. 103–27 (Westport, CT: Greenwood Press, 1990); J. Kuypers, *Presidential crisis rhetoric and the press in the post-cold war world* (Westport, CT: Praeger, 1997).

## Chapter 3 A "mission" and a "moment," time and again

1. For the reaction among some members of the press, see R. W. Apple, Jr., No middle ground. *New York Times*, 14 September 2001, p. A-1; J. Battenfeld and A. Miga, Bush vows a global pursuit of terrorists: America prepares wartime campaign. *Boston Herald*, 14 September 2001, p. 5; J. Heath, Emotions get better of Bush: public display is rare moment for U.S. president. *Atlanta Journal and Constitution*, 14 September 2001, p. A-4; M. Kelley, Attacks transform Bush's presidency. *Omaha World-Herald*, 18 September 2001, p. A-1.

2. See C. B. Strozier, *Apocalypse: on the psychology of fundamentalism in America* (Boston: Beacon Press, 1994). Strozier claims that the "dual message of immediacy and uncertainty" is a centerpiece of fundamentalism.

3. For insight into journalists' emphasis on strategy and competition, see T. E. Patterson, *Out of order* (New York: Vintage, 1994); J. N. Cappella and K. H. Jamieson, *Spiral of cynicism: the press and the public good* (New York: Oxford University Press, 1997).

4. The heavy reliance of mainstream journalists on the White House early in crises is a point of focus in J. Zaller and D. Chiu,

"Government's little helper: U.S. press coverage of foreign policy crises, 1945–1991," *Political Communication* 13 (1996): 385–405.

5.  Two people analyzed the news content and editorials. Following their analysis, a random selection of news articles was re-read. Agreement was found on 113 of 124 evaluations of source emphases (an inter-coder agreement rate of 91 percent, which was 87 percent after controlling for agreement by chance), which showed that the two people were evaluating the material consistently, and in practically the same way. All editorials were read twice; there were no disagreements about the viewpoints therein.

6.  Several steps were taken to make certain that analysis of the administration communications and the news coverage was highly consistent and accurate. One person analyzed Bush and Ashcroft's communications about the U.S.A. Patriot Act. A second person then read approximately half of the texts. For "time urgency," there was an inter-coder agreement rate of 94 percent, which was 88 percent after controlling for agreement by chance. For "calls on Congress to act," there were no disagreements. One person analyzed Bush's communications about the Department of Homeland Security, and a second person read approximately 10 percent of the texts. For "time urgency," there was an inter-coder agreement rate of 87 percent, 74 percent after controlling for chance. For "calls on Congress to act," there were no disagreements. One person also analyzed news coverage. A second person read approximately 15 percent of newspaper articles, editorials, and television news stories about the U.S.A. Patriot Act. For "time urgency," there was an inter-coder agreement rate of 91 percent, which was 83 percent after controlling for chance. For "calls on Congress to act," there was an inter-coder coefficient of 87 percent, which was 74 percent after controlling for chance. For the Department of Homeland Security texts, a second person read approximately 10 percent of newspaper editorials and television stories. For "time urgency," there was an inter-coder agreement rate of 88 percent, 76 percent after controlling for chance. For "calls on Congress to act," there were no disagreements.

7.  M. Kirk, *Frontline: the war behind closed doors* [television broadcast] (Boston: Public Broadcasting Corporation, 20 February 2003).

8.  For news discussion about this leak, see M. Gordon, U.S. nuclear plan sees new targets and new weapons. *New York Times*, 10 March 2002, p. A-1; J. Hoagland, Nuclear preemption. *Washington Post*, 17 March 2002, p. B-9.

9.  G. W. Bush, "Graduation address at United States Military Academy, West Point, New York," 1 June 2003, retrieved 6 July 2003 from http://www.whitehouse.gov/news/releases/2002/06

10. National Security Council, "The national security strategy of the

United States of America," 17 September 2002, retrieved 6 July 2003 from http://www.whitehouse.gov/nsc/print/nssall.html

11. For discussion of the administration's emphasis on the "battle" of Iraq, including the comments of Karl Rove, see R. Hutcheson, "White House now says Iraq is a battle, not a war," Knight Ridder Newspapers, 1 June 2003, retrieved 1 June 2003 from www.seattletimes.com; J. Witcover, Standing out from the crowd. *Baltimore Sun*, 12 May 2003, p. A-11, retrieved from Nexis database 4 July 2003.

12. Details about the administration's development of the U.S.A. Patriot Act, in particular the role of Attorney General John Ashcroft, can be found in S. Brill, *After: how America confronted the September 12 era* (New York: Simon & Schuster, 2003).

13. Perhaps members of the news media were nationalistically willing to accept the proposed law and department, but because the changes might affect the profession itself—possibly encroaching upon rights such as freedom of the press, speech, and privacy—some members of the press were reluctant to buy into Bush's fast-track political language. Nevertheless, many in the news industry did echo.

14. Public opinion data drawn from Gallup, "Poll topics and trends: terrorist attacks and the aftermath," 2002, retrieved 14 January 2002 from http://www.gallup.com/poll/topics/terror.asp

15. See United States Commission on National Security/21st Century, *Road map for national security: imperative for change*, February 2001, retrieved 15 July 2003 from http://www.nssg.gov/PhaseIIIFR.pdf

16. Analysis of the U.S. Senate debates can be found in E. Graham, D. Domke, K. Coe, S. L. John, and T. Coopman, *Follow the leader: the Bush administration, news media, and passage of the U.S.A. Patriot Act*. Paper presented to the Association for Education in Journalism and Mass Communication annual convention, August 2003, Kansas City, MO.

## Chapter 4 The universal gospel of freedom and liberty

1. On the centrality of freedom in American discourse, see, for example, V. Beasley, "The rhetoric of ideological consensus in the United States: American principles and American pose in presidential inaugurals," *Communication Monographs* 68/2 (2001): 169–83; A. Calabrese and B. Burke, "American identities: nationalism, the media and the public sphere," *Journal of Communication Inquiry* 16/2 (1992): 52–73; J. Hutchinson, *Modern nationalism* (Glasgow: Harper Collins, 1994); E. L. Tuveson, *Redeemer nation: the idea of America's millennial role* (Chicago: University of Chicago Press, 1968); E. Foner, "The meaning of freedom in the age of emancipation," *Journal of American History* 81 (1994): 435–60.

2. On the concept of national identity, see also W. Bloom, *Personal identity, national identity and international relations* (Cambridge: Cambridge University Press, 1990); Hutchinson, *Modern nationalism*; R. Poole, *Nation and identity* (London: Routledge, 1999).

3. On the movement of Christian fundamentalists toward support of a strong military and conservative foreign policy, see N. T. Ammerman, "North American Protestant fundamentalism," in M. E. Marty and R. S. Appleby (eds), *Fundamentalisms observed*, pp. 1–65 (Chicago: University of Chicago Press, 1991); A. J. Reichley, "The evangelical and fundamentalist revolt," in R. J. Neuhaus and M. Cromartie (eds), *Piety and politics: evangelicals and fundamentalists confront the world*, pp. 69–95 (Washington, D.C.: Ethics and Public Policy Center, 1987); M. Weiler and W. B. Pearce, "Ceremonial discourse: the rhetorical ecology of the Reagan administration," in M. Weiler and W. B. Pearce (eds), *Reagan and public discourse in America*, pp. 11–42 (Tuscaloosa, AL: University of Alabama Press, 1992).

4. See also Tuveson, *Redeemer nation*.

5. All appearances suggest that Bush's beliefs about God's will regarding freedom and liberty were held with strong conviction. For example, in his final press conference of 2003, Bush said: "I believe, firmly believe—and you've heard me say this a lot, and I say it a lot because I truly believe it—that freedom is the Almighty God's gift to every person, every man and woman who lives in this world. That's what I believe. And the arrest of Saddam Hussein changed the equation in Iraq. Justice was being delivered to a man who defied that gift from the Almighty to the people of Iraq" (see Bush, 2003g). Notably, these kinds of claims by Bush closely paralleled some made in the 1980s by Ronald Reagan, who also successfully converged conservative religion and politics.

6. On the cynicism among political reporters toward politicians' religious statements, see E. J. Dionne, Jr., Religion and politics. *Washington Post*, 28 December 1999, p. A-23, retrieved from Nexis database on 6 August 2003.

7. One person analyzed the presidential addresses and newspaper editorials. As a check of the accuracy of this analysis, a second person read approximately 10 percent of presidential paragraphs and 10 percent of editorials. Results from this self-check test showed that analysis of the documents was highly consistent and accurate. For presidential paragraphs, there were no disagreements for the analysis of "freedom/liberty" discourse; the universal norms analysis yielded an inter-coder agreement rate (i.e. the extent of accuracy across textual analyses) of 96 percent, which was 92 percent after controlling for agreement by chance; and there were no disagreements for the analysis of claims regarding God's desire. For editorials, there were no

disagreements for the analysis of "freedom/liberty" discourse; the universal norms analysis yielded an inter-coder agreement rate of 91 percent, 82 percent after controlling for chance; and there were no disagreements for the analysis of claims regarding God's desire.

8. G. W. Bush, "Graduation address at United States Military Academy, West Point, New York," 1 June 2002, retrieved 6 July 2003 from http://www.whitehouse.gov/news/releases/2002/06

9. National Security Council, "The national security strategy of the United States of America," 17 September 2002, retrieved 6 July 2003 from http://www.whitehouse.gov/nsc/print/nssall.html

10. Statistical tests indicated that "freedom/liberty" discourse was significantly more prevalent after September 11 in both presidential addresses ($X^2$ = 6.9, d.f. = 1, $p<.05$) and newspaper editorials ($X^2$ = 5.3, d.f. = 1, $p<.05$).

11. The address-by-address correlation between the president and editorials for "freedom/liberty" discourse was .31 ($n$ = 17, $p$ = .11).

12. Statistical tests indicated that claims of freedom or liberty as universal norms were significantly more prevalent after September 11 in both presidential addresses ($X^2$ = 4.7, d.f. = 1, $p<.05$) and newspaper editorials ($X^2$ = 2.8, d.f. = 1, $p<.10$).

13. The address-by-address correlation between the president and editorials for claims of freedom or liberty as universal norms was .17 ($n$ = 17, n.s.).

14. Statistical tests indicated that the president's addresses were much more likely to include "freedom/liberty" discourse generally ($X^2$ = 9.2, d.f. = 1, $p<.05$) and claims that these values represented universal norms ($X^2$ = 5.8, d.f. = 1, $p<.05$) during the "Iraq war" period.

15. Statistical tests indicated that the newspaper editorials were more likely, although not significantly so, to include "freedom/liberty" discourse generally ($X^2$ = 1.2, n.s.) and much more likely to include claims that these values represented universal norms ($X^2$ = 4.4, d.f. = 1, $p<.05$) during the "Iraq war" period.

16. To cite just one example of the civil liberties infringements enacted by the U.S.A. Patriot Act, this legislation allows the arrest and detainment of individuals, including U.S. citizens, for indeterminate periods without provision of a lawyer. For example, Brooklyn-born citizen Jose Padilla was arrested in early May 2002 on suspicion of building a radioactive "dirty bomb" and was held without public knowledge until his arrest was announced on June 10 (see Brill, 2003). Attorney General Ashcroft subsequently transferred Padilla from the federal legal system to a military tribunal that the president had implemented after September 11, in which Padilla continued to languish when a federal appeals court in December 2003 said the administration must either charge him with a crime or release him. The Supreme Court

announced in January 2004 that it would take up the issue and rule on whether the president has the constitutional authority to bypass the courts and hold U.S. citizens in military custody (see Savage, 2004). The decision is expected to be delivered in summer 2004.

17. See Ammerman, "North American Protestant fundamentalism."

18. In regard to the willingness of fundamentalists to impose their beliefs on others, see also H. Cox, "Fundamentalism as an ideology," in R. J. Neuhaus and M. Cromartie (eds), *Piety and politics: Evangelicals and fundamentalists confront the world*, pp. 289–301 (Lanham, MD: University Press of America, 1987).

19. On the contribution of news media to U.S. national identity, see also H. Gans, *Deciding what's news* (New York: Vintage Books, 1979); D. Hallin, "Hegemony: the American news media from Vietnam to El Salvador, a study of ideological change and its limits," in D. Paletz (ed.), *Political Communication Research*, pp. 3–25 (Norwood, NJ: Albex, 1987); J. Lule, "Myth and terror on the editorial page: the *New York Times* responds to September 11, 2002," *Journalism and Mass Communication Quarterly* 79/2 (2002): 275–93.

## Chapter 5 Unity, or else

1. This story about the U.S.A. Patriot Act is told in S. Brill, *After: how America confronted the September 12 era* (New York: Simon & Schuster, 2003), p. 174.

2. Public opinion data drawn from Pew Research Center, Terror coverage boost news media's images, 28 November 2001, retrieved 26 August 2003 from http://people-press.org/reports

3. On the administration's emphasis on political civility upon arriving in Washington D.C., see F. Bruni and D. E. Sanger, Bush, taking office, calls for civility, compassion, and "nation of character." *New York Times*, 20 January 2001, p. A-1, retrieved from Nexis database on 21 July 2003; D. Milbank and J. Eilperin, They never promised him a Rose Garden. *Washington Post*, 1 May 2001, p. A-1, retrieved from Nexis database on 21 July 2003; P. Shenon, House votes haunt retreat meant to spur collegiality. *New York Times*, 11 March 2001, p. A-32, retrieved from Nexis database on 21 July 2003.

4. On the response to Maher's comments, see C. Billhartz, Maher's comments lead to show's suspension. *St. Louis Post-Dispatch*, 22 September 2001, p. A-15, retrieved from Nexis database on 21 July 2003; B. Carter and F. Barringer, Speech and expression: in patriotic time, dissent is muted. *New York Times*, 28 September 2001, p. A-1; T. Cooper, 2 TV stations yank "Politically Incorrect." *Omaha World-Herald*, 22 September 2001, p. B-8, retrieved from Nexis database on 21 July 2003.

5. For evidence of the link between religious fundamentalism and authoritarianism, see, for example, B. Altemeyer, *Enemies of freedom: understanding right-wing authoritarianism* (San Francisco: Jossey-Bass, 1988); B. Altemeyer and B. Hunsberger, "Authoritarianism, religious fundamentalism, quest, and prejudice," *International Journal for the Psychology of Religion* 2 (1992): 113–33; H. Danso, B. Hunsberger, and M. Pratt, "The role of parental religious fundamentalism and right-wing authoritarianism in child-rearing goals and practices," *Journal for the Scientific Study of Religion* 36/4 (1997): 496–511; L. Wylie and J. Forest, "Religious fundamentalism, right wing authoritarianism and prejudice," *Psychology Report* 71(1992): 1291–8.

6. On Karl Rove, see also N. Lemann, The controller. *New Yorker*, 12 May 2003, pp. 68–83; L. Dubose, J. Reid, and C. M. Cannon, *Boy genius: Karl Rove, the brains behind the remarkable political triumph of George W. Bush* (New York: Public Affairs, 2003); J. Moore and W. Slater, *Bush's brain: how Karl Rove made George W. Bush presidential* (New Jersey: Wiley, 2003).

7. On public unity among administration officials, see J. M. Broder, A nation at war: the commander. *New York Times*, 23 March 2003, p. B-4; D. Horsey, Serving up the GOP agenda. *Seattle Post-Intelligencer*, 16 February 2003, p. G-1. There were some exceptions, of course. One, discussed in Chapter 6, occurred in late summer 2002 when disagreements within the administration and more broadly among Republicans about how to approach Iraq were publicly aired for a short time. Another occurred in January 2003 when Colin Powell publicly disagreed with the president after Bush criticized affirmative action policies in the administration's unusual action of submitting a brief for a Supreme Court case. In this instance, Condaleezza Rice, the administration's other high-ranking African American, spoke out on behalf of the president's position. In both of these instances, the public disagreement was downplayed by administration officials and soon disappeared from news coverage.

8. The preference among news media for conflict is a point of emphasis in J. N. Cappella and K. H. Jamieson, *Spiral of cynicism: the press and the public good* (New York: Oxford University Press, 1997); T. E. Patterson, *Out of order* (New York: Vintage, 1994).

9. Several steps were taken to make certain that analysis of the administration communications and the news coverage was highly consistent and accurate. One person analyzed Bush and Ashcroft's communications about the U.S.A. Patriot Act. A second person then read approximately half of the texts, producing an inter-coder agreement rate of 88 percent, which was 76 percent after controlling for agreement by chance. One person analyzed Bush's communications about the Department of Homeland Security, and a second person

read approximately 10 percent of the texts; there were no disagreements. One person also analyzed the communications by Bush, Powell, and Rumsfeld about Iraq, and approximately 10 percent of the texts were re-read; there were no disagreements. News coverage also was analyzed by one person. A second person read approximately 15 percent of newspaper articles, editorials, and television news stories about the U.S.A. Patriot Act, producing an inter-coder agreement rate of 87 percent, 74 percent after controlling for chance. For Department of Homeland Security texts, a second person read approximately 10 percent of newspaper editorials and television stories, producing an inter-coder agreement rate of 93 percent, 86 percent after controlling for chance. For the Iraq texts, a second person read approximately 10 percent of newspaper editorials and television stories, producing an inter-coder agreement rate of 91 percent, 82 percent after controlling for chance.

10. See J. Ashcroft, "Testimony of Attorney General John Ashcroft, before the U.S. Senate Committee on the Judiciary," 6 December 2001, retrieved 21 July 2003, from http://www.usdoj.gov/ag/testimony.html

11. See G. W. Bush, "Remarks to the community in Trenton, New Jersey," 23 September 2002, retrieved 22 July 2003 from http://www.access.gpo.gov

12. As noted earlier in the chapter, Bush discussed both the Department of Homeland Security and Iraq threat/resolutions in a number of his addresses. For this analysis, there are 56 texts in common. These texts are included in both categories since they are contributions to each discourse.

13. For the *Washington Post* story that brought the president's comments to the attention of Democrats, see D. Milbank, In president's speeches, Iraq dominates, economy fades. *Washington Post*, 25 September 2002, p. A-1, retrieved from Nexis database on 24 July 2003.

14. The administration's public criticisms of political adversaries not only helped to silence potential critics, they also functioned to keep supporters in line. For example, on the day that the *Washington Post* published the president's criticisms of Senator Daschle in September 2002 (the same day in which Daschle fired back), the Republican National Committee sent an email to 2 million party supporters that contained Bush's claim that the Senate "is not interested in the security of the American people." The email also included an Internet link allowing people to make political donations. See M. Allen and J. VandeHei, Bush: Unity soon on Iraq; Democrats seek more negotiation on war resolution. *Washington Post*, 27 September 2002, p. A-1, retrieved from Nexis database on 24 July 2003.

15. For Rumsfeld's comment, see D. Rumsfeld, "Secretary Rumsfeld briefs at the foreign press center, 22 January 2003," retrieved 18 July 2003,

from http://www.defense.gov/news/Jan2003. The mobilizing effects of the administration's calls for unity and squelching of dissent reached an absurd peak when France was symbolically admonished by Representative Bob Ney. Because the French voiced opposition to Bush's policy on Iraq, Ohio Republican Ney called for a renaming of food, specifically the French fries and French toast served in the congressional cafeteria. Ney suggested that "Freedom" fries and "Freedom" toast was much more appropriate for the House of Representatives menu. See S. G. Stolberg, An order of fries, please, but do hold the French. *New York Times*, 12 March 2003, p. A-1.

16. Regarding the reliance of mainstream journalists on conflict between the executive and legislative branches of government, see T. E. Cook, *Governing with the news* (Chicago: University of Chicago Press, 1998).
17. The request of Rice and the news media's response are noted in Carter and Barringer, Speech and expression: in patriotic time, dissent is muted. *New York Times*, 28 September, 2001, p. A-1.
18. See H. Kurtz, CNN chief orders "balance" in war news: reporters are told to remind viewers why U.S. is bombing. *Washington Post*, 31 October 2001, p. C-1, retrieved from Nexis database on 8 August 2003.
19. The response to Dan Rather's interview of Saddam Hussein and the national mood of the time is discussed in F. Rich, The spoils of war coverage. *New York Times*, 13 April 2003, retrieved 18 April 2003, from http://www.nytimes.com
20. On Arnett's firing, see E. Jensen, War with Iraq: Arnett fuming at loss of NBC job. *Los Angeles Times*, 2 April 2003, retrieved 18 April 2003 from http://web.lexis-nexis.com
21. On the Baseball Hall of Fame's disinvitation of Tim Robbins, see I. Berkow, The Hall of Fame will tolerate no dissent. *New York Times*, 11 April 2003, p. S-4, retrieved from Nexis database on 8 August 2003.

## Chapter 6 Political fundamentalism, the press, and Democrats

1. On the latter point see G. Lawson, George W.'s personal Jesus. *Gentlemen's Quarterly*, September 2003, pp. 330–5, 394–96, 399; R. Suskind, Why are these men laughing? *Esquire*, January 2003, pp. 96–105.
2. The desire of the administration to capitalize on the Iraq conflict in the 2002 elections is a point of emphasis in R. L. Berke, Bush adviser suggests war as campaign theme. *New York Times*, 19 January 2002, p. A- 15; M. Dowd, Secrets of the Yo-Yo's. *New York Times*, 16 June 2002, p. A-13.
3. Public opinion data derived from CBS News Poll, conducted 22–23 September 2002, retrieved from Public Opinion Online database, Roper Center at University of Connecticut; CBS News Poll, conducted

9–12 May 2003, retrieved from Public Opinion Online database, Roper Center at University of Connecticut.

4. For evidence regarding the reaction of news media after September 11, see M. A. Billeaudeaux, D. Domke, P. Garland, and J. Hutcheson, "The Bush administration, the 'war on terrorism,' and editorial voices of the New York *Times* and Washington *Post*," *Newspaper Research Journal* 24 (2003): 166–84; J. Hutcheson, D. Domke, M. A. Billeaudeaux, and P. Garland, "U.S. national identity, political elites, and a patriotic press following September 11," *Political Communication 21* (2004): 27–51; J. Lule, "Myth and terror on the editorial page: the *New York Times* responds to September 11, 2002," *Journalism and Mass Communication Quarterly* 79 (2002): 275–93.

5. See Pew Research Center, Terror coverage boost news media's images, 28 November 2001, retrieved 26 August 2003, from http://people-press.org/reports

6. See R. Bellah, *The broken covenant: American civil religion in time of trial* (Chicago: University of Chicago Press, 2nd ed., 1992).

7. These numbers about membership and churches were found on the Southern Baptist Convention's website (http://www.sbc.net/).

8. D. Milbank, Religious right finds its center in oval office: Bush emerges as movement's leader after Robertson leaves Christian Coalition. *Washington Post*, 24 December 2001, p. A-2.

9. See S. L. Althaus, J. A. Edy, R. M. Entman, and P. Phalen, "Revising the indexing hypothesis: Officials, media, and the Libya crisis," *Political Communication* 13 (1996): 407–21; W. L. Bennett and J. B. Manheim, "Taking the public by storm: information, cueing, and the democratic process in the gulf conflict," *Political Communication* 10 (1993): 331–52; H. Gans, *Deciding what's news* (New York: Vintage Books, 1979); E. S. Herman and N. Chomsky, *Manufacturing consent: the political economy of the mass media* (New York: Pantheon, 1988); S. D. Reese, A. Grant, and L. H. Danielian, "The structure of news sources television: a network analysis of 'CBS News,' 'Nightline,' 'MacNeil/Lehrer,' and 'This Week with David Brinkley,'" *Journal of Communication* 44/2 (1994): 84–107; L. V. Sigal, *Reporters and officials* (Lexington, MA: D. C. Heath, 1973).

10. For evidence that mainstream journalists become even more reliant on the presidential administration for sourcing during times of crisis, see J. Zaller and D. Chiu, "Government's little helper: U.S. press coverage of foreign policy crises, 1945–1991," *Political Communication* 13 (1996): 385–405.

11. See T. E. Cook, *Governing with the news* (Chicago: University of Chicago Press, 1998); J. Mermin, "Television news and American intervention in Somalia: the myth of a media-driven foreign policy," *Political Science Quarterly* 112 (1997): 385–403.

12. For discussion and evidence about journalists' cultural values serving as central filters in the coverage of news, see Gans (*Deciding what's news*); D. Hallin, "Hegemony: the American news media from Vietnam to El Salvador, a study of ideological change and its limits," in D. Paletz (ed.), *Political communication research*, pp. 3–25 (Norwood, NJ: Ablex, 1987); N. K. Rivenburgh, "Social identity and news portrayals of citizens involved in international affairs," *Media Psychology* 2 (2000): 303–29.

13. See also T. E. Patterson, *Out of order* (New York: Vintage, 1994); R. Lawrence, "Game-framing the issues: tracking the strategy frame in public policy news," *Political Communication* 17 (2000): 93–114.

14. This point about conflict within the administration is drawn from R. M. Entman, "Cascading activation: contesting the White House's frame after 9/11," *Political Communication* 20 (2003): 415–32.

15. In regard to the public's perception of a "liberal media," see M. Watts, D. Domke, D. Shah, and D. Fan, "Elite cues and media bias in presidential campaigns," *Communication Research* 26 (1999): 144–75.

16. Data on Fox News Channel's ratings are drawn from J. Getlin, Fox news' patriotic fervor sets it apart in ratings race. *Los Angeles Times*, 11 April 2003, p. A-16; B. Lowry, For cable networks, 2002 was solid year. *Los Angeles Times*, 1 January 2002, part 5, p. 4.

17. See J. Zengeri, Fiddling with the reception. *New York Times*, 17 August 2003, retrieved from Nexis database on 5 September 2003.

18. On conservative talk radio, see D. A. Jones, "The polarizing effect of news media messages," *International Journal of Public Opinion Research* 14 (2002): 158–74; J. Leland, Why the right rules the radio waves. *New York Times*, 8 December 2002, retrieved 1 July 2003, from Nexis database.

19. For data on the public's news sources, see Pew Research Center, Public confidence in war effort falters, 25 March 2003, retrieved May 22 2003, from http://people-press.org/reports

20. The desire for a network of talk radio hosts became a particular concern among political liberals after Republican Party success in the 2002 elections, an outcome that some pundits said was spurred in part by the predominance of political conservatives on talk radio. In January 2004, newly formed Progress Media, whose owners have ties to the Democratic Party, announced plans to launch a radio network, with comedian and author Al Franken as its flagship host. This network, under the name Air America Radio, was launched in late March in New York, Los Angeles, and Chicago. See J. Frey, A liberal haven on the radio dial; talk network plans to begin national broadcast in spring. *Washington Post*, 14 January 2004, p. C-1, retrieved from Nexis database on 16 January 2004. J. Steinberg, The media business; liberal talk radio network to start up in three cities. *New York Times*, 11 March 2004, retrieved 18 March 2004, from

Nexis database; R. Shorto, Al Franken, seriously so. *New York Times*, 21 March 2004, retrieved 21 March 2004, from Nexis database.

21. The concept of "value hierarchy" is drawn from the research and writings of psychologist Milton Rokeach. See M. Rokeach, *The nature of human values* (New York: Free Press, 1973).

22. See P. E. Tetlock, "Cognitive style and political ideology," *Personality Processes and Individual Differences 45* (1983): 118–26; P. E. Tetlock, J. Bernzweig, and J. L. Gallant, "Supreme Court decision making: cognitive style as a predictor of ideological consistency of voting," *Journal of Personality and Social Psychology* 48 (1985): 1227–39; P. E. Tetlock, K. Hannum, and P. Micheletti, "Stability and change in senatorial debate: testing the cognitive versus rhetorical style hypothesis," *Journal of Personality and Social Psychology* 46 (1984): 979–90.

23. See G. Lakoff, *Moral politics: what conservatives know that liberals don't* (Chicago: University of Chicago Press, 1996).

24. Public opinion data drawn from Pew Research Center, Religion and politics: contention and consensus, 24 July 2003, retrieved 18 August 2003, from http://people-press.org/reports

25. For opposition to the U.S.A. Patriot Act, see E. Lichtblau, Ashcroft's tour rallies supporters and detractors. *New York Times*. 8 September 2003, p. A-14. B. Whitaker, Even Patriot Act politics is local. *New York Times*, 14 March 2004, retrieved 19 March 2004, from Nexis database.

26. For ACLU membership information, see R. Carr, ACLU watches membership soar since 9/11; group attributes record growth to Ashcroft policies. *Atlanta Journal and Constitution*, 11 June 2003, p. A-16.

27. In regard to diminishing international support for the United States since September 11, see Pew Research Center, America's image further erodes, Europeans want weaker ties, 18 March 2003, retrieved 3 September 2003 from http://people-press.org/reports. Pew Research Center, A year after Iraq war: Mistrust of America in Europe ever higher, Muslim anger persists, 16 March 2004, retrieved 19 March 2004 from http://people-press.org/reports

## Chapter 7 Renewing democracy

1. Cultural and political critic Tariq Ali argues that: "the most dangerous 'fundamentalism' today—the 'mother of all fundamentalisms' is American imperialism," a viewpoint that he declares "has been amply vindicated over the last eighteen months." See T. Ali, *The clash of fundamentalisms* (London: Verso, 2002), p. xiii.

2. The administration's unwillingness to include others in the policy formation process can be seen in the development of the Department of Homeland Security legislation, which the president proposed in a national address on June 6, 2002. After September 11 the

administration dismissed less comprehensive but similarly targeted Democratic proposals, then convened its own small, tightly held group during spring 2002 to craft a proposal kept secret until the day before the president's address. See S. Brill, *After: how America confronted the September 12 era* (New York: Simon & Schuster, 2003).

3.  In the second presidential debate in autumn 2000, Bush was asked to describe his philosophy for projecting U.S. power. He said:

    If we're an arrogant nation, they'll resent us. If we're a humble nation, but strong, they'll welcome us. And our nation stands alone right now in the world in terms of power. And that's why we've got to be humble and yet project strength in a way that promotes freedom. So I don't think they [other nations] ought to look at us in any way other than what we are. We're a freedom-loving nation. And if we're an arrogant nation, they'll view us that way, but if we're [a] humble nation, they'll respect us.

    See The 2000 campaign: Second presidential debate between Gov. Bush and Vice President Gore. *New York Times*, 12 October 2000, p. A-22.

4.  It is noteworthy that the president's desire to transform the entire Middle Eastern region is consistent with a religious fundamentalist desire to rid the Holy Lands of threats to Judeo-Christian faithful—a conclusion given traction by the president's caught-on-tape comments about his "divine mission" to bring peace to the Middle East during a closed-door meeting with then-Palestinian prime minister Mahmoud Abbas. See G. Lawson, George W.'s personal Jesus. *Gentlemen's Quarterly*, September 2003, pp. 330–5, 394–6, 399.

5.  There is no indication that the administration's others-be-damned approach might dissipate. In the 2004 State of the Union address, Bush said: "From the beginning, America has sought international support for operations in Afghanistan and Iraq, and we have gained much support. There is a difference, however, between leading a coalition of many nations, and submitting to the objections of a few. America will never seek a permission slip to defend the security of our people" (Bush, 2004). While the nation clearly has the right to protect its security, the president's rhetoric leaves little room for working with others.

6.  It is not uncommon for governments to benefit from terrorist acts. Several nations, such as the United States, Great Britain, Israel, and South Korea, have gained much ideological power by opposing and combating terrorism, and their respective private sectors, which include think tanks, institutes and lobbying organizations, have employed many. Instead of deflating the violence inflicted, the state creates "the terrorism industry." See E. S. Herman and G. O'Sullivan, *The terrorism industry: the experts and institutions that shape our view of terror* (New York: Pantheon Books, 1989).

7. On the Joseph Wilson situation, see Justice Department opens probe into leak of CIA agent's name. *Wall Street Journal*, 29 September 2003, p. A-3.

8. On this commercial theme, see CNN Time, "AllPolitics Ad Archive, 1997," retrieved 13 January 2004 from http://www.cnn.com/ALLPOLITICS/1996/candidates/ad.archive/

9. This action is presented in detail by Brill (*After*, pp. 173–6). James Sensebrenner, a fellow Republican from Wisconsin who was chair of the Judiciary Committee, said, "The Speaker [Hastert] said to me that we had to do this for the sake of the country, so I reluctantly agreed." Hastert only allowed House members a few hours to read the Ashcroft version of the bill before forcing a vote, which nonetheless still was 337–79 in favor. Some of the dissenters pointed out that the House had never passed a bill related to criminal procedure and the Constitution that had not been cleared through the Judiciary Committee. Another Hastert maneuver paved the way for the Homeland Security Department to sail through the House in summer 2002: he appointed a nine-person select committee to evaluate the administration's proposal, a move that again bypassed the traditional congressional committee structure (see Brill, p. 504).

10. Bush's lack of vetoes stands in contrast to Bill Clinton's 37 vetoes during his eight years in office, the 44 issued by George H. W. Bush during his single term, and the 78 issued by Ronald Reagan over eight years. See J. Abrams, Bush may get through term with no vetoes. Associated Press, 6 January 2004, retrieved from Nexis database on 16 January 2004.

11. For example, the editions of *Time* and *Newsweek* magazines published in the weeks after September 11 were among the highest selling issues in the history of these publications. See S. Sutel, Attacks boosted news magazines' newsstand sales. *Associated Press*, 15 February 2002.

12. In fact, some media scholars have argued that terrorism is only made possible because the news media cover it. Many terrorists realize that in order to be effective—that is, to generate widespread fear in the masses—they must utilize the greatest amplifier: mass media. And terrorism, as a political act comprised of violence and drama, is a perfect fit for breaking news. In the words of Nacos (1994), "By resorting to ever more spectacular and brutal deeds and thereby heightening the threshold of violence, terrorists are assured press coverage and public attention—otherwise, as one terrorist put it, 'we would throw roses if it worked'" (p. 8). See B. L. Nacos, *Terrorism and the media: from the Iran hostage crisis to the World Trade Center bombing* (New York: Columbia University Press, 1994); S. Livingston, *The terrorism spectacle* (Boulder, CO: Westview Press, 1994); D. E. Long, *The anatomy of terrorism* (New York: Macmillan International, 1990).

# Bibliography

The 2000 campaign; Second presidential debate between Gov. Bush and Vice President Gore (2000, October 12) *New York Times*, p. A-22. Retrieved from Nexis database on February 20, 2004.

Abrams, J. (2004, January 6) Bush may get through term with no vetoes. Associated Press. Retrieved from Nexis database on January 16, 2004.

Ali, T. (2002) *The clash of fundamentalisms*. London: Verso.

Allen, M. (2003, February 3) Comforting words as a matter of faith, *Washington Post*. Retrieved from washingtonpost.com on February 3, 2003.

Allen, M. and VandeHei, J. (2002, September 27) Bush: Unity soon on Iraq; Democrats seek more negotiation on war resolution, *Washington Post*, p. A-1. Retrieved from Nexis database on July 24, 2003.

Altemeyer, B. (1988) *Enemies of freedom: understanding right-wing authoritarianism*. San Francisco: Jossey-Bass.

Altemeyer, B. and Hunsberger, B. (1992) "Authoritarianism, religious fundamentalism, quest, and prejudice," *International Journal for the Psychology of Religion* 2, 113–33.

Althaus, S. L., Edy, J. A., Entman, R. M., and Phalen, P. (1996) "Revising the indexing hypothesis: officials, media, and the Libya crisis," *Political Communication* 13, 407–21.

Altman, K. E. and Nakayama, T. K. (1991) "A difficult dialogue," *Journal of Communication* 41(4), 116–28.

American Council of Trustees and Alumni (2001, November) *Defending civilization: how our universities are failing America and what can be done about it*. Washington, D.C.: American Council of Trustees and Alumni.

Ammerman, N. T. (1991) "North American Protestant Fundamentalism," in M. E. Marty and R. S. Appleby (eds), *Fundamentalisms observed* (pp. 1–65). Chicago: University of Chicago Press.

Anderson, B. (1991) *Imagined communities: reflections on the origin and spread of nationalism* (rev. ed.). New York: Verso.

Apple, Jr., R. W. (2001, September 14) No middle ground, *New York Times*, p. A-1.

"A sampler: invoking an even higher authority" (2001, September 3) *New York Times*. Retrieved from Nexis database on July 6, 2003.

Ashcroft, J. (2001a, September 17) Press briefing with FBI director Robert Mueller. Retrieved from http://www.usdoj.gov/ag/ speeches2001.html on July 23, 2003.

Ashcroft, J. (2001b, October 4) Attorney General Ashcroft and FBI Director Mueller transcript, media availability with state and local law enforcement officials. Retrieved from http://www.usdoj.gov/ag/speeches2001. html on August 18, 2003.

Ashcroft, J. (2001c, September 25) Prepared remarks before Senate Committee on the Judiciary. Retrieved from http://www.usdoj.gov/03press/ 03_2.html on January 26, 2003.

Ashcroft, J. (2001d, October 2) John Ashcroft holds media availability with Canadian Solicitor General Lawrence MacAulay. Retrieved from http:// www.usdoj.gov/03press/03_2.html on January 26, 2003.

Ashcroft, J. (2001e, October 12) Man indicted for false statements to FBI regarding attacks. Retrieved from http://www.usdoj.gov/03press/ 03_2.html on January 26, 2003.

Ashcroft, J. (2001f, October 18) Attorney General John Ashcroft press conference. Retrieved from http://www.usdoj.gov/ 03press/03_2.html on January 26, 2003.

Ashcroft, J. (2001g, December 6) Testimony of Attorney General John Ashcroft, before the U.S. Senate Committee on the Judiciary. Retrieved from http://www.usdoj.gov/ag/testimony.html on July 21, 2003.

Baker, W. D. and Oneal, J. R. (2001) "Patriotism or opinion leadership: the nature and origins of the "rally 'round the flag" effect," *Journal of Conflict Resolution* 45, 661–87.

Baldasty, G. (1992) *The commercialization of news in the nineteenth century*. Madison, WI: University of Wisconsin Press.

Balz, D. (2002, November 17) Democrats in search of a leader, *Washington Post*, p. A-4.

Barr, J. (1977) *Fundamentalism*. Philadelphia: Westminster Press.

Battenfeld, J. and Miga, A. (2001, September 14) Bush vows a global pursuit of terrorists; America prepares wartime campaign, *Boston Herald*, p. 5.

Beasley, V. (2001) "The rhetoric of ideological consensus in the United States: American principles and American pose in presidential inaugurals," *Communication Monographs,* **68**(2), 169–83.

Becker, E. (1975). *Escape from evil*. New York: Free Press.

Bellah, R. (1974) Civil religion in America, in R. E. Richey and D. G. Jones (eds), *American Civil Religion* (pp. 21–44). New York: Harper & Row.

Bellah, R. (1992) *The broken covenant: American civil religion in time of trial* (2nd ed.). Chicago: University of Chicago Press.

Bennett, W. L. (1988) *News: the politics of illusion* (2nd ed.). New York: Longman.

Bennett, W. L. (1990) "Toward a theory of press–state relations in the United States," *Journal of Communication* 36(2), 103–25.

Bennett, W. L. (2003) *News: the politics of illusion* (5th ed.). New York: Longman.

Bennett, W. L. and Manheim, J. B. (1993) "Taking the public by storm:

information, cueing, and the democratic process in the gulf conflict," *Political Communication* 10, 331–52.

Berger, P. and Luckmann, T. (1966) *The social construction of reality*. New York: Doubleday.

Berke, R. L. (2002, January 19) Bush adviser suggests war as campaign theme, *New York Times*, p. A-15.

Berkow, I. (2003, April 11) The Hall of Fame will tolerate no dissent, *New York Times*, p. S-4. Retrieved from Nexis database on August 8, 2003.

Berlet, C. and Lyons, M. N. (2000) *Right-wing populism in America: too close for comfort*. New York: Guilford Press.

Billeaudeaux, M. A., Domke, D., Garland, P., and Hutcheson, J. (2003) "The Bush administration, the 'war on terrorism,' and editorial voices of the *New York Times* and *Washington Post*," *Newspaper Research Journal* 24, 166–84.

Billhartz, C. (2001, September 22) Maher's comments lead to show's suspension, *St. Louis Post-Dispatch*, p. A-15. Retrieved from Nexis database on July 21, 2003.

Bing, J. M. and Bergvall, V. L. (1996) "The question of questions: beyond binary thinking," in V. L. Bergvall, J. M. Bing, and A. F. Freed (eds), *Rethinking language and gender research: theory and practice* (pp. 1–30). New York: Longman.

Blitzer, W. and Kurtz, H. (2001, September 22) Dan Rather speaks out, *CNN Tonight*. Retrieved from Nexis database on December 16, 2003.

Bloom, W. (1990) *Personal identity, national identity and international relations*. Cambridge: Cambridge University Press.

Brands, H. W. (1999) "The idea of national interest," *Diplomatic History* 23, 239–62.

Brill, Steven (2003) *After: how America confronted the September 12 era*. New York: Simon & Schuster.

Brock, D. (2002) *Blinded by the right: the conscience of an ex-conservative*. New York: Crown.

Broder, D. S. (2003, April 27) Bush's leadership pinnacle, *Washington Post*, p. B-7.

Broder, J. M. (2003, March 23) A nation at war: the commander, *New York Times*, p. B-4.

Brody, R. A. (1991) *Assessing the president*. Stanford, CA: Stanford University Press.

Brown, T. (2003, September 10) Author Al Franken, former assistant secretary of Defense for public affairs, Victoria Clarke, and reporter Christiane Amanpour discuss the war. *Topic A with Tina Brown*, CNBC. Retrieved from Nexis database on December 16, 2003.

Brownstein, R. (2003, June 21) Centrists losing ground in Democratic tug of war, *Los Angeles Times*, p. A-16.

Bruce, S. (1987) "The Moral Majority: the politics of fundamentalism in secular society," in L. Caplan (ed.), *Studies in religious fundamentalism* (pp. 177–94). London: Macmillan.

Bruni, F. and Sanger, D. E. (2001, January 20) Bush, taking office, calls for civility, compassion, and "nation of character," *New York Times*, p. A-1. Retrieved from Nexis database on July 21, 2003.

Burke, K. (1969) *A grammar of motives*. Berkeley: University of California Press (original work published in 1945).

Bush exudes strength (2001, September 21) *San Francisco Chronicle*. Retrieved from http://web.lexis-nexis.com/universe on March 30, 2003.

Bush, G. W. (2001a, September 11) Address to the nation on the terrorist attacks. Retrieved from http://www.access.gpo.gov on January 26, 2003.

Bush, G. W. (2001b, September 13) Remarks on the terrorist attacks at Barksdale Air Force Base, Louisiana. Retrieved from http://www. access.gpo.gov/nara/nara003.html on September 11, 2003.

Bush, G. W. (2001c, September 14) Remarks at the National Day of Prayer and Remembrance Service. Retrieved from http://www.access.gpo.gov/ nara/nara003.html on August 18, 2003.

Bush, G. W. (2001d, September 19) Remarks following a meeting with congressional leaders and an exchange with reporters. Retrieved from http://www.access.gpo.gov/nara/nara003.html on July 23, 2003.

Bush, G. W. (2001e, September 20) Address before a joint session of the Congress on the United States response to the terrorist attacks of September 11. Retrieved from http://www.access.gpo.gov/nara/ nara003.html on January 26, 2003.

Bush, G. W. (2001f, September 25) Remarks to Federal Bureau of Investigation employees. Retrieved from http://www.access.gpo.gov/nara/ nara003.html on January 26, 2003.

Bush, G. W. (2001g, September 27) Remarks to airline employees in Chicago, Illinois. Retrieved from http://www.access.gpo. gov/nara/nara003.html on January 26, 2003.

Bush, G. W. (2001h, October 7) Address to the nation announcing strikes against Al Qaida training camps and Taliban military installations in Afghanistan. Retrieved from http://www.access.gpo.gov/nara/nara 003.html on August 7, 2003.

Bush, G. W. (2001i, November 8) Address to the nation on homeland security from Atlanta. Retrieved from http://www.access.gpo.gov/nara/ nara003.html on January 26, 2003.

Bush, G. W. (2002a, January 29) Address before a joint session of the Congress on the state of the union. Retrieved from http://www.access. gpo.gov/nara/nara003.html on January 9, 2003.

Bush, G. W. (2002b, June 1) Graduation address at United States Military Academy, West Point, New York. Retrieved from http://www.white house.gov/news/releases/2002/06 on July 6, 2003.

Bush, G. W. (2002c, June 7) Remarks at the World Pork Expo in Des Moines,

Iowa. Retrieved from http://www.access.gpo.gov/nara/ nara003.html on January 23, 2003.

Bush, G. W. (2002d, July 26) Remarks on proposed legislation to establish the Department of Homeland Security. Retrieved from http://www.access.gpo.gov on August 18, 2003.

Bush, G. W. (2002e, August 3) Remarks at a reception for Senator Susan Collins in Prout's Neck, Maine. Retrieved from http://www.access.gpo.gov on July 16, 2003.

Bush, G. W. (2002f, August 7) Remarks at Madison Central High School in Madison, Mississippi. Retrieved from http://www. access.gpo.gov on August 18, 2003.

Bush, G. W. (2002g, September 2) Remarks at a United Brotherhood of Carpenters and Joiners Labor Day Picnic on Neville Island, Pennsylvania. Retrieved from http://www.access.gpo.gov on August 18, 2003.

Bush, G. W. (2002h, September 11) Address to the nation on the anniversary of the terrorist attacks of September 11 from Ellis Island, New York. Retrieved from http://www.access.gpo.gov on August 7, 2003.

Bush, G. W. (2002i, September 12) Address to the United Nations General Assembly in New York City. Retrieved from http://www. access.gpo.gov on July 23, 2003.

Bush, G. W. (2002j, September 18) Remarks following a meeting with Congressional leaders and an exchange with reporters. Retrieved from http://www.access.gpo.gov on August 18, 2003.

Bush, G. W. (2002k, September 23) Remarks to the community in Trenton, New Jersey. Retrieved from http://www.access.gpo.gov on 22 July 2003.

Bush, G. W. (2002l, September 26) Remarks at a reception for Senatorial candidate John Cornyn in Houston, Texas. Retrieved from http://www.access.gpo.gov on August 18, 2003.

Bush, G. W. (2002m, October 3) Remarks calling for Congressional action on terrorism insurance legislation. Retrieved from http://www.access.gpo.gov on May 8, 2003.

Bush, G. W. (2002n, October 5) Remarks to the community in Manchester, New Hampshire. Retrieved from http://www.access.gpo.gov on February 21, 2003.

Bush, G. W. (2002o, October 12) The President's radio address. Retrieved from http://www.access.gpo.gov on August 18, 2003.

Bush, G. W. (2002p, October 14) Remarks at a dinner for Congressional candidate Thaddeus McCotter in Dearborn, Michigan. Retrieved from http://www.access.gpo.gov on August 18, 2003.

Bush, G. W. (2002q, October 18) Remarks at Southwest Missouri State University in Springfield, Missouri. Retrieved from http://www.access.gpo.gov on August 18, 2003.

Bush, G. W. (2002r, October 28) Remarks in Alamogordo, New Mexico. Retrieved from http://www.access.gpo.gov on February 21, 2003.

Bush, G. W. (2003a, January 28) Address before a joint session of the Congress on the State of the Union. Retrieved from http://www.access. gpo.gov on May 22, 2003.

Bush, G. W. (2003b, February 7) Remarks at the National Prayer Breakfast. Retrieved from http://www.access.gpo.gov on July 15, 2003.

Bush, G. W. (2003c, March 17) Address to the nation on Iraq. Retrieved from http://www.access.gpo.gov on July 17, 2003.

Bush, G. W. (2003d, March 19) Address to the nation on Iraq. Retrieved from http://www.access.gpo.gov on July 17, 2003.

Bush, G. W. (2003e, May 1) Address to the nation on Iraq from the U.S.S. Abraham Lincoln. Retrieved from http://www.access. gpo.gov on June 21, 2003.

Bush, G. W. (2003f, February 1) Address to the nation on the loss of Space Shuttle Columbia. Retrieved from http://www.gpoaccess.gov/wcomp/ index.html on September 9, 2003.

Bush, G. W. (2003g, December 15) The president's news conference. Retrieved from http://www.gpoaccess.gov/wcomp/index.html on January 8, 2004.

Bush, G. W. (2004, January 20) Address before a joint session of the Congress on the State of the Union. Retrieved from http://www.access. gpo.gov on February 20, 2004.

Calabrese, A. and Burke, B. (1992) "American identities: nationalism, the media and the public sphere," *Journal of Communication Inquiry* 16(2), 52–73.

Canes-Wrone, B. (2001) "The president's legislative influence from public appeals," *American Journal of Political Science* 45, 313–29.

Cappella, J. N. and Jamieson, K. H. (1997) *Spiral of cynicism: the press and the public good.* New York: Oxford University Press.

Carpenter, J. A. (1997) *Revive us again: the reawakening of American fundamentalism.* New York: Oxford University Press.

Carr, A. and Zanetti, L. A. (1999) "Metatheorizing the dialectic of self and other: the psychodynamics in work organizations," *American Behavioral Scientist* 43(2), 324–45.

Carr, R. (2003, June 11) ACLU watches membership soar since 9/11: group attributes record growth to Ashcroft policies, *Atlanta Journal and Constitution*, p. A-16.

Carter, B. and Barringer, F. (2001, September 28) Speech and expression: in patriotic time, dissent is muted, *New York Times*, p. A-1.

CBS News (2002, September 9) Poll: America, a changed country. CBS News/*New York Times* poll. Retrieved from http://www. cbsnews.com/ stories/2002/09/07/september 11/main521173. shtml on June 20, 2003.

CBS News Poll (2002) Poll question about involvement of Saddam Hussein in September 11 attacks. Retrieved from Public Opinion Online database, Roper Center at University of Connecticut. Poll conducted

September 22–23.

CBS News Poll (2003) Poll question about involvement of Saddam Hussein in September 11 attacks. Retrieved from Public Opinion Online database, Roper Center at University of Connecticut. Poll conducted May 9–12.

Cirksena, K. and Cuklanz, L. (1992) "Male is to female as _____ is to _____: a guided tour of five feminist frameworks for communication studies," in L. F. Rakow (ed.), *Women making meaning: new feminist directions in communication* (pp. 18–44). New York: Routledge.

Clymer, A. (2003a, May 25) Buoyed by resurgence, G.O.P. strives for an era of dominance, *New York Times*, p. A-1.

Clymer, A. (2003b, May 26) Democrats seek a stronger focus, and money. *New York Times*, p. A-1.

CNN Time (1997) AllPolitics Ad Archive. Retrieved from http://www. cnn.com/ALLPOLITICS/1996/candidates/ad.archive/ on January 13, 2004.

Cohen, R. (2001, September 22) Taking command, *Washington Post*, p. A-29.

Conason, J. and Lyons, G. (2000) *The hunting of the president: the ten-year campaign to destroy Bill and Hillary Clinton*. New York: St. Martin's Press.

Conger, K. H. and Green, J. C. (2002, February) "Spreading out and digging in: Christian conservatives and state Republican parties," *Campaigns & Elections* 23(1): 58–60, 64–5.

Cook, T. E. (1998) *Governing with the news*. Chicago: University of Chicago Press.

Cooper, T. (2001, September 22) 2 TV stations yank "Politically Incorrect," *Omaha World-Herald*, p. B-8. Retrieved from Nexis database on July 21, 2003.

Cox, H. (1987) "Fundamentalism as an ideology," in R. J. Neuhaus and M. Cromartie (eds), *Piety and politics: evangelicals and fundamentalists confront the world* (pp. 289–301). Lanham, MD: University Press of America.

Cristi, M. (2001) *From civil to political religion: the intersection of culture, religion and politics*. Waterloo, Ontario: Wilfrid Laurier University Press.

Crowley, C. (2001, April 25) President Bush vows to defend Taiwan if necessary, Cable News Network, in *CNN Live Today* program.

Dalby, S. (1990) *Creating the second cold war: the discourse of politics*. London: Pinter.

Dalton, R. J., Beck, P. A., and Huckfeldt, R. (1998) "Partisan cues and the media: information flows in the 1992 presidential election," *American Political Science Review* 92, 111–26.

Danso, H., Hunsberger, B., and Pratt, M. (1997) "The role of parental religious fundamentalism and right-wing authoritarianism in child-rearing goals and practices," *Journal for the Scientific Study of Religion* 36(4), 496–511.

Daschle, T. A. (2002, September 25) *Congressional Record—Senate*. Volume 148, No. 123, S 9186.

Derrida, J. (1981) *Positions*, trans. A. Bass. Chicago: University of Chicago Press (original work published in 1972).

Deutsch, K. (1953) *Nationalism and social communication*. Cambridge, MA: M.I.T. Press.

Deutsch, K. and Merritt, R. (1965) "Effects of events on national and international images," in H. Kelman (ed.), *International behavior: a social psychological analysis* (pp. 130–87). New York: Holt, Rinehart and Winston.

Diamond, S. (1989) *Spiritual warfare: the politics of the Christian Right*. Boston: South End Press.

Dionne, Jr., E. J. (1999, December 28) Religion and politics, *Washington Post*, p. A-23. Retrieved from Nexis database on August 6, 2003.

Dionne, Jr., E. J. (2003, February 14) When presidents talk of God, *Washington Post*, p. A-31. Retrieved from washingtonpost.com on August 26, 2003.

"Divine intervention" (May/June 2003) *Foreign Policy*, 136, 14.

Domke, D., Watts, M., Shah, D., and Fan, D. (1999) "The politics of conservative elites and the liberal media argument," *Journal of Communication* 49(4), 35–58.

Donnelly, J. (2003, February 16) Fighting terror/theologians, *Boston Globe*, p. A-20.

Dougherty, D. and Krone, K. (2000) "Overcoming the dichotomy: cultivating standpoints in organizations through research," *Women's Studies in Communication* 23(1), 16–39.

Dowd, M. (1999, December 15) Playing the Jesus card, *New York Times*, p. A-23. Retrieved from Nexis database on August 6, 2003.

Dowd, M. (2002, June 16) Secrets of the Yo-Yo's, *New York Times*, p. A-13.

Dubose, L., Reid, J., and Cannon, C. M. (2003) *Boy genius: Karl Rove, the brains behind the remarkable political triumph of George W. Bush*. New York: Public Affairs.

Easton, N. (2000) *Gang of five: leaders at the center of the conservative ascendancy*. New York: Simon & Schuster.

Easton, N. J. (2002, May 20) "The power and the glory: who needs the Christian Coalition when you've got the White House? The religious right's covert crusade," *The American Prospect* 13(9), 20–3.

Edel, W. (1987) *Defenders of the faith: religion and politics from the pilgrim fathers to Ronald Reagan*. New York: Praeger.

Edwards, L. (1999) *The conservative revolution: the movement that remade America*. New York: Free Press.

Entman, R. M. (1989) *Democracy without citizens: media and the decay of American politics*. New York: Oxford University Press.

Entman, R. M. (1991) "Framing U.S. coverage of international news:

contrasts in narratives of the KAL and Iran Air incidents," *Journal of Communication* **41**(4), 6–27.

Entman, R. M. (2003) "Cascading activation: contesting the White House's frame after 9/11," *Political Communication* **20**, 415–32.

Entman, R. M. and Rojecki, A. (1993) "Freezing out the public: elite and media framing of the U.S. anti-nuclear movement," *Political Communication* **10**, 155–73.

Excerpts from president's remarks on investigation into attack (2001, September 14) *New York Times*, p. A-18.

Fairclough, N. (1992) *Discourse and social change.* Cambridge: Polity Press.

Fan, D. P. 1988. *Predictions of public opinion from the mass media.* Westport, CT: Greenwood Press.

Ferguson, T. and Rogers, J. (1986) *Right turn: the decline of the Democrats and the future of American politics.* New York: Hill and Wang.

Fineman, H. (2003, March 10) Bush and God, *Newsweek,* 22–30.

Fleischer, A. (2001, September 26) White House press briefing by Ari Fleischer. Retrieved from http://www.whitehouse.gov/news/releases/2001/09/20010926-5.html on July 21, 2003.

Fleischer, A. (2003, March 18) White House press briefing by Ari Fleischer. Retrieved from http://www.whitehouse.gov/news/releases/2003/03/20030318-4.html on February 20, 2004.

Foner, E. (1994) "The meaning of freedom in the age of emancipation," *Journal of American History* **81**: 435–60.

For ABC, a winning season, at least on paper (2001, September 27) *Washington Post*, p. C-7.

Frey, J. (2004, January 14) A liberal haven on the radio dial; talk network plans to begin national broadcast in spring, *Washington Post*, p. C-1. Retrieved from Nexis database on January 16, 2004.

Frum, D. (2003) *The right man: the surprise presidency of George W. Bush.* New York: Random House.

Gallagher, J. and Bull, C. (1996) *Perfect enemies: the religious right, the gay movement, and the politics of the 1990s.* New York: Crown.

Gallup (2002) Poll topics and trends: terrorist attacks and the aftermath. Retrieved from http://www.gallup.com/poll/topics/ terror.asp January 14, 2002.

Gallup (2003) Poll question on Bush's leadership. Retrieved from Public Opinion Online database, Roper Center at University of Connecticut. Poll conducted April 8–11, 2003.

Gamson, W. A. (1988) "The 1987 distinguished lecture: a constructionist approach to mass media and public opinion," *Symbolic Interaction* **11**, 161–74.

Gans, H. (1979) *Deciding what's news.* New York: Vintage.

Garvey, J. H. (1993) "Introduction: fundamentalism and politics," in M. E.

Marty and R. S. Appleby (eds), *Fundamentalisms and the state* (pp. 13–27). Chicago: University of Chicago Press.

Geertz, C. (1966) "Religion as a cultural system," in M. Banton (ed.), *Anthropological approaches to the study of religion* (pp. 1–46). London: Tavistock.

Gerbner, G. (1964) "Ideological perspectives and political tendencies in news reporting," *Journalism Quarterly* **41**, 495–508.

Getlin, J. (2003, April 11) Fox News' patriotic fervor sets it apart in ratings race, *Los Angeles Times*, p. A-16.

Gettleman, J. (2003, November 13) He'd do it again, says the "Ten Commandments Judge," *New York Times*, p. A-18.

Gordon, M. (2002, March 10) U.S. nuclear plan sees new targets and new weapons, *New York Times*, p. A-1.

Graber, D. A. (1997) *Mass media and American politics* (5th ed.). Washington, D.C.: Congressional Quarterly.

Grady, S. (1999, December 29) Jesus holds all the cards in 2000 campaign, *Milwaukee Journal Sentinel*, p. A-18. Retrieved from Nexis database on August 6, 2003.

Graham, E., Domke, D., Coe, K., John, S. L., and Coopman, T. *Follow the leader: the Bush administration, news media, and passage of the U.S.A. Patriot Act.* Paper presented to the Association for Education in Journalism and Mass Communication annual convention, August 2003, Kansas City, MO.

Green, J. C., Kellstedt, L. A., Smidt, C. E., and Guth, J. L. (1998) "The soul of the south: religion and the new electoral order," in C. S. Bullock III and M. J. Rozell (eds), *The new politics of the Old South: an introduction to Southern politics* (pp. 261–76). Lanham, MD: Rowman and Littlefield.

Greene, D. L. (2003, February 10) Bush turns increasingly to language of religion, *Baltimore Sun*, p. A-1.

Hall, S. (1979) Culture, the media and the "ideological effect," in J. Curran, M. Gurevitch, and J. Woollacott (eds), *Mass communication and society* (pp. 315–48). Beverly Hills: Sage.

Hall, S. (1982) "The rediscovery of 'ideology': return of the repressed in media studies," in M. Gurevitch, T. Bennett, J. Curran, and J. Woollacott (eds), *Culture, society and the media* (pp. 56–90). London: Methuen.

Hallin, D. (1987) "Hegemony: the American news media from Vietnam to El Salvador, a study of ideological change and its limits," in D. Paletz (ed.), *Political communication research* (pp. 3–25). Norwood, NJ: Ablex.

Hallin D. C., Manoff, R. K., and Weddle, J. K. (1993) "Sourcing patterns of national security reporters," *Journalism Quarterly* **70**, 753–66.

Harding, S. (1994) "Imagining the last days: the politics of apocalyptic language," in M. E. Marty and R. S. Appleby (eds), *Accounting for fundamentalisms* (pp. 57–78). Chicago: University of Chicago Press.

Harper, J. (2003, January 30) Bush's speech resonates with public, polls show, *Washington Times*. Retrieved from http://www.washtimes.com/national on April 11, 2003.

Hawkins, B. D. (2002, September/October) Condaleezza Rice's secret weapon, ChristianityToday.com. Retrieved from http://www.christianitytoday.com/cr/2002/005/1.18.html on May 22, 2003.

Heath, J. (2001, September 14) Emotions get better of Bush; public display is rare moment for U.S. president. *Atlanta Journal and Constitution*, p. A-4.

Herman, E. S. and Chomsky, N. (1988) *Manufacturing consent: the political economy of the mass media*. New York: Pantheon.

Herman, E. S. and O'Sullivan, G. (1989) *The terrorism industry: the experts and institutions that shape our view of terror*. New York: Pantheon.

Hertsgaard, M. (1988) *On bended knee: the press and the Reagan presidency*. New York: Farrar Straus Giroux.

Hitchens, C. (2003, August) God and man in the White House, *Vanity Fair*, 76–81.

Hoagland, J. (2002, March 17) Nuclear preemption, *Washington Post*, p. B-9.

Horsey, D. (2003, February 16) Serving up the GOP agenda, *Seattle Post-Intelligencer*, p. G-1.

Huckin, T. N. (2002) "Textual silence and the discourse of homelessness," *Discourse & Society* 13(3), 347–72.

Hughes, W. J. (1995) The "not-so-genial" conspiracy: the *New York Times* and six presidential "honeymoons," *Journalism and Mass Communication Quarterly* 72, 841–50.

Hunsberger, B. (1996) Religious fundamentalism, right-wing authoritarianism, and hostility toward homosexuals in non-Christian religious groups, *International Journal for the Psychology of Religion* 6(1), 39–49.

Hutcheson, J., Domke, D., Billeaudeaux, M. A., and Garland, P. (2004) "U.S. national identity, political elites, and a patriotic press following September 11," *Political Communication* 21, 27–51.

Hutcheson, R. (2003, June 1) White House now says Iraq is a battle, not a war, Knight Ridder Newspapers. Retrieved from www.seattletimes.com on June 1, 2003.

Hutchinson, J. (1994) *Modern nationalism*. Glasgow: HarperCollins.

Ivie, R. (1980) "Images of savagery in American's justifications for war," *Communication Monographs* 47(4), 279–94.

Ivie, R. (1990) "Metaphor and the rhetorical invention of cold war 'idealists,'" in M. Medhurst et al., *Cold war rhetoric: strategy, metaphor, and ideology* (pp. 103–27). Westport, CT: Greenwood Press.

Iyengar, S. and Kinder, D. R. (1987) *News that matters*. Chicago: University of Chicago Press.

Jensen, E. (2003, April 2) War with Iraq; Arnett fuming at loss of NBC job, *Los Angeles Times*. Retrieved from http://web.lexis-nexis.com on April 18, 2003.

[ 223 ]

Jones, D. A. (2002) "The polarizing effect of news media messages," *International Journal of Public Opinion Research* **14**(2), 158–74.

Justice Department opens probe into leak of CIA agent's name (2003, September 29) *Wall Street Journal*, p. A-3.

Kagan, D., Schmitt, G., and Donnelly, T. (2000) *Rebuilding America's defenses: strategy, forces and resources for a new century,* Project for the New American Century. Retrieved from www.new americancentury.org on December 5, 2003.

Kaplan, L. (1992) "Introduction," in L. Kaplan (ed.), *Fundamentalism in comparative perspective* (pp. 3–14). Amherst, MA: University of Massachusetts Press.

Keller, B. (2003a, January 26) The radical presidency of George W. Bush, *New York Times*. Retrieved from Nexis database on July 6, 2003.

Keller, B. (2003b, May 17) God and George W. Bush, *New York Times*, p. A-17. Retrieved from Nexis database on June 6, 2003.

Kelley, M. (2001, September 18) Attacks transform Bush's presidency, *Omaha World-Herald*, p. A-1.

Kernell, S. (1997) *Going public: new strategies of presidential leadership* (3rd ed.). Washington, D.C.: Congressional Quarterly.

Kiefer, F. (2002, September 6) The private faith of a public man, *Christian Science Monitor*, p. 1.

King, A. and Anderson, F. (1971) "Nixon, Agnew, and the 'silent majority': a case study in the rhetoric of polarization," *Western Speech* **35**(4), 243–55.

Kirk, M. (2003, February 20) *Frontline: the war behind closed doors* (television broadcast). Boston: Public Broadcasting Corporation.

Kirkpatrick, L., Hood, Jr., R. W., and Hartz, G. (1991) "Fundamentalist religion conceptualized in terms of Rokeach's theory of the open and closed mind: new perspectives on some old ideas," *Research in the Social Scientific Study of Religion* 3, 157–79.

Kovach, B. and Rosenstiel, T. (1999) *Warp speed: America in the age of mixed media*. New York: Century Foundation Press.

Kress, G. (1985) "Ideological structures in discourse," in T. van Dijk (ed.), *Handbook of discourse analysis,* vol. 4 (pp. 27–42). London: Academic Press.

Kristof, N. D. (2003, March 4) God, Satan, and the media, *New York Times*, p. A-25.

Krosnick, J. A. and Brannon, L. (1993) "The media and the foundations of presidential support: George Bush and the Persian Gulf conflict," *Journal of Social Issues* **49**, 167–82.

Kunhenn, J. (2003, March 18) With U.S. on brink of war, Democrats fire salvos at Bush, Knight Ridder/Tribune News Service. Retrieved from Nexis database on July 28, 2003.

Kurtz, H. (2001a, February 5) Doing something right: Fox News sees ratings soar, critics sore, *Washington Post*, p. C-1.

Kurtz, H. (2001b, October 31) CNN chief orders "balance" in war news; reporters are told to remind viewers why U.S. is bombing, *Washington Post*, p. C-1. Retrieved from Nexis database on August 8, 2003.

Kurtz, H. (2003, March 5) Protest letters to MSNBC draw Savage response, *Washington Post*, p. C-1.

Kuypers, J. (1997) *Presidential crisis rhetoric and the press in the post-cold war world*. Westport, CT: Praeger.

Lakoff, G. (1996) *Moral politics: what conservatives know that liberals don't*. Chicago: University of Chicago Press.

Lakoff, G. and Johnson, M. (1980) *Metaphors we live by*. Chicago: University of Chicago Press.

Lawrence, B. (1989) *Defenders of God: the fundamentalist revolt against the modern age*. San Francisco, CA: Harper & Row.

Lawrence, R. (2000) "Game-framing the issues: tracking the strategy frame in public policy news," *Political Communication* 17, 93–114.

Lawson, G. (2003, September) George W.'s personal Jesus, *Gentlemen's Quarterly*, 330–5, 394–6, 399.

Leege, D. C. and Kellstedt, L. A. (1993) "Religious worldviews and political philosophies: capturing theory in the grand manner through empirical data," in D. C. Leege and L. A. Kellstedt, *Rediscovering the religious factor in American politics* (pp. 216–31). Armonk, NY: M. E. Sharpe.

Leland, J. (2002, December 8) Why the right rules the radio waves, *New York Times*. Retrieved from Nexis database on July 1, 2003.

Lemann, N. (2003, May 12) The controller, *New Yorker*, pp. 68–83.

Letter to President Clinton on Iraq (1998) Project for the New American Century. Retrieved from www.newamericancentury.org/iraqclinton letter.htm on December 5, 2003.

Lichtblau, E. (2003, September 8) Ashcroft's tour rallies supporters and detractors, *New York Times*, p. A-14.

Lienesch, M. (1993) *Redeeming America: piety and politics in the new Christian right*. Chapel Hill, NC: University of North Carolina Press.

Lind, M. (2001, December 9) The right still has religion, *New York Times*. Retrieved from Nexis database on July 1, 2003.

Livingston, S. (1994) *The terrorism spectacle*. Boulder, CO: Westview Press.

Long, D. E. (1990) *The anatomy of terrorism*. New York: Macmillan International.

Lowry, B. (2002, January 1) For cable networks, 2002 was solid year, *Los Angeles Times*, Part 5, p. 4.

Lule, J. (2002) "Myth and terror on the editorial page: the *New York Times* responds to September 11, 2002," *Journalism and Mass Communication Quarterly* 79(2), 275–93.

MacDougall, C. (1982) *Interpretative reporting*. New York: Macmillan.

Maltese, J. A. (1994) *Spin control: the White House Office of Communication and the management of presidential news* (2nd ed.). Chapel Hill: University of North Carolina Press.

Manheim, J. B. (1991) *All of the people, all of the time: strategic communication and American politics.* Armonk, NY: M. E. Sharpe.

Manheim, J. B. (1994) "Strategic public diplomacy," in W. L. Bennett and D. L. Paletz (eds), *Taken by storm: the media, public opinion, and U.S. foreign policy in the Gulf War* (pp. 131–48). Chicago: University of Chicago Press.

Marinucci, C. and Wildermuth, J. (2002, September 24) Gore blasts Bush's cowboy Iraq policy: global goodwill already squandered, he tells S.F. boosters, *New York Times*, p. A-1. Retrieved from Nexis database on July 24, 2003.

Marsden, G. M. (1980) *Fundamentalism and American culture.* New York: Oxford University Press.

Marty, M. E. (1987) *Religion and republic: the American circumstance.* Boston: Beacon Press.

Marty, M. E. (1992) "Fundamentals of fundamentalism," in L. Kaplan (ed.), *Fundamentalism in comparative perspective* (pp. 15–23). Amherst, MA: University of Massachusetts Press.

Marty, M. E. (2003, March 10) The sin of pride, *Newsweek*, pp. 32–3.

Marty, M. E. and Appleby, R. S. (1991a) "The fundamentalism project: a user's guide," in M. E. Marty and R. S. Appleby (eds), *Fundamentalisms observed* (pp. vii–xiii). Chicago: University of Chicago Press.

Marty, M. E. and Appleby, R. S. (1991b) "Conclusion: an interim report on a hypothetical family," in M. E. Marty and R. S. Appleby (eds), *Fundamentalisms observed* (pp. 814–42). Chicago: University of Chicago Press.

Marty, M. E. and Appleby, R. S. (1992) *The glory and the power: the fundamentalist challenge to the modern world.* Boston: Beacon Press.

Marty, M. E. and Appleby, R. S. (1993) "Introduction," in M. E. Marty and R. S. Appleby (eds), *Fundamentalisms and the state* (pp. 1–9). Chicago: University of Chicago Press.

Marty, M. E. and Appleby, R. S. (2002) "Fundamentalism," *Foreign Policy*, January/February, **128**, 16–22.

McDaniel, M. (2001, September 19) "Politically Incorrect" comes under fire for comments about terrorists, *Houston Chronicle*, p. A-10. Retrieved from Nexis database on July 21, 2003.

Medhurst, M. J. (2000) "Text and context in the 1952 presidential campaign: Eisenhower's 'I shall go to Korea' speech," *Presidential Studies Quarterly* 30(3), 464–84.

Mermin, J. (1997) "Television news and American intervention in Somalia: the myth of a media-driven foreign policy," *Political Science Quarterly* **112**, 385–403.

Milbank, D. (2001, December 24) Religious right finds its center in Oval

Office: Bush emerges as movement's leader after Robertson leaves Christian Coalition, *Washington Post*, p. A-2.

Milbank, D. (2002, September 25) In president's speeches, Iraq dominates, economy fades, *Washington Post*, p. A-1. Retrieved from Nexis database on July 24, 2003.

Milbank, D. (2003, February 10) Bush links faith and agenda in speech to religious group, *Washington Post*, p. A-2.

Milbank, D. and Eilperin, J. (2001, May 1) They never promised him a Rose Garden, *Washington Post*, p. A-1. Retrieved from Nexis database on July 21, 2003.

Moore, J. and Slater, W. (2003) *Bush's brain: how Karl Rove made George W. Bush presidential*. New Jersey: Wiley.

Mueller, J. E. (1970) "Presidential popularity from Truman to Johnson," *American Political Science Review* 64, 18–33.

Myers, S. L. (1999, September 21) Federal commission predicts increasing threat of terrorism, *New York Times*, p. A-7.

Nacos, B. L. (1994) *Terrorism and the media: from the Iran hostage crisis to the World Trade Center bombing*. New York: Columbia University Press.

Nagata, J. (2001) "Beyond theology: toward an anthropology of 'fundamentalism,'" *American Anthropologist* 103(2), 481–98.

Names and Faces (2004, January 3) *Washington Post*, p. C-3. Retrieved from Nexis database on January 3, 2004.

National Security Council (2002, September 17) The national security strategy of the United States of America. Retrieved from http://www.whitehouse.gov/nsc/print/nssall.html on July 6, 2003.

Naugle, D. K. (2002) *Worldview: the history of a concept*. Grand Rapids, MI: W. B. Eerdmans.

NBC News Poll (2001) Poll question about reaction to speech by President George W. Bush. Retrieved from Public Opinion Online database, Roper Center at University of Connecticut. Poll conducted September 20, 2001.

*Newsweek* Poll (2001) Poll question about reaction to speech by President George W. Bush. Retrieved from Public Opinion Online database, Roper Center at University of Connecticut. Poll conducted September 20–21, 2001.

*Newsweek* Poll (2002) Poll question about view of government leaders' expression of faith in God. Retrieved from Public Opinion Online database, Roper Center at University of Connecticut. Poll conducted June 27–28, 2002.

Niebuhr, R. (1967) "The social myths of the Cold War," in J. Farrell and A. Smith (eds), *Image and reality in world politics* (pp. 40–67). New York: Columbia University Press.

Nye, J. (2002) *The paradox of American power: why the world's only superpower can't go it alone*. New York: Oxford University Press.

Page, S. (2003, March 17) War may realign world and define a presidency, *USA Today*, p. A-1.

Pan, Z. and Kosicki, G. M. (1997) "Priming and media impact on the evaluation of the President's performance," *Communication Research* 24, 3–30.

Patterson, T. E. (1994) *Out of order*. New York: Vintage.

Perea, J. F. (1997) "The black/white binary paradigm of race: the 'normal science' of American racial thought," *California Law Review* 85(5), 1213–58.

Perkin, H. (2000) "American fundamentalism and the selling of God," in D. Marquand and R. L. Nettler (eds), *Religion and Democracy* (pp. 79–89). Oxford: Blackwell.

Peterson, G. R. (2001) "Religion as orienting worldview," *Zygon* 36(1), 5–19.

Pew Research Center (2000, September 20) Religion and politics: the ambivalent majority. Retrieved from http://people-press.org/reports on June 20, 2003.

Pew Research Center (2001a, September 19) American psyche reeling from terror attacks. Retrieved from http://people-press.org/reports on May 22, 2003.

Pew Research Center (2001b, December 18) Terrorism transforms news interest. Retrieved from http://www.people-press.org on June 8, 2002.

Pew Research Center (2001c, November 28) Terror coverage boost news media's images. Retrieved from http://people-press.org/reports on August 26, 2003.

Pew Research Center (2002a, June 27) Domestic concerns will vie with terrorism in fall. Retrieved from http://people-press.org/reports on May 22, 2003.

Pew Research Center (2002b, December 12) Public more internationalist than in 1990s. Retrieved from http://people-press.org/reports on May 22, 2003.

Pew Research Center (2003a, February 20) U.S. needs more international backing. Retrieved from http://people-press.org/reports on June 11, 2003.

Pew Research Center (2003b, March 19) Different faiths, different messages. Retrieved from http://people-press.org/reports on June 25, 2003.

Pew Research Center (2003c, March 25) Public confidence in war effort falters. Retrieved from http://people-press.org/reports on May 22, 2003.

Pew Research Center (2003d, March 28) TV combat fatigue on the rise. Retrieved from http://people-press.org/reports on June 11, 2003.

Pew Research Center (2003e, April 9) War coverage praised but public hungry for other news. Retrieved from http://people-press.org/reports on April 10, 2003.

Pew Research Center (2003f, April 18) Modest Bush approval rating boost at war's end. Retrieved from http://people-press.org/reports on July 25, 2003.

Pew Research Center (2003g, July 24) Religion and politics: contention and consensus. Retrieved from http://people-press.org/reports on August 18, 2003.

Pew Research Center (2003h, March 18) America's image further erodes, Europeans want weaker ties. Retrieved from http://people-press.org/reports on September 3, 2003.

Pew Research Center (2003i, November 5) The 2004 political landscape: evenly divided and increasingly polarized. Retrieved from http://people-press.org/reports on December 16, 2003.

Pew Research Centre (2004, March 16) A year after Iraq war: Mistrust of America in Europe ever higher, Muslim anger persists. Retrieved from http://people-press.org/reports on March 19, 2004.

Pierard, R. V. (1988) Civil religion and the presidency. Grand Rapids, MI: Academic Books.

Pinkus, S. (2001) Poll analysis: psychological effects of September 11, Los Angeles Times. Retrieved from http://www.latimes.com/news/custom/timespoll on May 22, 2003.

Poole, R. (1999) Nation and identity. London: Routledge.

Potter, J. and Wetherell, M. (1987) Discourse and social psychology. London: Sage.

Powell, C. (2002a, September 13) Interview on CBS's This Morning. Retrieved from http://www.state.gov/secretary/rm/2002 on July 18, 2003.

Powell, C. (2002b, September 13) Interview on CNN's American Morning. Retrieved from http://www.state.gov/secretary/rm/2002 on July 18, 2003.

Powell, C. (2002c, September 19) The Administration's position with regard to Iraq. Retrieved from http://www.state.gov/secretary/ rm/2002 on July 18, 2003.

Powell, C. (2002d, October 9) Interview on CNN's Larry King Live. Retrieved from http://www.state.gov/secretary/rm/2002 on July 18, 2003.

Powell, C. (2002e, October 28) Roundtable with European journalists. Retrieved from http://www.state.gov/secretary/rm/2002 on July 18, 2003.

Powell, C. (2002f, November 4) Interview by selected print journalists from UN Security Council member countries. Retrieved from http://www.state.gov/secretary/rm/2002 on July 18, 2003.

Powell, C. (2002g, November 7) Interview by the Associated Press. Retrieved from http://www.state.gov/secretary/rm/2002 on July 18, 2003.

Powlick, P. J. (1995) "The sources of public opinion for American foreign policy officials," International Studies Quarterly 39, 427–51.

Price, V. and Tewksbury, D. (1997) "News values and public opinion: a theoretical account of media priming and framing," in G. Barnett and F. J. Boster (eds), Progress in communication sciences (pp. 173–212). Greenwich, CT: Ablex.

Prokhovnik, R. (1999) Rational woman: a feminist critique of dichotomy. New York: Routledge.

Purdum, T. (2003, February 23) Focus groups? To Bush, the crowd was a blur, *New York Times*. Retrieved from Nexis database on September 8, 2003.

Raum, R. and Measell, J. (1974) "Wallace and his ways: a study of the rhetorical genre of polarization," *Central States Speech Journal* 25, 28–35.

Reagan, R. (1981, January 20) Inaugural address of President Ronald Reagan, in *Weekly compilation of presidential documents* 17(4), 1–5. Washington D.C.: United States Government Printing Office.

Reagan, R. (1984, January 25) The State of the Union, in *Weekly compilation of presidential documents* 20(4), 87–94. Washington D.C.: United States Government Printing Office.

Reagan, R. (1985, February 6) The State of the Union, in *Weekly compilation of presidential documents* 21(6), 140–6. Washington D.C.: United States Government Printing Office.

Reese, S. D., Grant, A., and Danielian, L. H. (1994) "The structure of news sources television: a network analysis of '*CBS News*,' '*Nightline*,' '*MacNeil/Lehrer*,' and '*This Week with David Brinkley*,'" *Journal of Communication* 44(2), 84–107.

Reichley, A. J. (1987) "The evangelical and fundamentalist revolt," in R. J. Neuhaus and M. Cromartie (eds), *Piety and politics: evangelicals and fundamentalists confront the world* (pp. 69–95). Washington, D.C.: Ethics and Public Policy Center.

Rich, F. (2003, April 13) The spoils of war coverage, *New York Times*. Retrieved from http://www.nytimes.com on April 18, 2003.

Riker, W. (1986) *The art of political manipulation*. New Haven: Yale University Press.

Ritter, K. and Henry, D. (1992) *Ronald Reagan: the great communicator*. Westport, CT: Greenwood Press.

Rivenburgh, N. K. (2000) "Social identity and news portrayals of citizens involved in international affairs," *Media Psychology* 2, 303–29.

Rokeach, M. (1973) *The nature of human values*. New York: Free Press.

Rosenblum, N. L. (2000, ed.) *Obligations of citizenship and demands of faith: religious accommodation in pluralist democracies*. Princeton: Princeton University Press.

Rottenberg, I. C. (2000, Summer–Fall) "The idea of a Judeo-Christian world-view: religiopolitical reflections," *Journal of Ecumenical Studies* 37(3–4), 401–20.

Rumsfeld, D. (2002a, September 18) Testimony of U.S. Secretary of Defense Donald H. Rumsfeld before the U.S. House Armed Services Committee regarding Iraq. Retrieved from http://www.defense.gov/speeches/2002 on July 18, 2003.

Rumsfeld, D. (2002b, September 21) Secretary Rumsfeld interview with the *Sunday Times* London. Retrieved from http://www.defense.gov/news/Sep2002 on July 18, 2003.

Rumsfeld, D. (2002c, October 7) DoD news briefing—Secretary Rumsfeld and Gen. Pace. Retrieved from http://www.defense. gov/news/Oct2002 on July 18, 2003.

Rumsfeld, D. (2003, January 22) Secretary Rumsfeld briefs at the foreign press center. Retrieved from http://www.defense.gov/ news/Jan2003 on July 18, 2003.

Rutenberg, J. (2001, December 3) Fox portrays a war of good and evil, and many applaud, *New York Times*. Retrieved from http://www.nytimes.com on December 3, 2001.

Savage, D. G. (2004, January 12) Justices to weigh presidential powers, *Los Angeles Times*, p. A-1. Retrieved from Nexis database on January 15, 2004.

Sawyer, K. (1984, December 25) Christian Right takes its place at center stage, *New York Times*, p. A-1. Retrieved from Nexis database on August 6, 2003.

Schaefer, T. M. (1997) "Persuading the persuaders: presidential speeches and editorial opinion," *Political Communication* 14(1), 97–111.

Schlesinger, P. (1991) "Media, the political order and national identity," *Media, Culture and Society* 13, 297–308.

Schuster, M. A., Stein, B. D., Jaycox, L. H., Collins, R. L., Marshall, G. N., Elliott, M. N., Zhou, A. J., Kanouse, D. E., Morrison, J. L., and Berry, S. H. (2001) "A national survey of stress reactions after the September 11, 2001, terrorist attacks," *New England Journal of Medicine* 345, 1507–12.

Scott, W. A. (1955) "Reliability of content analysis: the case of nominal scale coding," *Public Opinion Quarterly* 19, 321–5.

Seelye, K. Q. (2001, August 9) The president's decision: the overview; Bush gives his backing for limited research on existing stem cells, *New York Times*, p. A-1. Retrieved from Nexis database on July 19, 2003.

Shah, D. V., Watts, M. D., Domke, D., and Fan, D. P. (2002) "News framing and cueing of issue regimes: explaining Clinton's public approval in spite of scandal," *Public Opinion Quarterly* 66, 339–70.

Shenon, P. (2001, March 11) House votes haunt retreat meant to spur collegiality, *New York Times*, p. A-32. Retrieved from Nexis database on July 21, 2003.

Shorto, R. (2004, March 21) Al Franken, seriously so, *New York Times*. Retrieved from http://www.nytimes.com on March 21, 2004.

Sigal, L. V. (1973) *Reporters and officials*. Lexington, MA: D. C. Heath.

Smith, N. (2001) "Scales of terror and the resort to geography," *Environment and Planning D: Society and Space* 19, 631–7.

Steinberg, J. (2004 March 11) The media business; liberal talk radio network to start up in three cities, *New York Times*. Retrieved from Nexis database on March 18, 2004.

Stiver, D. R. (1996) *The philosophy of religious language: sign, symbol, and story*. Cambridge, MA: Blackwell.

Stolberg, S. G. (2003, March 12) An order of fries, please, but do hold the French, *New York Times*, p. A-1.

Strozier, C. B. (1994) *Apocalypse: on the psychology of fundamentalism in America*. Boston: Beacon Press.

Stuckey, M. E. (1995) "Competing foreign policy visions: rhetorical hybrids after the Cold War," *Western Journal of Communication* 59(3), 214–27.

Suskind, R. (2003, January) Why are these men laughing? *Esquire*, 96–105.

Sutel, S. (2002, February 15) Attacks boosted news magazines' newsstand sales, Associated Press.

Swarns, R. L. and Cardwell, D. (2003, December 6) Democrats try to regain ground on moral issues, *New York Times*, p. A-11.

Tetlock, P. E. (1983) "Cognitive style and political ideology," *Personality Processes and Individual Differences* 45, 118–26.

Tetlock, P. E. (1989) "Structure and function in political belief systems," in A. R. Pratkanis, S. J. Breckler, and A. G. Greenwald (eds), *Attitude structure and function* (pp. 129–51). Hillsdale, NJ: Lawrence Erlbaum.

Tetlock, P. E., Bernzweig, J., and Gallant. J. L. (1985) "Supreme Court decision making: cognitive style as a predictor of ideological consistency of voting," *Journal of Personality and Social Psychology* 48, 1227–39.

Tetlock, P. E., Hannum, K., and Micheletti, P. (1984) "Stability and change in senatorial debate: testing the cognitive versus rhetorical style hypothesis," *Journal of Personality and Social Psychology* 46, 979–90.

Tuchman, G. (1978) *Making news: a study in the construction of reality*. New York: Free Press.

Turner, G. (1992) *British cultural studies: an introduction*. New York: Routledge.

Tuveson, E. L. (1968) *Redeemer nation: the idea of America's millennial role*. Chicago: University of Chicago Press.

United States Commission on National Security/21st Century (2001, February) *Road map for national security: imperative for change*. Retrieved from http://www.nssg.gov/PhaseIIIFR.pdf on July 15, 2003.

van der Vyver, J. D. (1996) "Religious fundamentalism and human rights," *Journal of International Affairs* 50(1), 21–40.

VandeHei, J. (2002, September 26) Daschle angered by Bush statement; President "politicizing" security issues, he says, *Washington Post*, p. A-1.

Vermeer, J. P. (2002) *The view from the states: national politics in local newspaper editorials*. Lanham, MD: Rowman & Littlefield.

Watts, M., Domke, D., Shah, D., and Fan, D. (1999) "Elite cues and media bias in presidential campaigns," *Communication Research* 26, 144–75.

Weiler, M. and Pearce, W. B. (1992) "Ceremonial discourse: the rhetorical ecology of the Reagan administration," in M. Weiler and W. B. Pearce (eds), *Reagan and public discourse in America* (pp. 11–42). Tuscaloosa, AL: University of Alabama Press.

Whitaker, B. (2004, March 14) Even Patriot Act politics is local, *New York Times*. Retrieved from Nexis database on March 19, 2004.

Whittle, J. (2002) "All in the family: top Bush administration leaders, religious right lieutenants plot strategy in culture 'war,'" *Church & State* 55(5), 4–8.

Wilcox, C. (2000) *Onward Christian soldiers? The religious right in American politics*. Boulder, CO: Westview Press.

Wilcox, C., DeBell, M., and Sigelman, L. (1999) "The second coming of the new Christian right: patterns of popular support in 1984 and 1996," *Social Science Quarterly* 80(1), 181–93.

Will, G. F. (2001, May 3) Bush's conservatism, *Washington Post*, p. B-7. Retrieved from Nexis database on August 6, 2003.

Williams, R. (1977) *Marxism and literature*. Oxford: Oxford University Press.

Wills, G. (2003, March 30) With God on his side, *New York Times*. Retrieved from Nexis database on June 6, 2003.

Witcover, J. (2003, May 12) Standing out from the crowd, *Baltimore Sun*, p. A-11. Retrieved from Nexis database on July 4, 2003.

Wylie, L. and Forest, J. (1992) "Religious fundamentalism, right wing authoritarianism and prejudice," *Psychology Reports* 71, 1291–8.

Wyman, L. M. and Dionisopoulos, G. N. (2000) "Transcending the virgin/whore dichotomy: telling Mina's story in Bram Stoker's *Dracula*," *Women's Studies in Communication* 23(2), 209–37.

Zaller, J. 1992. *The nature and origins of mass opinion*. Cambridge: Cambridge University Press.

Zaller, J. (1994a) "Elite leadership of mass opinion: new evidence from the Gulf War," in W. L. Bennett and D. L. Paletz (eds), *Taken by storm: the media, public opinion and U.S. foreign policy in the Gulf War* (pp. 186–209). Chicago: University of Chicago Press.

Zaller, J. (1994b) "Strategic politicians, public opinion, and the Gulf crisis," in W. L. Bennett and D. L. Paletz (eds), *Taken by storm: the media, public opinion and U.S. foreign policy in the Gulf War* (pp. 250–74). Chicago: University of Chicago Press.

Zaller, J. and Chiu, D. (1996) "Government's little helper: U.S. press coverage of foreign policy crises, 1945–1991," *Political Communication* 13, 385–405.

Zengeri, J. (2003, August 17) Fiddling with the reception, *New York Times*. Retrieved from Nexis database on September 5, 2003.

# Index

perpetrators of 4, 118, 179
Saddam Hussein involvement
156
scope of 13, 137
trauma effects 13–14, 56
visual images 14, 19, 21
*see also* crisis: September 11
Stahl, Lesley 20–21
strategic communication
Bush administration, by
18–19, 21, 23, 31–4, 37,
56–60, 61–6, 76–7, 86–90,
92–4, 108, 115–17, 119–22,
127, 146–50, 154–62,
170–1, 177–82
language and construction of
reality 17–18, 170, 193n61
political leaders, presence
among 11, 18
Reagan administration, by 8,
19–21
similarity of Reagan and Bush
administrations 8, 19, 21,
156–8, 202n5
structures of feeling 6–7, 155
Suskind, Ron 120
Swarns, Rachel L. 173

**T**
talk radio 8, 22, 169, 209n20
television audiences 1, 31, 158
Tetlock, Philip E. 171
Tewksbury, David 165
Truman, Harry 116, 175

**U**
United Nations 25, 59, 116, 130

*see also* Iraq: resolutions
unity *see* dissent

**V**
van der Vyver, Johan D. 147
Vietnam War 164, 182

**W**
"war on terrorism"
creation 65, 66–8, 71–5, 88,
118, 153, 158
duration 67, 72–7, 87
metaphor, as 19, 64, 193n61
"mission" of U.S. nation, as
16, 26, 64, 74–7, 83, 86, 88,
178–80, 211n4
Watergate 182
*Weekly Compilation of Presidential
Documents* 38, 68–9, 123
Wildermuth, John 141
Williams, Raymond 6–7, 155
Wilson, Woodrow 175
Wolfowitz, Paul 71, 153
worldview, religious
Bush administration, of 5–7,
25–8, 160–2, 172, 174,
177–83
definition 4–5
difficulty of identification 5,
160

**Z**
Zahn, Paula 168
Zaller, John 22, 35
Zanetti, Lisa A. 33